DATE DUE

Prescription Drug Abuse

Books in the **Contemporary World Issues** series address vital issues in today's society such as genetic engineering, pollution, and biodiversity. Written by professional writers, scholars, and nonacademic experts, these books are authoritative, clearly written, up-to-date, and objective. They provide a good starting point for research by high school and college students, scholars, and general readers as well as by legislators, businesspeople, activists, and others.

Each book, carefully organized and easy to use, contains an overview of the subject, a detailed chronology, biographical sketches, facts and data and/or documents and other primary source material, a forum of authoritative perspective essays, annotated lists of print and nonprint resources, and an index.

Readers of books in the Contemporary World Issues series will find the information they need in order to have a better understanding of the social, political, environmental, and economic issues facing the world today.

Prescription Drug Abuse

A REFERENCE HANDBOOK

David E. Newton

ABC-CLIO™

An Imprint of ABC-CLIO, LLC
Santa Barbara, California • Denver, Colorado

Library of Congress Cataloging-in-Publication Data

Newton, David E., author.

Prescription drug abuse : a reference handbook / David E. Newton.

p. ; cm. — (Contemporary world issues)

Includes bibliographical references and index.

ISBN 978-1-4408-3978-8 (alk. paper) —

ISBN 978-1-4408-3979-5 (ebook)

I. Title.   II. Series: Contemporary world issues.

[DNLM: 1. Substance-Related Disorders.   2. Prescription Drugs—adverse effects. WM 270]

RC564

362.29—dc23   2015030401

ISBN: 978-1-4408-3978-8

EISBN: 978-1-4408-3979-5

20 19 18 17 16   1 2 3 4 5

This book is also available on the World Wide Web as an eBook. Visit www.abc-clio.com for details.

ABC-CLIO

An Imprint of ABC-CLIO, LLC

ABC-CLIO, LLC

130 Cremona Drive, P.O. Box 1911

Santa Barbara, California 93116-1911

This book is printed on acid-free paper ∞

Manufactured in the United States of America

"Monitoring the Future" is an ongoing study about student behaviors, values, and attitudes about drugs conducted by the Survey Research Center at the University of Michigan for the National Institute on Drug Abuse. The study began in 1975 and focused entirely on two legal substances, alcohol and tobacco, and a number of illegal drugs, such as marijuana, heroin, and cocaine. No mention during the early years of the survey was made of the nonmedical use of prescription drugs, such as OxyContin, Vicodin, and Percocet, presumably because the rate of misuse and abuse of those drugs was so low. In 2002, the survey began including questions about the nonmedical use of prescription drugs in its study of 12th graders, and, later, of 8th and 10th graders also. The data on these questions in the 21st century have been astounding. The number of high school students who admit to using prescription drugs for nonmedical purposes has increased by anywhere from 100 percent to 300 percent, depending on the age group and the drug involved. No wonder that substance abuse experts are now referring to the misuse of prescription drugs by young adults as an *epidemic* (the title of one of the most important recent studies on the issue).

Prescription drug abuse is, however, by no means a problem of childhood and adolescence only. Indeed, it has become a matter of concern also among the elderly, many of whom regularly take four, five, six, or more prescription drugs every day, a practice that can lead to a variety of problems, including confusion over drug doses and drug use, and physical dependence on and addiction to some drugs. Individuals having to deal with severe pain issues and other recalcitrant health problems may also become dependent on or addicted to prescription drugs.

One of the reasons for the increasing rate of nonmedical use of prescription drugs is, of course, the desire for more individuals to try new substances that will produce an artificial "high," "low," or some other unusual mental state. But another reason for the growing problem is also the advance in the number, type, and efficacy of drugs available for treating legitimate medical problems. One of the reasons that OxyContin and Vicodin have become drugs of choice for recreational purposes is that those substances are so effective at producing the effects for which they are designed, escape from unpleasant feelings (e.g., pain) associated with injuries or disease. For a healthy person, that "escape" may be nothing other than a form of relaxation and release.

Prescription Drug Abuse explores the history of drug use in general, and prescription drug use, in particular. The use of both natural and synthetic substances to cure disease, bring relief from pain, control fever, and produce other positive medical benefits can be traced to the earliest eras of human civilization. As science has developed over the centuries, so has the range of substances available for dealing with such problems.

But substances used for medical reasons have never been limited *just* to those applications. They have also been employed in religious and cultural ceremonies, and very often just to intentionally produce altered mental and emotional states for those looking for such experiences. The epidemic of prescription drug abuse today, then, is not so much an entirely new problem as it is a new variation on an issue with which human societies have had to deal for many centuries.

Chapter 1 of the book provides a historical background to the role of drugs in human society from earliest civilizations to the modern day. Chapter 2 focuses more specifically on the issues about prescription drug abuse with which modern Americans and citizens of other nations in the world are now dealing, how those problems arose, what their consequences can be, how they can be prevented, and how prescription drug abuse can be treated. These two chapters are intended as introductions to the issue of prescription drug abuse on which readers can base further research in the topic, if that is their interest, or simply as a better basis for understanding those issues.

Chapter 3 provides an opportunity for individuals with a special interest in the field to offer short essays on some specific topic in the field, such as developments in current research, effects of various prescription drugs, factors involved in the development of dependence on and addiction to prescription drugs, programs of prevention, and methods of treatment.

Chapters 4–8 provide a compendium of resources to which readers can turn for more information and additional tools for advancing their own studies of prescription drug abuse. These tools include biographical and descriptive sketches of individuals and groups with special relevance to or interest in prescription drug abuse issues (Chapter 4), a collection of relevant data and documents on the topic (Chapter 5), an extensive annotated bibliography of books, articles, reports, and Internet sources on the subject (Chapter 6), a chronology of prescription drug abuse events over the centuries (Chapter 7), and a glossary of useful terms in the field (Chapter 8).

Chapters 1 and 2 also contain extensive references for quotations, data and statistics, and other information provided in those chapters. These references are also a rich source of additional readings that will be helpful to the reader who is pursuing further research on the topic of prescription drug abuse.

Prescription Drug Abuse

1 Background and History

Andy found the bottle of Tramadol in the bathroom medicine cabinet only by chance. She knew her mother had been taking the drug to relieve the pain that continued after her recent operation. And she had heard kids at school talking about "trammies." But she didn't really know what they were or what effect they had on a person who took them. So she decided to try a pill and see what happened. What a great feeling! She found almost like she was floating on a cloud. She didn't feel all that good a day later. But she wanted to experience that "high" again. So she took one more pill the next day.

And another pill the next day.
And another pill the day after that.
And she was hooked.

Andy's story is not a new one. Nor is it very unusual among teenagers today (or adults, for that matter). Many experts are now saying that the use of prescription medications for other than medical reasons has become an epidemic in the United States and other parts of the world. According to the most recent data available from the National Survey on Drug Use and Health, 52 million people over the age of 12 had used prescription drugs for nonmedical purpose at least once in their lifetime, and just over 6 million had used them in the month prior to the survey. Misuse of prescription drugs is now classified as

The flowers on the crown of this statue of the Minoan "Poppy Goddess" are thought to be poppy heads. (CM Dixon/Print Collector/Getty Images)

3

the second most serious substance abuse problem, after marijuana, in the United States today. The problem is especially severe among young adults with just over a quarter of all 12th graders having reported that they had used one or more prescription drugs in the year preceding the survey ("Prescription Drug Addiction" 2015).

The United States stands out among other nations of the world with respect to prescription drug abuse. According to the 2011 World Drug Report, published by the United Nations Office on Drugs and Crime, the percentage of people who use prescription drugs for nonmedical purposes in the United States is somewhere between 5 and 5.60. By comparison, the rate of illicit prescription drug use in other nations of the world ranges from 0 percent to less than 1 percent. That rate for Canada, for example, is estimated to be about 0.50 percent and for Mexico, less than 0.1 percent. In only a handful of nations for which these data are available does prescription drug abuse approach even a quarter of the U.S. rate. As examples, the rate in New Zealand is estimated to be between 0.70 and 1.30, in Costa Rica, 2.80, and in Estonia, between 0.42 and 1.77 (UNODC 2011, Table 6.1.1: Opiates, 210–12; data are not available for many countries).One reason that prescription drug abuse is largely an issue for the United States is that such drugs are generally widely available in the United States, especially in comparison with less wealthy nations, where prescription drugs are generally less readily available for legitimate medical reasons, and thus certainly less available also for nonmedical purposes. The significant difference in the nonmedical use of prescription drugs in other developed nations, such as those in the European Union, is less clear and is the subject of some research.

Why do people use prescription drugs for purposes other than the medical purposes for which they are intended? Even though researchers are not entirely sure what the answer(s) to that question may be, a number of reasons have been suggested. One of the most common reasons is that some prescription drugs, like other illicit drugs, provide pleasant feelings of well-being, reduction in stress, and increased relaxation. Other prescription drugs may help in weight loss, increase alertness and mental acuity, and improve work or scholastic performance. These qualities may be especially attractive since many users believe that prescription drugs were originally developed for sound medical reasons and that they are, therefore, safe to use. While that may be true when used for legitimate medical reasons, abuse of prescription drugs occurs easily, and one can soon become addicted to such medications.

Drug Use in the Ancient World

Humans have been using drugs almost since the beginning of civilization. As used in this book, the term *drug* refers to any natural or synthetic substance which, when ingested by an animal, has a physiological effect on that animal. Humans have used drugs for a variety of purposes, including the amelioration or cure of a disease, the relief of pain, the production of pleasant emotional responses, and participation in religious ceremonies or experiences. A drug can consist of plant or animal material, a mineral, or a synthetic substance.

It is probably impossible to say with any certainty when and where humans first started using drugs. At least some researchers are convinced, however, that humans have been using drugs for at least five millennia before the birth of Christ, and possibly much longer. For example, Spanish anthropologist Ellisa Guerra-Doce published a review article in 2015 in which she summarized the evidence for the use of various types of drugs in prehistoric societies. In commenting about the presence of opium plant material in some archaeological digs, she concluded that "[a]part from its use as a food plant, there is also uncontested evidence for the exploitation of its narcotic properties." She dates the earliest known use of opium for such purposes to about 4000 BCE (Gray 2015; Guerra-Doce 2015). Other researchers have made similar claims for other cultures.

In 2010, for example, a team of archaeologists led by Vanderbilt researcher Tom Dillehay argued that evidence found in the Nanchoc Valley of Peru suggested that residents of the area were chewing coca leaves, presumably for their psychoactive effects, at least 8,000 years ago (Dillehay et al. 2010).

The rise of relatively advanced new civilizations at the end of the New Stone Age (Neolithic) period in the Middle East sometime before about 2000 BCE provided somewhat more reliable evidence about the use of drugs for medical, religious, and recreational purposes. Such civilizations tended to have developed written alphabets, making possible permanent written records of the use of various types of drugs for a number of purposes. Some scholars point, for example, to the frequent use of the phrase *hul gil* in Sumerian texts dating perhaps to as early as 3400 BCE to describe the opium plant. The term translates as the *joy* ("hul") *plant* ("gil"), suggesting that it may have been used to produce psychoactive states of ecstasy. (This hypothesis was first suggested by Terry 1931.)

Sculptures and other artifacts also provide hints about the possible use of a variety of drugs in early societies of the Middle East. For example, one of the most frequently mentioned examples of artwork that may provide a hint of drug use for its psychedelic effects is the so-called Minoan goddess of the narcotics, a terra-cotta figure dating to about 1300 BCE. The statue appears to have fruit capsules from the opium plant inserted into her hair, along with a facial expression (closed eyes and fixed smile), that seem to suggest a state of intoxication. Other figurines of a similar age appear to have similar characteristics that seem to suggest the use of opium as an intoxicant among inhabitants of the time (see, e.g., Kritikos and Papadaki 1967; note, however, that there is considerable doubt as to the precise significance of some of these archaeological findings; for a discussion of this point, see Escohotado 2010, 93).

Probably the best clue available to the types of drugs used by ancient societies and the ways in which they were used is a number of clay tablets that provide good information about these facts. Of particular importance is a clay tablet dated at 2100 BCE that contains a commentary about the use of opium for surgical anesthesia, thought to be among "the world's oldest recorded list of medical prescriptions" (Norn, Kruse, and Kruse 2005, citing Kramer 1954). Such prescriptions are especially important for archaeologists because they list the substances used in medical care and the methods used in preparing them for use.

A prescription is simply a set of directions for preparing and administering some type of treatment for a patient. During the earliest period of human history, the acts of examining a patient, making a diagnosis, deciding how to treat a medical condition, and administering that treatment were probably all carried out by a single individual, such as a medicine man (or woman), priest, wise woman, or witch doctor. However, some division of responsibility probably also began to occur early on, with the examination, diagnosis, and treatment falling to the skills of someone whom we might today call a physician, while the preparation (and sometimes administration) of the treatment to a person whom we might call a pharmacist.

A considerable number of instructions for medical treatment, which can only be called prescriptions, remain from the second and third millennium BCE in the Middle East. One such prescription has been dated to the last quarter of the third millennium BCE and is generally acknowledged as being the oldest prescription known. The tablet on which it was found actually consists of three sets of instructions, one for making a poultice (a warm medicated dressing), one for treating gastrointestinal disorders, and one whose purpose is not entirely understood. The instructions that make up the second of these groups of prescriptions, for example, say to "pour strong beer over the resin of the [unknown] plant; heat over a fire; put this liquid in river bitumen oil, and let the sick person drink" (Clarke 1999).

These early prescriptions were often a complex mixture of trial-and-error semiscientific knowledge, magic incantations, social customs, and religious beliefs. In fact, the modern terms *pharmacy* and *pharmacist* derive originally from the Greek word *pharmacos*, which referred to the process by which an individual was cast out of society (either by being killed or by exiled) as a way of treating social disasters such as famine or disease ("'Pharmakon': The Cure or the Poison?" 2009). The prescriptions made use of an impressive variety of materials, including some 250 vegetable products and 120 mineral drugs during the time of King Ashurbanipal of Assyria (685 BCE–627 BCE), according to one source (Kremers, Urdang, and Sonnedecker 1976, 5). Among the herbs commonly used in these early prescriptions were asafetida, calamus, cannabis, castor, crocus, galbanum, glycyrrhiza, hellebore, mandragora, mentha, myrrh, opium, pine turpentine, styrax, and thymus (Janick 2003). A number of excellent references are available on the nature of medicine in the ancient Near East (see, e.g., Biggs 2006; "Medicine in Ancient Mesopotamia" 2015).

Other ancient civilizations developed pharmacopeia and medical practices similar to those in Middle East societies, differing largely with regard to the types of plants and minerals available in the area. (The term *pharmacopeia* refers to a list of medicinal drugs along with their properties, effects, and directions for use.) Many archaeologists believe that medical principles and practices involving the use of drugs probably migrated from Mesopotamia and other parts of the Middle East to Egypt, where they became integrated into medical practices there. As in the Middle East, descriptions of those practices are often found on clay tablets or the walls of temples and other buildings. (You can read at Cribiore, Davoli, and Ratzan 2008 about one interesting discovery of an ancient Egyptian school with a lesson in drug use inscribed on its walls.)

One of the most interesting herbs used by the Egyptians, especially for nonmedical purposes, was a type of water lily called the sacred narcotic water lily of the Nile *(Nymphaea caerulea* Sav.). The plant was apparently widely known and used as early as the beginning of the third millennium BCE. It was used primarily for its narcotic powers, according to one expert, "in order to provoke the shamanic state of ecstasis among a priestly caste in ancient Egypt" (Emboden 1979). One of the most interesting features of the plant was that a very close relative also grows in South America, where it was also used by the Mayans at a somewhat later date for essentially the same purposes as was the case in Egypt (Emboden 1981). Some questions remain about this interpretation of the water lily's use as a drug, however (see, e.g., Pommerening, Marinova, and Hendrickx 2011, fn 97).

In ancient China, one of the most widely used medicinal drugs was *ephedra*, a term that refers either to the complete plant whose scientific name is *Ephedra sinica* or to the leaves and branches from which a medical concoction is made. The Chinese name for the drug is *ma huang*, which translates to English literally as "yellow hemp." Ephedra has been used in traditional Chinese medicine for at least 2,000 years, and probably long before that, for the treatment of headaches, colds, and general body aches and pains. It is also used in combination with other herbs to treat a variety of other medical complaints.

The primary active ingredient in ephedra, an amine known as ephedrine, was first discovered and isolated from the plant in 1885 by Japanese chemist Nagai Nagayoshi. By the late 1920s, ephedrine was being manufactured synthetically and sold on the open market, often in the form of a tea that was recommended as a "pick-me-up" that provided a person with extra energy. In this format, it eventually became popular as recently as the 19th century in the United States, where ephedrine concoctions became known as Mormon tea or Indian tea for the two groups of people who most enjoyed them, the Mormons and Native Americans.

Since the late 1990s, concern about the harmful effects of ephedra and ephedrine increased in the United States and other nations, eventually resulting in a ban on the sale of dietary supplements containing either product. The ban was proposed originally by the U.S. Food and Drug Administration

(FDA) in response to a number of reports of serious side effects among individuals who used such supplements for nonmedical reasons. Certain concoctions of ma huang in the form of teas are, however, legally available for sale (Gaeddert 2015; McKenna, Jones, and Hughes 2002, 271–320).

The history of drugs in ancient India is similar to that of other parts of the world, with accounts of medicinal herbs available, according to one source "as far back as history can take us" (Chopra 1958, 1). Specifically, the Indian materia medica (the collected body of knowledge about drugs and other medicines) dates back to a fundamental medical work, the Rigveda, which was written between 4500 and 1600 BCE. The most prominent drug mentioned in that work was a concoction called *soma*, often referred to as "the elixir of immortality" and "the drink of the Gods." The drink was made by crushing the stems and leaves of the soma plant and then passing the juice through wool. There is no certain knowledge as to what precisely the soma plant was, and scholars have proposed a number of theories over the years. Interestingly enough, one of the most widely accepted hypotheses today is that the soma plant may well have been the same ephedrine plant that was popular in China, *Ephedra sinica* (Khan 2014).

A Short History of Opium

Of the hundreds of herbs and minerals used by ancient peoples in all parts of the globe, only one remains of interest in a discussion about the misuse of prescription drugs in the modern world: opium. All other substances in the ancient materia medica have faded into oblivion in the medical world, are still being used (usually without evidence for their efficacy), or have been banned as too dangerous for human therapeutic and/or recreational use. By contrast, opium has been an essential part of the world's pharmacopeia around the world for well over 2,000 years. And the misuse of compounds containing opium or one of its derivatives is one of the most serious problems in the fight against prescription drug abuse.

Opium is a term used to describe the dried exudate (the liquid excreted when a plant is cut) from the unripe capsules of the *Papaver somniferum* plant. The material consists of about 25 psychoactive drugs (drugs that cause changes in brain functions), such as morphine, codeine, papaverine, noscapine, and thebaine. A typical analysis shows a composition of about 2.3 percent morphine, 2.6 percent codeine, 4.7 percent papaverine, and 10.2 percent noscapine (with no detectable thebaine) (Panicker, Wojno, and Ziska 2007). These values vary somewhat depending on the source of the opium being studied. The complex nature of opium was not known to the ancients and was discovered over a period of time beginning with the isolation of the first constituent, morphine, by German chemist Friedrich Sertürner in 1803.

The oldest evidence for the growth of the *P. somniferum* plant dates to Neolithic villages in Switzerland in about 5700 BCE. Additional evidence suggests that the plant was being grown in a number of locations in central and southern Europe for at least the next six millennia. These data suggest that a previous hypothesis that the plant originated in the Middle East may well be incorrect and that what probably happened was that the opium plant originated in central Europe and then was transmitted over the centuries to Sumeria, Assyria, Babylon, and other Middle Eastern cultures (Merlin 2003, Table 1, 304–8; Zohary, Hopf, and Weiss 2012, 109–11). From there, transmission continued to the East, probably carried by Arab traders, to Persia, China, and Japan (Chopra 1958, 204–5; Li and Fang 2013, 190–91).

The evolution of the role of opium in Chinese society is particularly interesting because it may well provide insight into similar patterns that have occurred in most (perhaps all) other cultures. At first, opium was used exclusively for medical purposes. In traditional Chinese medicine, the plant is thought to control the balance of bodily fluids and to preserve qi, the vital energy needed to maintain normal bodily function. Opium had long been known also as a soporific (a substance that induces sleep) and as a powerful pain reliever. Some historians have also suggested that the Chinese gave opium to their warriors to increase their strength and determination in battle, a practice that has been documented in other cultures also ("A Century of International Drug Control" 2009, 19).

At first, the use of opium appears to have been restricted almost entirely to physicians and the upper classes, the former because of its health benefits, and the latter, more often, because of its psychoactive effects. Over time, however, it was the latter application that grew in popularity, and opium began to attain the role of emotional enhancement by which it is perhaps as well known today as is its medical benefits. Eventually, the psychoactive charms of opium began to expand beyond the upper classes and among commoners. One observer has noted that "[b]y the late Ming [1368–1644], opium was no longer the province of royal dabbling but a court necessity, and was working its way into the commoners' purview" (Diaz 2008). Perhaps one of the most interesting confirmations of this change in Chinese attitudes toward the use of opium came with a modification of the term used to describe the drug during the Ming dynasty, from *yao* ("medicine") to *chun yao* ("spring drug" or, more accurately, "aphrodisiac"). The new term was meant to refer to the drug's ability to "induce sexual desire, vitalise intercourse and control ejaculation or emission." It thus came to be associated less with, or at least equally valuable as, a symbol of "lust and regeneration" (Zheng 2005, 12).

The impact of opium on Chinese history by the early 18th century had become profound. An important factor in this event was the introduction of smoked opium to the Chinese by Dutch companies that imported the product to China from plantations in India. The use of opium for recreational purposes eventually became so widespread and so serious a problem that the Chinese emperor Yongzheng issued an edict in

1729 prohibiting the use of the drug for any purpose other than medicinal. Yongzheng's action did not solve the problem of opium addiction in China, however, and one of his successors, the Qianlong Emperor, eventually banned the use of opium entirely in 1799 (Greenberg 1951, 29; for an excellent discussion on the role of opium in Chinese society during this period, see UNODC 2008 World Drug Report, Section 2: A Century of International Drug Control; also see Figure 2, page 175, for trends in opium imports during the 17th through 19th centuries.)

The use of opium and its role in national economics and politics eventually became such a matter of importance that it led to two of the world's most famous drug-related wars, the Opium Wars of 1839–1842 and 1856–1860, over the Chinese government's attempt to restrict or completely ban the importation of opium into the country. The final result of these wars was the eventual opening of China to the importation not only of opium, but also of other products (for a detailed discussion of the opium wars, see Lovell 2015; for a briefer discussion, see Vassilev 2010; for an excellent detailed history of opium in all parts of the world, see Booth 1998).

A Multitude of Opium Products

Laudanum

While physicians and pleasure-seekers around the world were using opium in ever-increasing amounts, researchers were trying to learn more about the composition of this "marvelous" drug and to find new uses for it. One of the first breakthroughs in this area was the discovery (or invention) of a new opium-containing substance called *laudanum* (supposedly from the Latin verb *laudare*, meaning "to praise"). Although the term was used for a fairly wide variety of concoctions, it is most commonly described as a tincture of opium, opium powder dissolved in alcohol. (A tincture is, in general, any solution in which alcohol is the solvent.)

Most histories of opium ascribe the discovery of laudanum to the Swiss-German alchemist and physician Paracelsus. They claimed that he discovered that opium is much more soluble in alcohol than in water, making it possible to produce a format (a tincture) that is easier to use than other forms. In fact, some recipes for laudanum recommend a high-quality wine as a solvent, to which are added a variety of herbs and spices to improve the otherwise harsh taste of the concoction. The laudanum produced as a tincture can also be reformulated in the form of pills, which can be taken as aspirin and other drugs are taken today. (The actual discovery of laudanum is probably a far more complex story than that found in most sources; for one of the best reviews of this history, see Ball 2007, 182–84.)

Whatever its precise origin, laudanum was a highly praised and eagerly sought-out medication. Paracelsus himself claimed almost endless benefits from the drug, with an ability to cure any disease whatsoever, with the one exception of leprosy. In fact, he said that laudanum could even raise the dead and, as his assistant once wrote, some patients who "seemed to be dead" "suddenly arose" after taking the drug (Ball 2007, 182).

The person who is usually credited with spreading information about laudanum is the English physician Thomas Sydenham, who lived from 1624 to 1689. Sydenham claimed his formulation for laudanum was based on Paracelsus's original recipe, although such was probably not the case. Sydenham's laudanum (usually known by just that name) consisted of a tincture of opium made with "good sherry wine," cinnamon, cloves, and saffron. Proponents of the concoction claimed nearly as many benefits as did Paracelsus for his original version of laudanum. Sydenham's formulation became widely popular although, in an interesting side note, it tended to fall out of use in regions where saffron was omitted from the recipe, raising questions as to what effect this particular herb had on the taste and/or efficacy of the drug (see "American Druggist and Pharmaceutical Record" 1906).

Because of its efficacy in the treatment of a wide range of physical complaints, laudanum remained popular in many parts of the world until the early 20th century. It probably reached its peak of popularity during the Victorian period in England, when it was particularly popular among women, who used the concoction for the treatment of menstrual cramps and other unspecified complaints. Among its other many uses were the treatment of pain; calming of the nerves; aid in sleeping; relief from colds and flu; and treatment of a number of more serious disorders and diseases, such as meningitis, cardiac disease, and yellow fever. The drug was also widely used by parents and nurses to reduce crying and fussiness among babies and young children (Cowell 2015; Delgado 2009; Diniejko 2002).

The history of laudanum use provides a useful insight into today's problem of prescription drug abuse. The drug was developed for the legitimate treatment of a number of serious medical problems, and its success in so doing led to its increased popularity among physicians and the general public. Over time, however, more and more people were using it for purposes other than medical treatment, to get "high" or to escape from one's daily worries and concerns. Because of its nature, the drug readily became addictive so that a whole new category of medical and social problems began to develop arising out of laudanum addiction. That was the story that was to be repeated over and over again throughout subsequent history, and especially during the early years of the 21st century ("Prescription Drug Abuse History" 2015; for an excellent history of laudanum, see Hodgson 2001).

Laudanum is still available by prescription in the United States, although it has been banned in other parts of the world. The most common use for the drug is the treatment of diarrhea and the treatment of babies born to women who are addicted to opium. The drug is not widely used because of its serious side effects (taken in excess, it can be fatal) and because other drugs are available for most applications that are much less dangerous than is laudanum itself ("Laudanum Addiction Treatment" 2015; "Opioid [Narcotic Analgesics Systemic]" 2001).

Morphine

The first quarter of the 19th century might well be called the Age of the Alkaloids. Alkaloids are organic (carbon-containing) compounds that contain the element nitrogen, are present in plants, and have physiological effects on humans. Some well-known alkaloids are caffeine, nicotine, morphine, strychnine, quinine, atropine, and curare. Prior to 1800, scientists knew virtually nothing about alkaloids. Although the plants from which alkaloids come (e.g., opium) had been known and used for centuries, their detailed composition was essentially unknown. One of the first major breakthroughs in the field of alkaloid research came in 1804 when French chemist Charles Derosne isolated a new compound from a sample of opium with psychoactive effects far more profound than those for opium itself. Derosne called his discovery (somewhat immodestly) *Sel narcotique de Derosne*, or "Derosne's narcotic salt." The compound was later shown to be the alkaloid noscapine, a primary component of opium (Anderson 1862, 446).

The first real advance in opium chemistry occurred, however, a few years later when a 19-year-old German pharmacist's assistant, Friedrich Sertürner, discovered another component of opium, morphine. Sertürner chose this name for his discovery because of its connection with the Greek god of dreams, Morpheus. Sertürner reported his discovery in the *Journal der Pharmacie fuer Aerzte und Apotheker* (*Journal of Pharmacy for Physicians and Pharmacists*) in 1806 (Huxtable and Schwarz 2001; also see Booth 1998, 68–69). The isolation of morphine was important not only in advancing human understanding of opium but also as the first real step in the new field of alkaloid chemistry.

Morphine is perhaps the best known and most efficacious of all opiates. At one time, the term *opiate* was used to refer to any alkaloid found in the opium plant, such as morphine or codeine. Another term used to describe opium-like substances is *opioid*, which originally referred only to synthetic or semisynthetic substances with narcotic (mood-changing) effects. The term *opioid* is sometimes reserved also for any substance that attaches to and activates cellular structures in the body known as *opioid receptors*. Some disagreement exists today as to the precise meaning of the terms *opiate* and *opioid*, with some authorities preferring to keep this original distinction, and other experts preferring to use the latter term for *all* opium-like substances, whether natural or synthetic. (For more on this debate, see "Opiates/Opioids" 2015; "Opiates and Opioids" 2014; "Opiate vs. Opioid—What's the Difference?" 2015.)

Morphine has a molecular structure very similar to that of other opiates and opioids, both natural and synthetic (see, e.g., Arnaud 2014, Diagram). Its primary application is in the treatment of both acute and chronic severe pain, such as those associated with myocardial infarction, severe and multiple injuries, and postoperative distress. Its value for these uses was apparent early on. In one of the most famous statements in the history of morphine use, the famous English physician William Osler wrote about his use of morphine during the most difficult years of his life-ending medical problems. "Shunt the whole pharmacopeia," he wrote, "except for opium. It alone in some form does the job. What a comfort it has been!" (Bliss 1999, 469). Elsewhere Osler referred to morphine by a term that has ever since been associated with it: "God's own medicine" (Bliss 1999, 365).

The two most serious problems associated with the use of morphine are its effects on the respiratory system and its tendency to be addictive. When consumed in excessive amounts, morphine can cause asphyxia (a severe deficiency of oxygen in the body) and respiratory depression that can lead to death. Sertürner himself was the first person to become aware of this dangerous side effect. Soon after he discovered morphine, he decided to test its effects on animals. He fed small amounts first to mice living in his basement, and then to some unwanted dogs in the neighborhood. In all cases, the animals died from eating the drug. Not to be deterred, Sertürner then decided to try the drug on himself and some of his friends. He soon found unpleasant effects similar to those described earlier and concluded that the level of morphine used with a human was critical to its effects—beneficial or harmful—to an individual (Altman 1987, 89–90). Sertürner's research and discoveries revealed the most basic facts about the use and misuse of morphine that is essential for anyone concerned with prescription drug abuse today.

Sertürner's discovery of morphine was truly one of the most significant events in the history of pharmacology. As news of his research began to spread through the medical community, reports came flooding in of successful treatments for pain that had never been possible before. By the 1820s, morphine had become routinely available and without prescription in Great Britain, the United States, and other countries. These advances were made possible at least in part by the development of commercial means for manufacturing morphine from its raw ingredients, one of the first products produced by the Merck company in 1827 ("Pharmaceutical Research by a Commercial House" 1906). The standardization of morphine manufacture meant that physicians could confidently prescribe very specific amounts of morphine to be taken ("take two pills twice a day") with the confidence that the patient was receiving the correct dosage that would help cure his or her problem without risking serious side effects (Booth 1998, 70; see a typical Merck ad for the drug at "Merck's Merits in the Manufacture of Morphine" 1907).

Even with the increased availability of morphine, opium remained popular among the medical profession, mainly because it was the most effective method for treating pain then known and, also of considerable importance, it was thought to have few, if any, serious long-term side effects (e.g., addiction). For these same reasons, opium became increasingly popular especially among the upper classes in Great Britain as a recreational drug. The list of opium users (some of whom, in spite of "common knowledge" about the drug's long-term effects, eventually became opium addicts) includes some of the best-known names in British literature, the arts, and other fields: abolitionist William Wilberforce; poets John Keats, Percy Bysshe Shelley, Lord Byron, and Elizabeth Barrett Browning; novelist Wilkie Collins; and, perhaps most famously of all, essayist Thomas De Quincey, whose best-known work was *Confessions of an Opium Eater* (Milligan 1995, 24–27).

The majority of these illustrious individuals experimented with opium or morphine, becoming addicted or not, not because of medical need, but as a means of pleasure-seeking. It was often thought of as a fruitful source of inspiration by poets, novelists, and other writers (Ruston 2015). But for the great majority of men and women who *did* become addicted to morphine in particular, the ultimate cause was not pleasure-seeking, but the need for treatment of pain and other medical problems. Perhaps the preeminent example of that fact was the American Civil War, fought between 1861 and 1865. Two of the most challenging problems with which physicians had to deal during the war (as had been the case with nearly all preceding wars) were dysentery and surgical pain. According to the data most commonly cited, 1,525,236 Union soldiers were admitted for medical care as a result of dysentery and diarrheal disorders (caused by agents such as *Salmonella*, *Shigella*, and *Amoeba*), resulting in a total of 37,794 deaths. A total of 224,586 men were killed by noncombat deaths, compared with 110,070 Union soldiers who died as a result of combat (Agnew 2014, 72).

Other Natural Opiates

Throughout the 19th century, chemists analyzed the composition of opium in greater detail, finding more than two dozen substances in addition to morphine present in the flower. Among these ingredients are codarnine, codeine, cryptopine, gnoscopine, lanthopine, laudanidine, narceine, narcotine (noscapine), neopine, papaverine, rhoeadine, and tebaine. The most common of these ingredients are morphine (typically about 20%), noscapine (about 5%), codeine (about 2%), papaverine (about 2%), and thebaine (about 1%) (Burdock 2010, 1717).

These substances are now known as *natural opiates* for the obvious reason that they occur naturally in the poppy seed. By contrast, researchers later developed other types of opiates consisting of artificially altered forms of natural opiates—the so-called *semisynthetic opiates* such as heroin, hydromorphone, oxymorphone, and oxycodone—and synthetic compounds prepared artificially with chemical structures similar to those of the natural opiates—the so-called *synthetic opiates* such as meperidine, fentanyl, and methadone. The most important examples of these natural opiates were codeine, discovered in 1832 by French chemist Pierre Robiquet; noscapine, discovered in 1803 by Derosne; thebaine, discovered in 1835 by French chemist Thiboumèry; papaverine, discovered by German chemist Georg Merck in 1848; and narceine, discovered by French chemist Pierre-Joseph Pelletier in 1832 (Dohme 1893; Kapoor 1995, Chapter 8).

Semisynthetic Opioids

By the mid-19th century, researchers were fascinated by the potential therapeutic possibilities of the natural opiates that had been discovered in the first half of the century. They were focusing, in particular, on two lines of research. First, they believed that the components of the poppy seed contained some fundamental chemical structure that conveyed the analgesic properties of opium and its natural components. They hoped to be able to identify that basic component and use it as the structure of synthetic compounds that would be even more efficacious than opium, morphine, codeine, or other natural opiates. Second, they wanted to create synthetic, or at least semisynthetic, products that were less addictive than the natural opiates. As time passed, it became increasingly clear that "God's own medicine" was not an entirely beneficent product. If not used carefully, opium, morphine, and other natural medicines could become addictive, causing medical problems at least as severe as and often far more harmful than the problems they were used to treat.

The first breakthrough in the search for semisynthetic forms of the opiates occurred at St. Mary's Hospital in London in 1874. C. R. Alder Wright, a chemist working at the hospital, was trying a variety of modifications of the morphine molecule to see if he could solve at least one of the two problems described previously. In one of these attempts, he added two acetyl groups to the morphine molecule, producing a new substance called *diacetylmorphine* or *morphine diacetate* (a comparison of the molecular structure of morphine and heroin is available at "Opium, Morphine, and Heroin" 2015).

Wright sent a sample of his product to a colleague, F. M. Pierce, for testing on animals. Pierce described the effect of the substance on young dogs and rabbits that were injected with it. The most noticeable effects, Pierce said, were

> great prostration, fear, and sleepiness speedily following the administration, the eyes being sensitive, and pupils dilated, considerable salivation being produced in dogs, and slight tendency to vomiting in some cases, but no actual emesis. Respiration was as first quickened, but subsequently reduced, and the heart's action was diminished, and rendered irregular. Marked want of co-ordinating power over the muscular movements, and loss of power in the pelvis and hind limbs, together with a diminution of temperature in the rectum of about 4°. (Wright 1874, 1043)

These results may at least partly account for the fact that Wright went no further with his research on diacetylmorphine, a substance that attracted no further attention for more than 20 years. Then, in 1897, a researcher at the Aktiengesellschaft Farbenfabriken pharmaceutical company (later to become the giant pharmaceutical manufacturer, Bayer), Felix Hoffmann, turned his attention to the same line of research as that pursued by Wright. He rediscovered essentially the same chemical and pharmacological properties as those observed by Wright and Pierce, but also saw the marketing potential for the new drug. Heroin was about twice as efficacious as morphine and it appeared at first to have none of the addictive properties of the natural opiate. Aktiengesellschaft Farbenfabriken began an aggressive advertising campaign for its new product (named *heroin*, after the German word *heroisch*, for "heroic") based on its efficacy and safety. It was recommended as a substitute for morphine and used as a constituent in cough syrups. In perhaps its most optimistic recommendation, the company even suggested that heroin could be used to wean morphine addicts off the natural opiate, a claim that very quickly turned out not to be true (Durlacher 2000).

Some other important semisynthetic opioids are buprenorphine, etorphine, hydrocodone, hydromorphone, oxycodone, oxymorphone. The oldest of these products is oxymorphone, first synthesized in Germany in 1914, but not made available in the United States until 1959. It is made from the opium constituent thebaine. A second semisynthetic opioid, oxycodone was also produced in Germany two years later by chemists Martin Freund and Edmund Speyer. Oxycodone was also first made from thebaine and became available in the United States in 1939. Hydrocodone was first prepared in 1920 by German chemists Carl Mannich and Helene Löwenheim. The drug was marketed by the pharmaceutical firm of Knoll four years later under the name of Dicodid. It was approved for sale in the United States in 1943. Both hydrocodone and oxycodone are derivatives of codeine.

Hydromorphone was first synthesized in 1924, also by researchers at Knoll, which marketed the drug under the name of Dilaudid two years later. Hydromorphone is a derivative of morphine, synthesized by adding hydrogen to one of the ketone groups in morphine. Etorphine was first produced in 1960. Its synthesis is somewhat unusual in that it is made from oripavine, a constituent of opium poppy straw, rather than from the poppy seed itself.

Etorphine is up to 3,000 times as strong as morphine and is currently legal in the United States only for veterinary uses. The discovery of buprenorphine was announced in 1972 as the result of a targeted research program at the Reckitt & Coleman pharmaceutical company (now Reckitt Benckiser) to find a safer version of heroin. The most important use of buprenorphine today is for the treatment of addiction to other opioids. (For a good general introduction to semisynthetic opioids, see "Opiates and Opioids" 2014.)

Synthetic Opioids

The first synthetic opioid to have been discovered was pethidine, also known as meperidine. It was first prepared by German chemist Otto Eisleb (also given as Eislib) in 1932. Eisleb was actually looking for an anticholinergic/antispasmodic agent (a substance that interrupts nerve action), and did not realize that his new drug might have other applications. The most important of those applications, as an opium-like analgesic agent, was later discovered by German chemist Otto Schaumann in 1939 (Michaelis, Schölkens, and Rudolphi 2007). The drug was given the trade name of Dolantin, but has since become better known as Demerol. Today, nearly 150 synthetic opioids have been discovered and described, including such familiar compounds as fentanyl, methadone, propoxyphene, sufentanil, and tramadol, a naturally occurring opioid that is almost always made synthetically for commercial purposes ("Overview: Opioids, Opioid Antagonists" 2015; "Synthetic, Opioids" 2015).

Rising Concerns about the Opioids

In spite of all the research on opioids taking place in the 19th century, the fact remained that morphine was generally the most accessible, the most efficacious, and the most popular drug used for chronic severe pain and for dysentery. Yet, it continued to become obvious that morphine and other opium products were far from being safe medications in many instances. This problem began to reach the halls of Congress at the turn of the century, as the volume of opium products being imported to the United States began to rise dramatically, and the number of men and women addicted to the drugs began to grow exponentially.

At a hearing before the Ways and Means Committee of the U.S. House of Representatives in December 1910 and January 1911, for example, committee members were astounded to hear experts on drug use recite the statistics of drug importation in preceding decades. According to one witness, Christopher Koch, vice president of the State Pharmaceutical Examining Board of Pennsylvania, the United States imported 1,425,196 pounds of opium in the decade from 1860 to 1869 and 6,435,623 pounds in the decade from 1900 to 1909, an increase of 351 percent. Between the same two periods, the U.S. population had grown by only 133 percent ("Importation and Use of Opium" 1911, 70). For purposes of comparison, Koch pointed out, the United States imported about 13 times as much opium per person during the period in question as the total amount of the drug imported by four countries in Europe (Austria, Germany, Italy, and the Netherlands) ("Importation and Use of Opium" 1911, 71).

Perhaps the most striking fact that was becoming apparent about the opium problem in the United States was the description of the average user. In the immediate years after the end of the Civil War, that user was most likely to be a veteran of the war who had become addicted to opium as a result of injuries or illness during the war. By some estimates, as many as 400,000 returning veterans were afflicted with opium addiction, a condition that came to be known as "the soldier's disease" ("Soldier's Disease" 2011). But before long, it became apparent that, as those veterans began to die off, opium addiction became a problem for another, quite unsuspected, group of individuals: women.

Opium Addiction among the Chinese and Other Immigrants

The turn-of-the-century characterization of opium users tended to focus on two groups, Chinese immigrants and Native Americans. Members of the first group began arriving on the West Coast of the United States in the mid-1850s, at first to pursue their fortunes in the gold rush taking place in California and Nevada, and later to take on many of the most difficult jobs in railroad construction. Not surprisingly, Chinese men brought with them the custom of smoking opium so popular in their native land. The problem became so serious among native Americans that local communities began passing laws prohibiting the smoking of opium, in general, and the existence of opium dens, where such activities took place, specifically. San Francisco was the first such municipality to adopt such a law when the board of supervisors adopted an opium ordinance on November 15, 1875, the first antidrug law in the United States. The law did not ban the sale, importation, or use of opium, but did restrict its use to so-called opium dens. Similar legislation was soon adopted by other municipalities with Chinese populations and, in 1879, the state of California adopted an amendment to its constitution prohibiting the hiring of Chinese men and women by both private and public entities (Ahmad 2000, 2011; Dial 2013).

A great deal has been written about the "Chinese opium problem" on the West Coast in the late 19th century. An important element in the story was the involvement of leading businessmen, politicians, members of the mass media, and other leaders of the community who, for reasons of their own, mounted a campaign against the foreign Chinese, employing their use of the "dread drug" opium to support their complaints. Perhaps the best-known example of this campaign was William Randolph Hearst, who entered the publishing business in 1887 when he acquired control of the *San Francisco Examiner*. Over the next decade, Hearst built a publishing empire of 30 newspapers with a circulation of more than 20,000,000 readers. He was so successful, at least in part, because of its promotion of so-called *yellow journalism*, a type of journalism that made use of bold statements that was not necessarily (and often was not) based on any factual information. Hearst's papers relied on bold, sometimes outrageous, headlines and striking cartoons to stake a position on controversial issues of the day.

In the case of the Chinese and opium smoking, Hearst's papers warned of the growing "yellow peril" resulting from the influx of Chinese laborers to the United States, who brought with them the socially and physically dangerous practice of opium smoke. They told horror stories of Chinese men crazed by opium attacking, molesting, and stealing white women for all types of immoral and unspeakable purposes. Such representations of the Chinese were, of course, a key factor in the ultimate imposition of prohibitions on opium use in many parts of the nation, along with a growing spread of racist attitudes about the Chinese who were thought to be responsible for the problem (Dormandy 2012, Chapter 18; Goldberg and Latimer 2014, Chapter 9; Hearst's papers were later to use the threat of marijuana addition to stoke resentment against and hatred of both Mexican immigrants and African Americans; see Herer 2010, Chapter 4).

The controversy occurring on the West Coast about the use of opium at the end of the 19th century was also being played out on the East Coast, sometimes involving Chinese immigrants, but also including immigrants from Europe. Many of these immigrants arrived in the United States with few, if any, chances for earning a living and adapting to their new homes.

One avenue of escape for what had become a hopeless way of life for many young immigrants from Ireland, Italy, and other parts of the continent was opium smoking (Courtwright 2001; "Medication-Assisted Treatment for Opioid Addiction in Opioid Treatment Programs" 2005).

The second group that drew attention for problems involving opium smoking were Native Americans, who were largely drawn into the habit through contact with Chinese entrepreneurs who saw an opportunity to make a living by means other than hard labor. The opium trade was also advantageous for Native Americans also, who were generally forbidden from purchasing alcohol or drugs through other channels, and essentially had no choice other than to do business with their Chinese compatriots (Hua 2012, 34).

Opium Addiction among Women

With the barrage of "news" from the press about opium addiction among the Chinese, Native Americans, and other immigrant groups, many Americans at the beginning of the 20th century might well have viewed that problem as someone else's concern, that is, an issue affecting men (usually) and women who had come to this country from another culture, bringing their drug habits with them. Opium addiction may not have appeared to be a problem for "real" Americans. Yet, scholars who had studied the problem of drug addiction already knew that such was not the case, that the typical opium addict in the United States was not a Chinese immigrant or a recent arrival from Ireland or Italy, but a middle-aged white woman living in a rural setting (Kandall 1998; Whitebread 1995).

The fact that women were generally more likely to become addicted to opium than men was a matter of great interest to researchers and other observers as early as the mid-19th century. A number of reasons were suggested for this pattern. Sometimes, it appeared that women were simply too tired, exhausted from a life of work greater than they could endure. As a result, they turned to opium for an escape from their reality. In

1867, for example, American author Fitz Hugh Ludlow mentioned "our weary sewing-women" as being prime candidates for opium addiction (Ludlow 1867, 387). Too often, observers suggested, women simply had to work so hard that they needed the relief of drugs to get through their lives. As one author put it, some women "whose business or whose vices make special demands on their nervous systems," such as "women obliged by their necessities to work beyond their strength," may eventually become abusers of opium (Day 1868, 7). In other instances, women may have a level of discouragement with their lives that they were not able to deal with without the crutch of addictive drugs. For example, Ludlow referred in his essay to the number of "disappointed wives" who turned to opium for consolation (Ludlow 1867, 387). Indeed, one of the findings that stand out most prominently is the frequency of opium addiction among middle-aged women in rural areas, women who had little or no social company and who perhaps saw little meaning in their own lives. As Dr. F. E. Oliver wrote in his report to the Massachusetts State Board of Health in 1872,

> Doomed, often, to a life of disappointment, and, it may be, of physical and mental inaction, and in the smaller and more remote towns, not unfrequently, to utter seclusion, deprived of all wholesome social diversion, it is not strange that nervous depression, with all its concomitant evils, should sometimes follow,-opium [sic] being discreetly selected as the safest and most agreeable remedy. (Oliver 1872)

Yet another factor leading to opium addiction among women was the use of the drug to treat a physical malady. Although many writers of the time felt that this etiology for opium addiction was understandable among women—after all, they were the weaker sex and subject to all manner of medical problems for which opium was a logical treatment—the number of cases of opium addiction due strictly to the medical use of the drug was surprisingly small (see, e.g., Terry and Pellens 1928, Chapter 3, Etiology).

(The study cited here, The Opium Problem, was one of the most important studies of opium addiction in the early-20th-century United States. It was conducted by physician Charles E. Terry and his wife, Mildred Pellens. Although it appeared somewhat later in the period [1928], the study revealed a host of information about the use and misuse of opium in the United States in the last decade of the 19th century and the first two decades of the 20th century. It attempted to determine the extent of "the opium problem" in the United States, how the problem developed, the problem's etiology (its causes), the general nature of opium addiction, its characteristic pathology, its symptomatology, the types of users, treatment modalities, and international, national, state, and local control of the problem. The authors of the report reviewed more than 4,000 distinct studies of all aspects of "the opium problem" in the United States and summarized their result in a document that ran more than a thousand pages in length. The study is an invaluable resource on almost all aspects of the opium problem in the United States during the time period discussed here.)

Opium Availability

One of the striking features of the opium problem in the late 1800s and early 1900s was the ready availability of opium and marijuana. For anyone living in the 2010s, it might be difficult to imagine a time when a person could walk into a drugstore and purchase opium products over the counter, without prescription or any other type of restriction. Yet there were no federal laws prohibiting the use of at least some forms of opium until 1970 (although state and local laws were enacted earlier than that) ("Laws" 2013). Physicians and pharmacists routinely gave out opium products, and private citizens could purchase such products at the local drugstore without a problem, providing at least one explanation as to why opium addiction appeared to be a growing problem at the beginning of the 20th century.

Statistics summarized by Terry and Pellens confirmed the ready availability of opium and opium products in the United States from the mid-19th century to the date of the report (1928). As Table 1.1 shows, imports of opium and opium products routinely ranged from a third of a million pounds to more than half a million pounds year after year from 1870 to 1915. Import numbers began to change at that point largely because of new federal legislation concerning the importation of opium, as discussed in the following table. (Note: The years with the highest volume of imports, not shown in the table, were 1897, with 1,072,914 pounds of raw opium imported, and 1920, with 730,272 pounds. See table reference.) Until federal legislation began to appear in the mid-1910s, there was obviously plenty of opium available for general use in the United States.

Patent Medicines

One of the most common methods by which an individual could obtain opium and opium products during the period under discussion was through patent medicines. The term *patent medicine* dates to at least the early 18th century when King George I of England granted a "letter patent" to a businessman named Benjamin Okell for the manufacture and sale of a product called Dr. Bateman's Pectoral Drops. As with all later patent medicines, the product consisted of a variable combination and concentration of substances, primarily opium, aniseed, and camphor (http://thequackdoctor.com/index.php/barclays-dr-batemans-pectoral-drops/2009). It was recommended for a number of complaints, including "Colds, Agues, Fevers, Colics, Melancholy, and Rickets; but also in curing those great and implacable Enemies of our Health and Ease, the Gout, Rheumatism, Jaundice, Stone, Gravel, and Astma's" ("A Short Treatise" 1725).

Patent medicines soon became popular both in Great Britain and in the United States, where they were sold over-the-counter

Table 1.1 Importation of Opium and Related Products, 1850–1925, in Pounds

Year	Crude Opium	Opium for Smoking	Opium for Consumption	Smoking Opium for Consumption	Morphine for Consumption	Other Opioids for Consumption
1850	130,349					
1855	111,229		107,632			
1860	119,525		116,686			
1865	110,470	13,703	96,099	31,918	172	
1870	254,609		121,185	12,603	3,187	
1875	305,136		188,239	62,775	4,252	
1880	533,451		243,211	77,196	19,386	
1885	351,609	37,475	351,609	37,475	20,310	
1890	473,095	34,465	380,621	58,982	19,954	
1895	358,455	139,765	357,981	115,709	16,029	
1900	544,938	142,479	537,004	129,335	26,208	
1905	594,680	159,380	456,523	144,997	21,390	
1910	449,239		439,378		13,082	22,970
1915	484,027		391,938		1,385	8,676
1920	211,277		225,528		4,000	6,522
1925	96,848		96,848			65,365

Source: Table V. Importation of Opium and Opium Preparations to the United States for the Years 1850–1924. The Opium Problem. http://babel.hathitrust.org/cgi/pt?id=mdp.39015006502523;view=1up;seq=70. Accessed on April 17, 2015.

(OTC) in drugstores without prescription as treatment for virtually every disease and medical condition that could be imagined. They became wildly popular among the general population, partly because of their perceived efficacy and partly because of the ingredients they contained (alcohol, opium, and cocaine, most commonly), which almost guaranteed some level of success among users. The most common component of most patent medicines was alcohol, which constituted anywhere from 10 to 44 percent of many popular patent medicines (Agnew 2014, 119). Opium was also present in the vast majority of patent medicines. As Terry and Pellens observed in their 1928 report,

> [p]ractically all remedies advertised for painful conditions, such as consumption [tuberculosis], coughs and colds, pelvic conditions of women, cancer, rheumatism and neuralgia, as well as soothing syrups for babies, and diarrhoea and cholera mixtures contained opium or some of its products and depended primarily on these drugs for such virtues as they possessed. (Terry and Pellens 1928, 75)

It was hardly surprising, the authors went on then, to find that "many persons became dependent on these preparations and later turned to the active drug itself when accidentally or otherwise they learned of its presence in the "medicine" they had been taking" (Terry and Pellens 1928, 75; patent medicines are a popular topic among researchers and many good sources are available; see, e.g., "Balm of America: Patent Medicine Collection" 2015; Hodgson 2001; Young 2015).

Legislative Responses

As noted earlier, some municipalities and states had adopted laws prohibiting or regulating the importation and/or use of opium as early as 1875. The federal government also made some desultory attempts at controlling the use of opium during the last quarter of the 19th century. The first such action came about in 1887 as the result of a treaty about the use of opium made with China seven years earlier. According to the 1887 law, Chinese residents of the United States were not allowed to import opium or morphine into this country, and Americans living in China were not allowed to import those products into China (Ahmad 2011, 78; Terry and Pellens 1928, 747–48). U.S. citizens living in the United States were exempt from the law's provisions. In 1890, the law was extended to prohibit the manufacture by Chinese in the United States of opium products for smoking, although the law again did not apply to American citizens ("The History of Drug Laws" 2015).

The first important breakthrough in legislation to deal with opium-related problems for all Americans was passage of the Pure Food and Drugs Act of 1906 (P.L. 59-384, 34 Stat. 768). The purpose of the law was to prevent "the manufacture, sale, or transportation of adulterated or misbranded or poisonous or deleterious foods, drugs, medicines, and liquors, and for regulating traffic therein" ("An Act of June 30, 1906" 1906). Among the reforms included in the law were new restrictions on the labeling of patent medicines, with the aim of letting consumers have a better idea as to the ingredients included in such drugs, along with more rigorous restrictions on the substances that could be used in the manufacture of patent medicines. Passage of the Pure Food and Drugs Act took 29 years, the first version of the bill having been introduced in 1879. However, as critical as the act turned out to be in many ways for most foods and drugs, it was only marginally successful in dealing with the problem of patent medicines, as manufacturers found ways to work around the new regulations to continue producing products with marginal efficacy and safety (Bailey 1930; Fee 2010; Goldberg 2003, 75). Possibly the most important long-term consequence of adoption of the Pure Food and Drugs Act was the creation of the FDA, which continues to be today the nation's single most important agencies dealing with all aspects of legal and illegal drug use.

Passage of the Pure Food and Drugs Act was an indication of the growing concerns in the United States about the harmful effects of opium, morphine, codeine, and other opiates. That concern eventually took on an international flavor as a small group of politicians and religious leaders petitioned President Theodore Roosevelt to call for an international conference about the growing threat of narcotic drugs to the United States and the need for international action to deal with this threat. As a result of this concern, Roosevelt called for the creation of an international commission on narcotics trade, scheduled to meet in Shanghai from February 5 to 26, 1909. The commission expected originally to deal primarily with the opium trade in China, although discussions very soon evolved to include a much broader canvas, essentially the problems of drug trade throughout the world. In addition, the commission expanded its original charge to include a new non-opioid drug of growing concern, cocaine ("A Century of International Drug Control" 2009; Lowes 1966).

(The strong moral flavor of the U.S. stance against opiates—in contrast to the many possible medical consequences—was reflected in the composition of the U.S. delegation to the Shanghai meeting. It consisted of Charles Henry Brent, Episcopalian bishop in western New York state and the Philippines, and physician Hamilton Wright and pharmacist Henry J. Finger, both of whom had been and continued to be strong advocates in the battle against all types of drug use in the United States, a campaign they conducted for the sake of retaining "ethnic purity" in the nation [see, e.g., Davenport-Hines 2002, Chapter 7; Downs 2013; Gieringer 2015]).

In planning for the Shanghai meeting, organizers were careful to point out that the session would not be a formal international conference with the authority to write a binding treaty, but an advisory group whose objective it was to learn more about the opium problem and to make recommendations for future actions. The follow-up to the Shanghai meeting, then, was just such a conference, the First International

Opium Convention, held at The Hague, the Netherlands, December 1, 1911, to January 23, 1912. On the latter date, attendees adopted a proposed treaty consisting of 6 chapters and 25 articles, dealing not only with opium and morphine, the original drugs of concern, but also with cocaine and heroin, which had received increasing attention during the Shanghai meeting. The conference was hardly an "international" event in the true sense of the word since it was attended by only 13 nations who were most affected by the Chinese opium problem, China itself, France, Germany, Italy, Japan, the Netherlands, Persia, Portugal, Russia, Siam, the United Kingdom, British India, and the United States. The treaty took effect in 1915 when it was ratified by the required five nations, China, Honduras, the Netherlands, Norway, and the United States. It was adopted by most other powers in 1919 when its provisions were incorporated into the Treaty of Versailles, ending World War I ("A Century of International Drug Control" 2009, 50–51; also see Bewley-Taylor 1999).

One of the provisions of the Hague treaty, mentioned in four different articles of the document, was a requirement that signatories to the treaty take such actions as might be necessary to control the manufacture, sale, use, importation, and exportation of opium, morphine, cocaine, and their respective salts ("Suppression of Abuse of Opium and Other Drugs" 1912). In the United States, this provision was met by means of an act of Congress known as the Harrison Narcotic Act of 1914. The act was proposed and adopted not only to meet the requirements of the treaty but also as the first step by the U.S. government to aggressively control the use of opium and opiates in the country.

The act itself seemed somewhat routine, laying out a system for monitoring and controlling the flow of opium products through the U.S. economy. It required anyone who handled opium products in any way—by importing, selling, prescribing, manufacturing, or exporting, for example—to license their business with the federal government and to pay a modest tax for conducting that business. It specifically confirmed the right of physicians to use opiate products in their own practice (King 1953).

Execution of the Harrison Act turned out to be an exercise entirely different from that laid out in the original bill and, perhaps, from the Congress's intention. The U.S. Department of Justice apparently decided to use the provisions of the act to *de facto* define opium and opiate addiction as a type of criminal behavior, rather than a medical problem. It systematically set out to violate the act's stated intent to allow physicians to use opium and opiates to treat addicts therapeutically and to make such behavior criminal behavior equivalent to that of opium patients. In one of the most passionate expressions of this interpretation of post-Harrison history, Rufus King, at the time special counsel to the subcommittee of the U.S. House Committee on the Judiciary to Investigate the Department of Justice and special counsel to the Investigations Subcommittee of the Senate Interstate Commerce Committee, wrote:

> In sum, the Narcotics Division succeeded in creating a very large criminal class for itself to police (i.e., the whole doctor-patient-addict-peddler community), instead of the very small one that Congress had intended (the smuggler and the peddler). Subsequent Division officials have sustained the enforcement-oriented propaganda barrage: the addict is a criminal, a criminal type, or laden with criminal tendencies. Addicts can only be dealt with by being tracked down and isolated from society in total confinement; the cure-all is more arrests and stiffer criminal penalties for all narcotics offenders; and anyone who raises a dissenting voice is most likely a bungling "dogooder" or one who wants to undermine the foundations of our society. (King 1953, unpaginated text)

This observation is of considerable importance because it clarifies the attitude that the U.S. government has, for the most part, taken about drug abuse, essentially since the adoption of the Harrison Act in 1914 (see also Brecher and the Editors of Consumer Reports 1972, Chapter 8; Hickman 2007, Chapter 4; Morgan 1981, Chapters 6 and 7).

The history of federal narcotics legislation in the 20th century, then, is a fascinating chronicle of efforts to reduce or eliminate the illegal (and sometimes legal) use of opium and its derivatives by a variety of mechanisms, sometimes just short of simply declaring the possession and use of those products as being against the law. Instead, the government usually took the course of banning the importation or exportation of opium and its derivatives, the manufacture or transportation of those products, or their sale or purchase. In addition, federal laws at first tended to make a distinction between opium and opiates that were intended for purely recreational purposes—that is, smoking—in contrast to its medicinal uses (although as the Harrison experience showed, such distinctions became more and more murky very early on).

The first federal law formulated on this approach was actually adopted shortly before the Harrison Act. It was the Smoking Opium Exclusion of 1909, which adopted in the spirit of negotiations occurring simultaneously at the Shanghai opium meetings. The act explained in the introduction that its purpose was to "prohibit the importation and use of opium for other than medicinal purposes," a goal it intended to achieve by banning the importation of any form of opium that could be used or converted into "smoking opium." At the same time, all medical uses of opium and opium products were specifically excluded from the act ("Comparison of the Tariffs of 1897 and 1909" 1910).

Throughout the rest of the century, the federal government struggled with a variety of ways for dealing with the nation's "drug problem." That problem gradually evolved over the years to involve a wider range of drugs, such as cocaine, heroin, marijuana, and a host of synthetic drugs, to which the government responded, usually with more severe penalties for trafficking and use, and sometimes with more aggressive treatment and prevention programs. Some of the most important laws that were adopted over this period were the following:

Heroin Act of 1924 banned the manufacture, importation, possession, and use of heroin for any reason whatsoever in the United States, including all medical applications. Heroin remains the only opiate drug that is banned for all purposes in the United States today (Davies 2001; hearings and testimony about the original bill are available at "Prohibiting the Importation of Opium for the Manufacture of Heroin," hearings before the Committee on Ways and Means of the House of Representatives, on H.R. 7079, April 3, 1924.)

Narcotic Drug Import and Export Act of 1922 extended the existing ban on the import and export of opium products, but added cocaine to the list of prohibited substances. A limited number of exceptions were allowed for legitimate medical use. The act also created the Federal Narcotics Control Board to carry out provisions of this and all previous drug control legislation (Quinn and McLaughlin 1973, 597; for provisions of the law, see "Regulations under the Narcotic Drugs Import and Export Act" 1939, 1064–84).

Uniform State Narcotic Act of 1932 was proposed and passed as an effort to bring drug laws in all states into conformity with each other. The law was drafted with the input of a number of medical and pharmaceutical organizations, but was largely shaped by the Federal Narcotics Control Board. The act was eventually adopted by all 50 states and has been updated and renewed a number of times since its adoption (Baumohl 2011; "Controlled Substances Act Summary" 2015).

Boggs Act of 1951 became law on November 2, 1951. It represented a dramatic increase in the severity of penalties for possession and use of and trafficking in narcotic drugs and, for the first time, marijuana. This was occasioned by general concern among legislators and the general public about the increase in illegal drug use after World War II. The act differed from preceding bills in a number of ways, one of which was the lumping of marijuana with opiate drugs for the first time. In addition, the penalties for illegal drug use were increased by about fourfold, with a minimum mandatory sentence of 2 years for simple possession of marijuana, cocaine, or heroin, with a maximum sentence of 5 years; a minimum of 5 years and a maximum of 10 years for a second offense; and a minimum of 10 years and a maximum of 15 years for a third offense. The act was also significant in that it provides, for the first time in federal law, mandatory minimum sentencing, removing from judicial discretion the possibility of any less severe punishments (Erlen and Spillane 2004, 76–92). Another effect of the Boggs Act was the passage by a number of states of similar "mini-Boggs" legislation over succeeding years, many of which imposed even more stringent penalties for drug use (Bonnie and Whitebread 1970, 1074–6). Finally, the Boggs Act was significant because it specifically recognized the growing threat of drug abuse by young people, a group of drug users who had largely been ignored prior to the time (Bonnie and Whitebread 1970, 1064–6).

Narcotic Control Act of 1956 continued the trend of increasingly severe penalties for trafficking in and use of illegal drugs. Also introduced by Representative Hale Boggs (Boggs Act of 1951), the Narcotic Control Act reflected congressional concern that judges were still being too lenient in sentencing drug abusers and eliminated the possibility of suspending sentences or granting parole. One authority in the field of drug history has called the law "the most punitive and repressive anti-narcotics legislation ever adopted by Congress" (McWilliams 1990, 116; also see Cameron and Dillinger 2011; King 1972, Chapter 16).

Drug Abuse Control Amendment of 1965 was passed primarily in response to concerns about the illicit use of certain types of drugs, such as depressants, stimulants, and hallucinogens that were then legal to use for medical purposes and had not yet been declared illegal for recreational purposes (King 1972, Chapter 26).

Controlled Substance Act of 1970

The Controlled Substance Act of 1970 is perhaps the most important single piece of drug legislation in the history of the United States. The immediate impetus for the legislation was a ruling by the U.S. Supreme Court that crucial parts of the Marihuana Tax Act of 1937 were unconstitutional. Although the Court's decision did not speak to opium control laws specifically, it did raise questions about the type of drug laws the Congress had been passing over the preceding decades. In commenting on the situation, President Lyndon Johnson remarked in a 1968 speech before Congress that "present Federal laws dealing with these substances are a crazy quilt of inconsistent approaches and widely disparate criminal sanctions" ("Special Message to the Congress on Crime and Law Enforcement" 1968).

In response to such concerns, the Congress passed the Comprehensive Drug Abuse Prevention and Control Act of 1970, which President Richard M. Nixon then signed on October 27, 1970. The act had three sections that dealt with rehabilitation programs, control and enforcement, and importation and exportation of drugs. The act was designed to simplify and clarify the morass of drug laws that had been accumulating over the previous six decades.

The initial section on rehabilitation programs was especially interesting, since that aspect of drug abuse had received relatively little attention in previous legislation. But the second section turned out to have the most significant impact on federal drug laws to the present day. In that section, five categories ("schedules") of drugs were created. Each drug was assigned to one of those five categories depending on three criteria: (1) a drug's potential for abuse, (2) its value in accepted medical treatment in the United States, and (3) its safety when used under medical supervision. Thus substances placed in Schedule I are those that (1) have a high potential for abuse, (2) have no currently accepted use for medical treatments in the

United States, and (3) cannot be safely used even under appropriate medical supervision. Drugs traditionally regarded as the most dangerous—cocaine, the opiates, marijuana—are classified under Schedule I of the act. Other examples of Schedule I drugs today are LSD (lysergic acid diethylamide), mescaline, peyote, and psilocybin.

In contrast to Schedule I drugs, substances listed in Schedule V: (1) have minimal potential for abuse, (2) have accepted medical applications in the United States, and (3) are generally regarded as safe to use under medical supervision (although they may lead to addiction). Examples of Schedule V drugs are certain cough medications that contain small amounts of codeine and products used to treat diarrhea that contain small amounts of opium. In the first announcement of scheduled drugs in the Federal Register in 1971, 59 substances were listed in Schedule I, 21 in Schedule II, 22 in Schedule III, 11 in Schedule IV, and 5 in Schedule V (Convention on Pscyhotropic Substances, 1971 2015). As of late 2015, there were 783 drugs on the schedules, 347 in Schedule I, 170 in Schedule II, 103 in Schedule III, 75 in Schedule IV, and 88 in Schedule V (Controlled Substances 2015).

The federal government has continued to adopt legislation dealing with all aspects of the drug abuse issue, some fine-tuning penalties for possession, use, and trafficking of illegal drugs, and others relating to the prevention and treatment of drug addiction and with programs of drug education. A useful summary of those laws can be found at "Laws" (2013). Individual states have also passed a very large number of drug laws that supplement federal laws. A good listing of those laws is available at "State Drug Possession Laws" (2015).

The Evolution of Prescription Drugs

If one defines a *prescription* as a set of written instructions for the preparation of a medicine or medical treatment, then prescriptions have existed since the beginning of human civilization.

As noted previously in this chapter, clay tablets dating back to at least 2600 BCE include dozens of prescriptions for the treatment of a variety of injuries and illnesses (Teall 2013). One of the best known of the ancient records is the so-called Ebers Papyrus in Egypt, dating to about 1500 BCE. That document contains more than 800 prescriptions that make use of at least 700 different drugs (Bender 1965, #2–#4); for an older, but highly recommended reference, also see Wall 1917; also see Greene and Watkins 2012 for a good historical review of the history of prescriptions). The abbreviation by which prescriptions are denoted even today, R_X, is thought to have originated in ancient Egypt, as an icon for the god Horus; in Greece, for the god Jupiter; or in Rome, as an abbreviation for the term *receptum*, meaning "recipe" or "receipt" (Greene and Watkins 2012, 5).

For much of early history, prescriptions were probably written out and executed by medicine men, shaman, wise women, physicians, pharmacists, druggists, apothecaries, and other specialists in the field of healing. In many cases, little distinction was made as to which individual or profession was responsible for which part of the writing and executing actions. Some historians date the separation of medicine (the writing of prescriptions) and pharmacy (the execution or "filling" of prescriptions) to the third century CE when twin brothers of Arabian descent, Cosmas and Damian (both later sanctified by the Roman Catholic Church) consolidated the fields of medicine (Cosmas) and pharmacology (Damian) (La Wall 1934).

The development of the field of pharmacy and the use of prescriptions and prescription drugs is a long and complex story, of limited relevance to this book. That is, such was the case until 1938, when the FDA was granted authority in the Federal Food, Drug, and Cosmetic Act of 1938 to more diligently monitor and regulate the release and use of new synthetic compounds, whether used in foods, drugs, or cosmetics. The congressional action was driven to a large extent by a medical disaster that occurred in 1937 when more than a hundred people in 15 states died after taking a new formulation of the antibiotic medicine prescribed for them, a product called Massengill's Elixir Sulfanilamide. As it later developed, the solvent used in making the drug, diethylene glycol, was deadly poisonous, although it had not been tested before the new drug was released (Ballentine 1981; "An Interview with Mr. George P. Larrick" 1968; Marks 1995). At least partly in response to this tragedy, the Congress gave the FDA a relatively free hand in doing whatever it felt was necessary to improve the safety of drugs (and foods and cosmetics) made available to the American public. In following what the FDA believed was Congress's intent to take a firmer stance on the prescribing of drugs (which it almost certainly was), the agency announced a new regulation in 1940 requiring all drugs deemed not safe for self-medication to be clearly labeled "Caution: To be used only by or on the prescription of a physician" ("History of Federal Regulation" 2015; similar actions had been taken somewhat earlier in Great Britain when the Venereal Disease Act of 1917 first defined the meaning of "prescription drugs" in the United Kingdom ["History of Pharmacy" 2015]).

The 1940 action by the FDA did not completely resolve the question about ensuring the safety of certain types of drugs. The problem was that some drug manufacturers were making and selling the same drug, sometimes as an OTC drug and sometimes as prescription drug. (Some companies were even producing the same drug under both designations.) Pharmacists themselves became concerned about their legal liability in such a confused state of affairs since they could be prosecuted for selling a drug that was designated as "prescription-only" but which had been supplied to them by a company as "OTC."

In 1948, Paul Dunbar, president of the National Association of Retail Druggists, brought this issue to the attention of his colleagues and of federal legislators. He pointed to the particular and growing problem of certain "prescription-only" drugs that were increasingly sold OTC, without prescription. The two classes of drugs that most commonly fell into this category were stimulant amphetamines and sedative barbiturates ("An Interview with Mr. George P. Larrick" 1968, 1). Dunbar called for new legislation that would definitively clarify the status of "prescription-only" drugs and the rights and responsibilities of dispensing pharmacists.

This call for action occurred at just the right time, as a court case of fundamental importance was working its way through the courts. That case involved pharmacist Mark Sullivan, owner of Sullivan's Pharmacy in Columbus, Georgia. Sullivan had purchased a supply of sulfathiazole which, at the time, was a very popular short-acting sulfa drug used against a wide range of gram-positive and gram-negative pathogenic microorganisms. Sullivan eventually resold sulfathiazole pills without including the cautionary label wording required by existing federal law. The case brought against him worked its way through the court system to the Supreme Court which, on January 19, 1948, ruled that Sullivan's actions were illegal (*United States v. Sullivan*, 332 U.S. 689 1948).

Pharmacists and legislators were still concerned that the status of "prescription-only" drugs was not entirely clear, relying only on administrative rules and the Supreme Court decision. As a consequence, the U.S. Congress took up legislation to clarify (finally?!) the status of such drugs. That legislation took the form of the Durham-Humphrey Amendment to the Food, Drug, and Cosmetics Act of 1938, an amendment that was passed in 1951 and took effect in 1952. The amendment first clarified the type of drug to which the legislation applied, namely one that is (1) a habit-forming drug, (2) not safe for use except under the supervision of a medical practitioner, or (3) limited to use under the professional supervision of a practitioner licensed by law to administer such drug. The amendment then specified the conditions under which such drugs could be sold, namely: (1) through a prescription written by a practitioner licensed by law to administer such drug, (2) by means of an oral prescription of such practitioner, which is reduced promptly to writing and filed by a pharmacist, or (3) by refilling any written or oral prescription that has been authorized by the prescriber ("The Durham-Humphrey Amendment" 1952; Strauss 1995, 158; a section of the Durham-Humphrey Amendment is reproduced in Chapter 5 of this book).

Prescription Drugs in the 21st Century

In the second decade of the 21st century, thousands of prescription drugs are available. These drugs can be classified into a number of categories based on the medical conditions for which their use is recommended. Some of those categories include drugs that can be used against a relatively wide variety of conditions, such as anti-infectives, antivirals, and gastrointestinal agents; others are designed to treat specific diseases, such as antimalarial agents, antituberculosis agents, and antiparkinsonian agents; still others are intended for specific body systems, such as cardiovascular agents, genitourinary tract agents, and dermatological agents; and others are recommended for the treatment of physical, mental, or emotional conditions, such as anticonvulsants, antipsychotics, and nutritional substances (for a complete list of prescription drugs, see "Drug Index A to Z" 2015).

Prescription drug use is now a common part of most Americans' lives, and is growing over the recent past. As Table 1.2 shows, nearly half of all Americans surveyed in the period between 2007 and 2010 said that they took at least one drug, with a third of them taking between one and four drugs and 10 percent taking five or more drugs on a daily basis. These data are very much age-related, with older individuals much more inclined to be taking prescription drugs on a regular basis.

The type of drugs now popular in the United States differs to some extent between those used by children and young adults and those used by older adults. One of the interesting trends apparent from Table 1.3 is the significant increase in the amount of antidepressants used by older adults (an increase of 381% among adults 19–64 years and 357% among adults

Table 1.2 Prescription Drug Use in the Past 30 Days in the United States during Three Time Periods (Percentage of Respondents)

Number of Drugs	1988–1994	1999–2002	2003–2006	2007–2010
No drugs	62.2	55.0	52.7	51.5
1–4 drugs	34.2	37.6	37.1	37.9
5 or more drugs	3.6	7.4	10.1	10.6

For 2007–2010

	Under 18 Years	18–44 Years	45–64 Years	Over 64 Years
No drugs	76.0	61.3	33.8	10.3
1–4 drugs	23.2	35.6	49.4	50.0
5 or more drugs	0.8	3.1	16.8	39.7

Source: Health, United States, 2013, With Special Feature on Prescription Drugs. 2014. Hyattsville, MD: National Center for Health Statistics, Data Table for Figure 22, 31.

Table 1.3 Prescription Drug Use in the Past 30 Days, by Age and Selected Drug Class: United States, 1988–1994 and 2007–2010

Age and Drug Class	1988–1994	2007–2010
Under 18 Years		
Antiasthmatics (asthma, allergies, breathing)	3.2	6.8
Antibiotics (bacterial infections)	10.1	6.1
Central nervous system stimulants (attention deficit disorder)	0.8	4.2
Analgesics (pain relief)	1.2	1.3
Antidepressants (depression and related disorders)	**	1.3
18–64 Years		
Cardiovascular agents (high blood pressure, heart disease, kidney disease)	10.0	17.7
Cholesterol-lowering drugs (high cholesterol)	1.6	10.7
Anti-acid reflux drugs (gastric reflux, ulcers)	3.0	9.0
Antidiabetic agents (diabetes)	2.4	5.3

Age and Drug Class	1988–1994	2007–2010
Anticoagulants (blood clot prevention)	0.7	1.8
Analgesics (pain relief)	8.6	10.5
Antidepressants (depression and related disorders)	2.2	10.6
65 Years and Over		
Cardiovascular agents (high blood pressure, heart disease, kidney disease)	51.5	70.2
Cholesterol-lowering drugs (high cholesterol)	5.9	46.7
Anti-acid reflux drugs (gastric reflux, ulcers)	7.5	21.5
Antidiabetic agents (diabetes)	9.0	18.4
Anticoagulants (blood clot prevention)	6.1	18.1
Analgesics (pain relief)	13.8	17.5
Antidepressants (depression and related disorders)	3.0	13.7

Source: Health, United States, 2013, With Special Feature on Prescription Drugs. 2014. Hyattsville, MD: National Center for Health Statistics, Data Table for Figure 21, 32.

over 65). Antidepressants are among the most popular prescription drugs now being used illegally by young adults.

An average of 435,891,857 prescriptions per month were written for drugs in the United States over the period from October 2013 through September 2014. The drug for which the greatest number of prescriptions were written in the United States during this period was the cholesterol-lowering drug rosuvastatin (Crestor; 22,279,247 prescriptions per month), which displaced the perennial leader in this category, levothyroxine (Synthroid; 22,258,461). The remaining drugs in the top 10 list were acid-reducer esomeprazole (Nexium; 17,763,935), asthma medications albuterol (Ventolin HFA; 17,745,136) and fluticasone propionate/salmeterol (Advair Diskus; 14,495,507), the insulin glargine injection (Lantus Solostar; 10,450,322), the attention-deficit drug lisdexamfetamine dimesylate (Vyvanse; 10,147,910), the antiepileptic drug pregabalin (Lyrica; 9,798,532), the chronic obstructive pulmonary disease medication tiotropium bromide (Spiriva Handihaler; 9,555,794), and the antihypertensive drug valsartan (Diovan; 9,470,735) (Brown 2014).

The list of most profitable drugs sold in the United States is very different from the list of most prescribed drugs because of the cost of individual drugs. In the period covered by the most recent report, the 10 drugs producing the greatest income for drug companies were the antipsychotic Abilify ($7,545,171,814 in sales), anti-inflammatory Humira ($6,732,549,721), hepatitis C antiviral Sovaldi ($6,707,188,529), Nexium ($6,140,633,073), Crestor ($5,771,965,582), the antiarthritic Enbrel ($5,294,762,089), Advair Diskus ($4,951,078,263), anti-inflammatory Remicade ($4,462,708,246), Lantus Solostar ($4,141,633,161), and anti-infective agent Neulasta ($3,773,342,168). The total amount spent on prescription drugs in the United States during the period of this study was $178,585,957,827 (Brown 2014).

For the purpose of this book, one of the most important statistics about prescription drug sales relates to the three categories most commonly abused, opioids, stimulants, and depressants. Between 1991 and 2011, the number of opioid prescriptions nearly tripled, from 76 million in the former year to 219 million in the latter year. The majority of those prescriptions were for hydrocodone and oxycodone (Volkow 2012, #8). During the same period of time, the number of prescriptions for stimulants—primarily methylphenidate and amphetamines—increased nearly 1,200 percent, from 4 million in 1991 to 51 million in 2011 (Volkow 2012, #12; comparable data are not available for depressants). The dramatic increase in the number of prescriptions written for these classes of drugs is almost certainly one factor in their role in the current prescription drug abuse problem.

Global figures for the number of prescriptions written and the profits made by various drugs vary somewhat from that for the United States, for the obvious reason that medical services and financial resources differ dramatically from country to country. According to the most recent data available, the top 10 prescription drugs worldwide, in terms of sales, were Humira (US$11.8 billion), Lantus (US$10.3 billion), Sovaldi (US$9.3 billion), Abilify (US$9.2 billion), Enbrel (US$8.7 billion), the antiasthmatic Seretide (US$8.6 billion), Crestor (US$8.4 billion), Remicade (US$8.1 billion), Nexium (US$7.6 billion), and the anticancer and antiautoimmune drug MabThera (US$6.5 billion) (Lindsley 2015).

Conclusion

The history of drugs is the story of efforts by members of the healing professions to find and use new substances that will bring relief to the myriad health problems to which humans are subject. Along with that endeavor has come the struggle to ensure that drugs are—to the extent possible—used for the purposes for which they were originally intended and not as the cause of additional medical and social problems with which humans have to deal, such as drug addiction. The story told in this chapter is a brief review of the gradual evolution of drug research, administrative rules, professional policies, legislative actions, and other methods of promoting the beneficial and legal uses of drugs and preventing or discouraging their recreational and harmful nonmedical uses. To a large extent, the barrier between these two applications of medicinal substances—curative and harmful—has gradually become more and more effective over time.

The early 21st century has seen a reversal in this trend. Probably for the first time in history, more and more individuals are finding ways to obtain and use drugs that have highly beneficial medical applications for purposes other than those intended by their manufacturers. Prescription drug abusers obtain from these medications most of the same mental, physical, and emotional experiences previously available only from illegal drugs such as heroin, opium, and cocaine. Unfortunately, they also experience a host of harmful side effects that may even include death. Chapter 2 of this book will explore in more detail the history of prescription drug abuse, its current status in the United States, its etiology and symptomology, and efforts that have been developed and recommended to deal with this new and serious issue of substance abuse.

References

"An Act of June 30, 1906, Public Law 59-384, 34 STAT 768, for Preventing the Manufacture, Sale, or Transportation of Adulterated or Misbranded or Poisonous or Deleterious Foods, Drugs, Medicines, and Liquors, and for Regulating Traffic Therein, and for Other Purposes." 1906. National Archives. http://research.archives.gov/description/5716297. Accessed on April 17, 2015.

Agnew, Jeremy. 2014. *Alcohol and Opium in the Old West: Use, Abuse, and Influence.* Jefferson, NC: McFarland & Company, Inc.

Ahmad, Diana. 2000. "Opium Smoking, Anti-Chinese Attitudes, and the American Medical Community, 1850–1890." *American Nineteenth Century History* 1 (2): 53–68.

Ahmad, Diana. 2011. *The Opium Debate and Chinese Exclusion Laws in the Nineteenth-Century American West.* Reno: University of Nevada Press.

Altman, Lawrence K. 1987. *Who Goes First?: The Story of Self-Experimentation in Medicine.* New York: Random House.

"American Druggist and Pharmaceutical Record." 1906. Google Digitized Version. https://books.google.com/book s?id=kFMgAQAAMAAJ&pg=RA1-PA135&lpg=RA1-PA 135&dq=laudanum+sydenham&source=bl&ots=GImKu UtSMq&sig=xWjjRk84jImA9QvDUUrPTYJtaiQ&hl=en

&sa=X&ei=3ZwqVejtCce5ogTPsoGICA&ved=0CEAQ6A
EwBQ#v=onepage&q=laudanum%20sydenham&f=false.
Accessed on April 12, 2015.

Anderson, Thomas. 1862. "On the Chemistry of Opium."
Journal of the Chemical Society 15: 446–55.

Arnaud, Celia Henry. 2014. "A Step toward Making
Painkillers without Poppies: Bioengineering: Modified
Yeast Produce Morphine and Semisynthetic Opioids
Starting from the Baine." *C&EN* 92 (35): 11.

Bailey, Thomas A. 1930. "Congressional Opposition to
Pure Food Legislation, 1879–1906." *American Journal of
Sociology* 36 (1): 52–64.

Ball, Philip. 2007. *The Devil's Doctor: Paracelsus and the World
of Renaissance Magic and Science*. London: Arrow.

Ballentine, Carol. 1981. "Taste of Raspberries, Taste of Death.
The 1937 Elixir Sulfanilamide Incident." *FDA Consumer
Magazine* 15: 18–21.

"Balm of America: Patent Medicine Collection."
2015. The National Museum of American History.
http://ahm.si.edu/collections/object-groups/balm-o
f-america-patent-medicine-collection?ogmt_page=balm-o
f-america-introduction. Accessed on April 17, 2015.

"Barclay's Dr. Bateman's Pectoral Drops." 2009. The
Quack Doctor. http://thequackdoctor.com/index.php/
barclays-dr-batemans-pectoral-drops/. Accessed on
April 17, 2015.

Baumohl, Jim. 2011. "Uniform State Narcotics Act." In Mark
A. R. Kleinman and James E. Hawdon, eds. *Encyclopedia of
Drug Policy*. Thousand Oaks, CA: Sage Publications.

Bender, George A. 1965. Great Moments in Pharmacy. *The
Stories and Paintings in the Series: A History of Pharmacy
in Pictures*. Detroit: Northwood Institute Press. http://
www.pharmacy.wsu.edu/history/A%20History%20

52 Prescription Drug Abuse

of%20Pharmacy%20in%20Pictures.pdf. Accessed on April 20, 2015.

Bewley-Taylor, David R. 1999. *The United States and International Drug Control, 1909–1997*. New York: Pinter.

Biggs, Robert D. 2006. "Medicine, Surgery, and Public Health in Ancient Mesopotamia." In Jack M. Sasson, ed. *Civilizations of the Ancient Near East*. Peabody, MA: Hendrickson Publishers. http://cis.uchicago.edu/outreach/summerinstitute/epidemics/readings/biggs_medicine.pdf. Accessed on April 9, 2015.

Bliss, Michael. 1999. *William Osler: A Life in Medicine*. Oxford; New York: Oxford University Press.

Bonnie, Richard J., and Charles H. Whitebread. 1970. "The Forbidden Fruit and the Tree of Knowledge: An Inquiry into the Legal History of American Marijuana Prohibition." *Virginia Law Review* 56 (6): 971–1203. http://www.votehemp.com/PDF/The_Forbidden_Fruit_and_The_Tree_of_Knowledge.pdf. Accessed on April 20, 2015.

Booth, Martin. 1998. *Opium: A History*. New York: St. Martin's Press.

Brecher, Edward M., and the Editors of Consumer Reports. 1972. *Licit and Illicit Drugs: The Consumers Union Report on Narcotics, Stimulants, Depressants, Inhalants, Hallucinogens, and Marijuana—Including Caffeine, Nicotine, and Alcohol*. Boston: Little, Brown.

Brown, Troy. 2014. "100 Most Prescribed, Best-Selling Branded Drugs through September." Medscape. http://www.medscape.com/viewarticle/834273. Accessed on April 22, 2015.

Burdock, George A. 2010. *Fenaroli's Handbook of Flavor Ingredients*, 6th ed. Boca Raton, FL: CRC Press/Taylor & Francis Group.

Cameron, Jennifer M., and Ronna J. Dillinger. 2011. "Narcotic Control Act." In Mark A. R. Kleinman and James E. Hawdon, eds. *Encyclopedia of Drug Policy.* Thousand Oaks, CA: Sage Publications.

"A Century of International Drug Control." 2009. United Nations Office on Drugs and Crime. http://www.unodc .org/documents/data-and-analysis/Studies/100_Years_of_ Drug_Control.pdf. Accessed on April 11, 2015.

Chopra, R. N. 1958. *Indigenous Drugs of India.* Calcutta: Dhur.

Comparison of the Tariffs of 1897 and 1909 in Parallel Columns. 1910. Washington, D.C.: Government Printing Office. https://archive.org/details/cu31924018727697. Accessed on April 19, 2015.

"Controlled Substances." 2015. Office of Diversion Control. Drug Enforcement Administration. http://www .deadiversion.usdoj.gov/schedules/orangebook/c_cs_alpha .pdf. Accessed on April 20, 2015.

"Controlled Substances Act Summary." 2015. Uniform Law Commission. http://www.uniformlaws.org/ActSummary .aspx?title=Controlled%20Substances%20Act. Accessed on April 19, 2015.

"Convention on Psychotropic Substances, 1971." 2015. https://www.unodc.org/pdf/convention_1971_en.pdf. Accessed on August 11, 2015.

Courtwright, David T. 2001. *Dark Paradise: A History of Opiate Addiction in America.* Cambridge, MA: Harvard University Press.

Cowell, Stephanie. 2015. "Poetry, Pain, and Opium in Victorian England." Wonders & Marvels. http://www .wondersandmarvels.com/2013/02/poetry-pain-and-opium- in-victorian-england-elizabeth-barrett-brownings-use-of- laudanum.html. Accessed on April 12, 2015.

Cribiore, Raffaella, Paola Davoli, and David M. Ratzan. 2008. "A Teacher's Dipinto [*painting*] from Trimithis (Dakhleh Oasis)." *Journal of Roman Archaeology* 21: 170–92.

Davenport-Hines, Richard. 2002. *The Pursuit of Oblivion: A Global History of Narcotics*. New York: Norton.

Davies, Nick. 2001. "Make Heroin Legal." Guardian. http://www.theguardian.com/politics/2001/jun/14/ drugsandalcohol.socialsciences. Accessed on April 19, 2015.

Day, Horace B. 1868. *The Opium Habit, with Suggestions as to the Remedy*. New York: Harper & Brothers.

Delgado, Maria Victoria. 2009. "Review of Three Centuries: Prescription and Over-the-Counter Drugs: Has Anything Changed?" http://www.benzos.une.edu/documents/ Littlehandout_Rx_article_mvd_08_03_09_MDA.pdf. Accessed on April 12, 2015.

Dial, Nick. 2013. "Prohibition: The War on Opium and the Chinese 'Yellow Peril.'" Law Enforcement Today. http://www.lawenforcementtoday.com/2013/07/13/ prohibition-the-war-on-opium-and-the-chinese- "yellow-peril"/. Accessed on April 16, 2015.

Diaz, Ernie. 2008. "China's Unofficial Opium Story." China Expat. http://www.chinaexpat.com/2008/12/11/ chinas-unofficial-opium-story.html/. Accessed on April 11, 2015.

Dillehay, Tom D., et al. 2010. "Early Holocene Coca Chewing in Northern Peru." *Antiquity* 84 (326): 939–53.

Diniejko, Andrzej. 2002. "Victorian Drug Use." The Victorian Web. http://www.victorianweb.org/victorian/ science/addiction/addiction2.html. Accessed on April 12, 2015.

Dohme, Alfred R. L. 1893. "The Constitution of the Alkaloids." The Pharmaceutical Journal and Transactions.

https://books.google.com/books?id=1kDOAAAAMAA
J&pg=PA551&lpg=PA551&dq=thiboumery+chemist+the
baine&source=bl&ots=aqCtNq0WMN&sig=f6hSFq7kV6
D3vDTCQmg5QfgojfE&hl=en&sa=X&ei=Qj4tVbjtDIay
oQS1_IDIAg&ved=0CCUQ6AEwAQ#v=onepage&q=
thiboumery%20chemist%20thebaine&f=false. Accessed on
April 14, 2015.

Dormandy, Thomas. 2012. *Opium: Reality's Dark Dream.*
New Haven, CT: Yale University Press.

Downs, David. 2013. "The Grand, Racist, Hundred-Year
History of Pot Prohibition in California." East Bay Express.
http://www.eastbayexpress.com/LegalizationNation/
archives/2013/01/23/racism-led-to-100-year-wa
r-on-pot-in-california. Accessed on April 18, 2015.

"Drug Index A to Z." 2015. Drugs.com. http://www.drugs
.com/drug_information.html. Accessed on April 21, 2015.

"The Durham-Humphrey Amendment." 1952. *Journal of the
American Medical Association* 149 (4): 371. http://jama
.jamanetwork.com/article.aspx?articleid=314797. Accessed
on April 21, 2015.

Durlacher, Julian. 2000. *Heroin: Its History and Lore.* London:
Carlton Books.

Emboden, William A., Jr. 1979. "Sacred Narcotic Water Lily
of the Nile: *Nymphaea caerulea* Sav." *Economic Botany* 33
(1): 395–407.

Emboden, William A., Jr. 1981. "Transcultural Use of
Narcotic Water Lilies in Ancient Egyptian and Maya Drug
Ritual." *Journal of Ethnopharmacology* 3 (1): 39–83.

Erlen, Jonathon, and Joseph F. Spillane. 2004. *Federal Drug
Control: The Evolution of Policy and Practice.* New York:
Pharmaceutical Products Press.

Escohotado, Antonio. 2010. *The General History of Drugs.*
Translated by G. W. Robinette. Valparaiso, Chile: Graffiti
Milante Press.

Fee, Elizabeth. 2010. "Samuel Hopkins Adams (1871–1958): Journalist and Muckraker." *American Journal of Public Health* 100 (8): 1390–91.

"59 - Special Message to the Congress on Crime and Law Enforcement: 'To Insure the Public Safety.'" 1968. American Presidency Project. http://www.presidency .ucsb.edu/ws/?pid=29237#axzz1k1QdB1Wg. Accessed on April 20, 2015.

Gaeddert, Andrew. 2015. "Ephedra (Ma Huang)." http:// www.longmontacupuncture.net/ephedra.html. Accessed on April 10, 2015.

Gieringer, Dale. 2015. "The 100 Years' Worldwide War on Drugs." http://www.drugsense.org/dpfca/100yrsworld .html. Accessed on April 18, 2015.

Goldberg, Jeff, with Dean Latimer. 2014. *Flowers in the Blood: The Story of Opium*. New York: Skyhorse Publishing.

Goldberg, Ray. 2003. *Drugs across the Spectrum*. Belmont, CA: Thomson/Wadsworth.

Gray, Richard. 2015. "No Wonder They Called It the Stone Age! Ancient Humans Were Taking Drugs—Including Magic Mushrooms and Opium—Up to about 10,600 Years Ago." Daily Mail. http://www.dailymail.co.uk/sciencetech/ article-2939830/No-wonder-called-stone-age-An cient-humans-taking-drugs-including-magic-mush rooms-opium-10-600-years-ago.html. Accessed on April 10, 2015.

Greenberg, Michael. 1951. *British Trade and the Opening of China, 1800–42*. Cambridge, UK: Cambridge University Press.

Greene, Jeremy A., and Elizabeth Siegel Watkins, eds. 2012. *Prescribed: Writing, Filling, Using, and Abusing the Prescription in Modern America*. Baltimore: Johns Hopkins University Press.

Guerra-Doce, Elisa. 2015. "Psychoactive Substances in Prehistoric Times: Examining the Archaeological Evidence." *Time and Mind* 8 (1): 91–112.

Herer, Jack. 2010. *The Emperor Wears No Clothes*. 12th ed. Austin, TX: Ah Ha Publishing.

Hickman, Timothy Alton. 2007. *The Secret Leprosy of Modern Days: Narcotic Addiction and Cultural Crisis in the United States, 1870–1920*. Amherst: University of Massachusetts Press.

"The History of Drug Laws." 2015. Schaffer Library of Drug Policy. http://www.druglibrary.org/schaffer/library/histdrug.htm. Accessed on April 17, 2015.

"History of Federal Regulation: 1902–Present." 2015. FDA Review.org. http://www.fdareview.org/history.shtml. Accessed on April 20, 2015.

"History of Pharmacy." 2015. Royal Pharmaceutical Society. http://www.rpharms.com/about-pharmacy/history-of-pharmacy.asp. Accessed on April 21, 2015.

Hodgson, Barbara. 2001. *In the Arms of Morpheus: The Tragic History of Laudanum, Morphine, and Patent Medicines*. Buffalo, NY: Firefly Books.

Hua, Jordan. 2012. " 'They Looked Askance': American Indians and Chinese in the Nineteenth Century U.S. West." http://history.rutgers.edu/honors-papers-2012/402-they-looked-askance-american-indians-and-chinese-in-the-nineteenth-century-u-s-west/file. Accessed on August 11, 2015.

Huxtable, Ryan J., and Stephan K. Schwarz. 2001. "The Isolation of Morphine—First Principles in Science and Ethics." *Molecular Interventions* 1 (4): 189–91.

"Importation and Use of Opium." 1911. Hearings before the Committee on Ways and Means of the House of Representatives. December 14, 1910 and January 11, 1911. https://books.google.com/books?id=HXGzAAAAQ

BAJ&pg=PA15&lpg=PA15&dq=opium+originated+in+t
igris+euphrates&source=bl&ots=HQ4vSOwrLa&sig=f0k
ADuDIfcZwmhCgHSlKM9asjEU&hl=en&sa=X&ei=O0
ooVZuLGZbhoASLpYGwCA&ved=0CCAQ6AEwAA#v
=onepage&q=opium%20originated%20in%20tigris%20
euphrates&f=false. Accessed on April 15, 2015.

"An Interview with Mr. George P. Larrick." 1968. http://
www.fda.gov/downloads/aboutfda/whatwedo/history/
oralhistories/selectedoralhistorytranscripts/ucm265382.pdf.
Accessed on April 20, 2015.

Janick, Jules. 2003. "Herbals: The Connection between
Horticulture and Medicine." *HortTechnology* 13 (2):
229–38. https://www.hort.purdue.edu/newcrop/herbals_
HortTech.pdf. Accessed on April 9, 2015.

Johnson, Clarke. 1999. "The Oldest Known
Prescription." http://www.uic.edu/classes/osci/
osci590/11_1OldestPrescription.htm. Accessed on
April 9, 2015.

Kandall, Stephan R. 1998. "Women and Addiction in the
United States—1850–1920." In Cora Lee Wetherington
and Adele B. Roman, eds. *Drug Addiction Research and
the Health of Women*. Rockville, MD: U.S. Department of
Health and Human Services, National Institutes of Health,
National Institute on Drug Abuse.

Kapoor, L. D. 1995. *Opium Poppy: Botany, Chemistry, and
Pharmacology*. New York: Food Products Press.

Khan, Hasan Javaid. 2014. "Closing in on Soma." http://
www.heritageinstitute.com/zoroastrianism/haoma/iic.htm.
Accessed on April 10, 2015.

King, Rufus. 1953. "The Narcotics Bureau and the Harrison
Act: Jailing the Healers and the Sick." *The Yale Law Journal*
62 (5): 784–87. http://druglibrary.org/special/king/king1.
htm. Accessed on April 18, 2015.

King, Rufus. 1972. *The Drug Hang-Up: America's Fifty Year Folly*. New York: Norton. http://druglibrary.org/special/king/dhu/dhumenu.htm. Accessed on April 20, 2015.

Kramer, Samuel Noah. 1954. "First Pharmacopeia in Man's Recorded History." *American Journal of Pharmacy and the Sciences Supporting Public Health* 126 (3): 76–84.

Kremers, Edward, George Urdang, and Glenn Sonnedecker. 1976. *Kremers and Urdang's History of Pharmacy*. Philadelphia: Lippincott.

Kritikos, P. G., and S. P. Papadaki. 1967. "The History of the Poppy and of Opium and Their Expansion in Antiquity in the Eastern Mediterranean Area." United Nations Office on Drugs and Crime. http://www.unodc.org/unodc/en/data-and-analysis/bulletin/bulletin_1967-01-01_3_page004.html. Accessed on April 9, 2015.

"Laudanum Addiction Treatment." 2015. Project Know. http://www.projectknow.com/research/laudanum/. Accessed on April 12, 2015.

La Wall, Charles H. 1934. "St. Cosmas and St. Damian, Patron Saints of Medicine and Pharmacy." *Journal of Chemical Education* 11 (10): 555–57.

"Laws." 2013. The National Alliance of Advocates for Buprenorphine Treatment. https://www.naabt.org/laws.cfm. Accessed on April 17, 2015.

Li, Xiaobin, and Qiang Fang. 2013. *Modern Chinese Legal Reform: New Perspectives*. Lexington: University Press of Kentucky.

Lindsley, Craig W. 2015. "2014 Global Prescription Medication Statistics: Strong Growth and CNS Well Represented." *ACS Chemical Neuroscience* 6 (4): 505–6.

Lovell, Julia. 2015. *Opium War: Drugs, Dreams, and the Making of Modern China*. New York: Overlook Press.

Lowes, Peter D. 1966. *The Genesis of International Narcotics Control*. Geneva: Librairie Droz.

Ludlow, Fitz Hugh. 1867. "What Shall They Do to Be Saved?" Harper's New Monthly Magazine 35 (207): 377–87. https://www.erowid.org/culture/characters/ludlow_fitz_hugh/ludlow_fitz_hugh_article2.shtml. Accessed on April 16, 2015.

Marks, Harry M. 1995. "Revisiting 'The Origins of Compulsory Drug Prescriptions.'" *American Journal of Public Health* 85 (1): 109–15.

McKenna, Dennis J., Kenneth Jones, and Kerry Hughes. 2002. *Botanical Medicines: The Desk Reference for Major Herbal Supplements*. New York: Haworth Herbal Press.

McWilliams, John C. 1990. *The Protectors: Harry J. Anslinger and the Federal Bureau of Narcotics, 1930–1962*. Newark: University of Delaware Press.

"Medication-Assisted Treatment for Opioid Addiction in Opioid Treatment Programs." 2005. Treatment Improvement Protocol (TIP) Series, No. 43. Rockville, MD: Substance Abuse and Mental Health Services Administration. http://www.ncbi.nlm.nih.gov/books/NBK64157/. Accessed on April 16, 2015.

"Medicine in Ancient Mesopotamia." 2015. http://www.indiana.edu/~ancmed/meso.HTM#target4. Accessed on April 9, 2015.

"Merck's Merits in the Manufacture of Morphine." 1907. The Merck Report, January 1907. https://books.google.com/books?id=bTlHAQAAMAAJ&pg=PA28&lpg=PA28&dq=merck+morphine+1827&source=bl&ots=hZez5WhuaV&sig=ABMfEDqZhTzVSNkUccnr7a0xJu0&hl=en&sa=X&ei=SugrVamYFMipogSWhIBQ&ved=0CD8Q6AEwBQ#v=onepage&q=merck%20morphine%201827&f=false. Accessed on April 13, 2015.

Merlin, M. D. 2003. "Archaeological Evidence for the Tradition of Psychoactive Plant Use in the Old World." *Economic Botany* 57 (3): 295–323.

Michaelis, Martin, Bernward Schölkens, and Karl Rudolphi. 2007. "An Anthology from Naunyn-Schmiedeberg's Archives of Pharmacology: O. Schaumann (1940) Über eine Neue Klasse von Verbindungen mit Spasmolytischer und Zentral Analgetischer Wirkung unter Besonderer Berücksichtigung des 1-methyl-4-phenyl-piperidin-4-carbonsäure-äthylesters (Dolantin). Archiv f. Experiment. Path. u. Pharmakol. 196: 109–36." *Naunyn-Schmiedeberg's Archives of Pharmacology* 375 (2): 81–84.

Milligan, Barry. 1995. *Pleasures and Pains: Opium and the Orient in Nineteenth-Century British Culture.* Charlottesville: University Press of Virginia.

Morgan, H. Wayne. 1981. *Drugs in America: A Social History, 1800–1980.* Syracuse, NY: Syracuse University Press.

Norn, Svend, Poul R. Kruse, and Edith Kruse. 2005. "Opiumsvalmuen og Morfin Gennem Tiderne." ["Opium and Morphine through the Ages."] *Dansk Medicinhistorisk Årbog* 33: 171–84. Original in Danish. Translation from Danish to English at http://translate.google.com/translate?hl=en&sl=da&u=http://www.jmhs.dk/PDF-files/Aarbog/2005/Norn171-184.pdf&prev=search.

Oliver, F. E. 1872. "The Use and Abuse of Opium." Massachusetts State Board of Health. Third Annual Report. Schaffer Library of Drug Policy. http://druglibrary.net/schaffer/History/1870/useandabuseofopium1872.htm. Accessed on April 16, 2015.

"Opiate vs. Opioid—What's the Difference?" 2015. *Opium.* http://opium.com/derivatives/opiate-vs-opioid-whats-difference/. Accessed on April 15, 2015.

"Opiates/Opioids." 2015. The National Alliance of Advocates for Buprenorphine Treatment. https://www .naabt.org/education/opiates_opioids.cfm. Accessed on April 12, 2015.

"Opioid." 2014. Mahalo. http://www.mahalo.com/ opioid#ref_38. Accessed on April 15, 2015.

"Opioid (Narcotic Analgesics Systemic)." 2001. Drugs.com. http://www.drugs.com/mmx/laudanum.html. Accessed on April 12, 2015.

"Opium, Morphine, and Heroin." 2015. http://www.ch.ic .ac.uk/rzepa/mim/drugs/html/morphine_text.htm. Accessed on April 14, 2015.

"Overview: Opioids, Opioid Antagonists." 2015. National Library of Medicine. http://livertox.nih.gov/Opioids.htm. Accessed on April 15, 2015.

Panicker, Sini, Heidi Wojno, and Lewis H. Ziska. 2007. "Quantitation of the Major Alkaloids in Opium from Papaver Setigerum DC." *Microgram Journal* 5 (1–4): 13–19.

"Pharmaceutical Research by a Commercial House." 1906. American Druggist and Pharmaceutical Record. February 26, 1906. https://books.google.com/books?id= U343AQAAMAAJ&pg=PA122-IA4&lpg=PA122-IA4& dq=history+of+merck+corporation+morphine+1827&so urce=bl&ots=5REjJlN0W3&sig=DtvTlQeD2XRlHWf XlFlEZ3wXcMk&hl=en&sa=X&ei=EvMrVYz6HpCQo QSf3YHgCg&ved=0CEgQ6AEwBw#v=onepage&q=hist ory%20of%20merck%20corporation%20morphine%20 1827&f=false. Accessed on April 13, 2015.

"'Pharmakon': The Cure or the Poison?" 2009. https://flutuante.wordpress.com/2009/08/01/ pharmakon-the-cure-or-the-poison/. Accessed on April 9, 2015.

Pommerening, Tanja, Elena Marinova, and Stan Hendrickx. 2011. "The Early Dynastic Origin of the Water-Lily Motif." *Chronique d'Egypte* 85 (169–70): 14–40.

"Prescription Drug Abuse History." 2015. Narconon International. http://www.narconon.org/drug-abuse/ prescription-drug-history.html. Accessed on April 12, 2015.

"Prescription Drug Addiction—Top 18 Facts for You and Your Family." Drugs.com. http://www.drugs.com/ slideshow/prescription-drug-addiction-1075#slide-1. Accessed on April 8, 2015.

Quinn, Thomas M., and Gerald T. McLaughlin. 1973. "The Evolution of Federal Drug Control Legislation." *Catholic University Law Review* 22 (3): 586–627. http://scholarship .law.edu/cgi/viewcontent.cgi?article=2622&context=law review. Accessed on April 19, 2015.

"Regulations under the Narcotic Drugs Import and Export Act." 1939. In The Code of Federal Regulations of the United States of America. Vol. 5. https://books.google .com/books?id=beuyAAAAIAAJ&pg=PA1065&lpg=PA10 65&dq=%2242+stat.+596%22+heroin&source=bl&ots=p 2Boe4f72s&sig=8cLwlV5zo3T0XOZkN8bEj65yFqc&hl= en&sa=X&ei=dyk0VaD8KMzUoATDvIDwBg&ved=0C DQQ6AEwBQ#v=snippet&q=%22narcotic%20drug%20 import%22&f=false. Accessed on April 19, 2015.

Ruston, Sharon. 2015. "Representations of Drugs in 19th-Century Literature." Discovering Literature—Romantics and Victorians. http://www.bl.uk/ romantics-and-victorians/articles/representations-of-drugs-in-19th-century-literature. Accessed on April 13, 2015.

A Short Treatise of the Virtues of Dr. Bateman's Pectoral Drops: The Nature of the Distempers They Cure, and the Manner of Their Operation. Publish'd by the King's Letters Patents under the Great Seal of Great Britain. 1725.

University of Oxford Text Archive. http://ota.ox.ac.uk/
text/5634.html. Accessed on April 17, 2015.

"Soldier's Disease." 2011. Providentia. http://drvitelli
.typepad.com/providentia/2011/02/soldiers-disease.html.
Accessed on April 15, 2015.

"State Drug Possession Laws." 2015. FindLaw. http://
statelaws.findlaw.com/criminal-laws/drug-possession.html.
Accessed on April 20, 2015.

Strauss, Steven. 1995. *Strauss's Pharmacy Law and
Examination Review*, 3rd ed. Lancaster, PA: Technomic
Publishing Company.

"Suppression of Abuse of Opium and Other Drugs." 1912.
United States Treaties. Library of Congress. http://www.loc
.gov/law/help/us-treaties/bevans/m-ust000001-0855.pdf.
Accessed on April 18, 2015.

"Synthetic, Opioids." 2015. Medscape. http://reference
.medscape.com/drugs/synthetic-opioids. Accessed on
April 15, 2015.

Teall, Emily K. 2013. "Medicine and Doctoring in Ancient
Mesopotamia." Grand Valley Journal of History. http://
scholarworks.gvsu.edu/cgi/viewcontent
.cgi?article=1056&context=gvjh. Accessed on
April 20, 2015.

Terry, Charles E. 1931. "The Development and Causes
of Opium Addiction as a Social Problem." *Journal of
Educational Sociology* 4 (6): 335–46.

Terry, Charles E., and Mildred Pellens. 1928. "The Opium
Problem." New York: The Committee on Drug Addictions
and The Bureau of Social Hygiene, Inc. http://babel
.hathitrust.org/cgi/pt?id=mdp.39015006502523;view=
1up;seq=16. Accessed on April 16, 2015.

United States v. Sullivan. 332 U.S. 689. 1948. Justia US
Supreme Court. https://supreme.justia.com/cases/federal/
us/332/689/case.html. Accessed on April 29, 2015.

UNODC. 2008. "World Drug Report." Vienna: United Nations Office on Drugs and Crime. http://www.unodc .org/documents/wdr/WDR_2008/WDR_2008_eng_web .pdf. Accessed on April 11, 2015.

UNODC. 2011. "World Drug Report." Vienna: United Nations Office on Drugs and Crime. http://www.unodc .org/documents/data-and-analysis/WDR2011/World_ Drug_Report_2011_ebook.pdf. Accessed on April 8, 2015.

Vassilev, Rossen. 2010. "China's Opium Wars: Britain as the World's First Narco-State." *New Politics* 13 (1): 75–80.

Volkow, Nora D. 2012. "Prescription Drug Abuse: It's Not What the Doctor Ordered." http://www.slideshare .net/OPUNITE/nora-volkow-final-edits. Accessed on April 23, 2015.

Wall, Otto A. 1917. *The Prescription, Therapeutically, Pharmaceutically, Grammatically and Historically Considered.* 4th and rev. ed. St. Louis: C. V. Mosby Company. https:// archive.org/details/prescriptionthe00wall. Accessed on April 20, 2015.

Whitebread, Charles. 1995. "The History of the Non-Medical Use of Drugs in the United States." Schaffer Library of Drug Policy. http://druglibrary.org/schaffer/history/ whiteb1.htm. Accessed on April 16, 2015.

Wright, C. R. A. 1874. "On the Action of Organic Acids and Their Anhydrides on the Natural Alkaloids. Part I." *Journal of the Chemical Society* 27: 1031–43. https://www .thevespiary.org/rhodium/Rhodium/Vespiary/talk/files/ 4132-On-the-action-of-organic-acids-and-their-anhydrides- on-the-natural-alkalo%C3%AFds.-Part-I6d99.pdf? topic=1698.0. Accessed on April 14, 2015.

Young, James Harvey. 2015. *The Toadstool Millionaires: A Social History of Patent Medicines in America before Federal Regulation.* Princeton, NJ: Princeton University Press.

Zheng, Yangwen. 2005. *The Social Life of Opium in China.* Cambridge, UK: Cambridge University Press.

Zohary, Daniel, Maria Hopf, and Ehud Weiss. 2012. *Domestication of Plants in the Old World: The Origin and Spread of Domesticated Plants in Southwest Asia, Europe, and the Mediterranean Basin.* Oxford, UK: Oxford University Press.

Most adults in the developed world have had the experience of obtaining a prescription drug. The process is usually a simple one. One visits a medical practitioner and describes the medical problem he or she is experiencing. The practitioner may then make a diagnosis and, often, write a prescription for a drug or procedure designed to deal with the patient's problem. In 2013, the most recent year for which data are available, about 4.208 billion prescriptions were filled at pharmacies in the United States, more than 10 million prescriptions per day on average ("Medicine Use and Shifting Costs of Healthcare" 2014, Appendix 2, p. 45). One then takes the prescription to a pharmacy or other dispensing service to have the prescription "filled" (i.e., the drug dispensed to the patient). In many cases, taking the prescribed medication brings relief from the medical problem. In this light, prescription drugs have become one of the most important factors for dealing with a person's medical problems.

Except that this simple story of prescription medications is no longer quite the positive medical experience it has been over the last century. Today, an increasing number of individuals, especially young adults, have taken to using prescription medications for purposes other than those for which they were intended, such as "getting high" or "spacing out." Not only is this practice illegal but it may also have harmful and sometimes very serious consequences, from relatively modest effects, such

---

In today's world, prescription drugs are often readily available, even to people who have no need of them for medical purposes. (Mocker/Dreamstime.com)

as sleepiness, confusion, and constipation, to far more serious consequences, such as respiratory disorders, addiction, and death ("Effects of Prescription Drug Abuse" 2015).

In a 2013 report and overview on the problem of prescription drug abuse, the Behavioral Health Coordinating Committee of the U.S. Department of Health and Human Service's Prescription Drug Abuse Subcommittee said that

> The United States is in the midst of an unprecedented drug overdose epidemic. Drug overdose death rates have increased five-fold since 1980. By 2009, drug overdose deaths outnumbered deaths due to motor vehicle crashes for the first time in the U.S. Prescription drugs, especially opioid analgesics, have been increasingly involved in drug overdose deaths. Opioid analgesics were involved in 30% of drug overdose deaths where a drug was specified in 1999, compared to nearly 60% in 2010. Opioid-related overdose deaths now outnumber overdose deaths involving all illicit drugs such as heroin and cocaine combined. In addition to overdose deaths, emergency department visits, substance treatment admissions and economic costs associated with opioid abuse have all increased in recent years. ("Addressing Prescription Drug Abuse in the United States: Current Activities and Future Opportunities" 2013)

What exactly does the term *prescription drug abuse* mean? What are the dimensions of the problem? What is its history in the United States and other parts of the world? How does prescription drug abuse occur in individuals, and what are its medical, social, emotional, psychological, economic, and other effects on a person? And what efforts are being made to deal with the problem of prescription drug abuse in the United States at the present time. These are some of the questions to be addressed in this chapter.

Demographics

Claims that prescription drug abuse is now an "epidemic" in the United States (see the previous discussion on the 2013 report of the Behavioral Health Coordinating Committee) are common in the scientific and general literature today. Publications by federal, state, local, and nongovernmental groups interested in drug issues frequently emphasize the number of men and women and boys and girls who use prescription drugs for nonmedical purposes and the many harmful consequences that result from this practice (see, e.g., "Popping Pill: Prescription Drug Abuse in America" 2014). For example, Dr. Nora D. Volkow, director of the National Institute on Drug Abuse, has noted that at least 52 million people are thought to have misused at least one prescription drug on at least one occasion in their lives. That number is about 20 percent of all Americans over the age of 12 (Volkow 2014). This statement suggests that prescription drug abuse can, in one sense at least, certainly be thought of as a widespread problem in the United States.

Nonmedical Use of Prescription Drugs: Statistics

Such warnings are supported by a number of studies of the extent of prescription drug abuse among the American population. One of the most comprehensive of these studies was completed in 2012 by the Behavioral Health Coordinating Committee of the Prescription Drug Abuse Subcommittee of the U.S. Department of Health and Human Services. That study found that the number of chronic prescription drug abusers (people who use the drug consistently over a long period of time) in the United States has increased over the period between 2002–2003 and 2009–2010 by more than 74 percent (from 2.2% to 3.8% of the population of all Americans over the age of 12). As shown in Table 2.1, that trend has been true for all age groups except for those between the ages of 12 and 17 and for both genders ("Addressing Prescription Drug Abuse

Table 2.1   Average Annual Rates of Past Year Chronic Nonmedical Use of
Opioid Analgesics among People 12 Years and Older by Age and
Sex, U.S. 2002–2003 and 2009–2010.

Characteristic	2002–2003	2009–2010	Percentage Change
All Nonmedical Users	2.2	3.8	74.6
Age			
12–17	4.0	3.0	–25.7
18–25	4.2	7.4	77.6
26–34	2.8	5.0	81.0
35–49	1.7	4.0	134.6
≥50	0.9	2.1	124.3
Sex			
Male	2.5	5.1	105.3
Female	1.9	2.6	36.4

Source: "Average Annual Rates of Past Year Chronic Non-Medical Use of Opioid Analgesics among People 12 Years and Older by Age and Sex, U.S. 2002-2003 and 2009-2010." [2013]. "Addressing Prescription Drug Abuse in the United States: Current Activities and Future Opportunities" 2013. Behavioral Health Coordinating Committee. Prescription Drug Abuse Subcommittee. U.S. Department of Health and Human Services. Table 1:, p. 10. http://www .cdc.gov/HomeandRecreationalSafety/pdf/HHS_Prescription_Drug_Abuse_ Report_09.2013.pdf. Accessed on April 23, 2015.

in the United States: Current Activities and Future Opportunities" 2013, Table 1, p. 10).

Another large and highly respected study, the National Survey on Drug Use and Health (NSDUH), reported in 2011 that 6.1 million people had reported using a prescription drug for nonmedical purposes in the month preceding the study, of which the largest number involved the use of pain-killing drugs (4.3 million), followed by tranquilizers (1.8 million), stimulants (1.0 million), and sedatives (0.3 million) ("Results from the 2011 National Survey on Drug Use and Health: Summary of National Findings" 2012, Figures 2.2 and 2.3).

The data for prescription drug abuse tend to vary by age group, gender, ethnicity, and other characteristics. As shown in Table 2.2, women tend to request treatment for prescription

Table 2.2   Prescription Pain Relievers as the Primary Substance of Abuse
among Substance Abuse Treatment Admissions Aged 12 or
Older, by Gender and Age, 2011*

Age Group	Males (%)	Females (%)
12–17	1.7	3.1
18–24	12.8	17.6
25–34	12.2	19.0
35–44	5.9	11.2
45–54	3.5	8.0
55–64	3.7	8.3
Over 65	2.8	7.2

* Percent of admissions to substance abuse treatment facilities.

Source: Prescription Pain Relievers as the Primary Substance of Abuse among Substance Abuse Treatment Admissions Aged 12 or Older, by Gender and Age: 2011. Gender Differences in Primary Substance of Abuse across Age Groups. http://www.samhsa.gov/data/sites/default/files/sr077-gender-differences-2014 .pdf. Accessed on April 24, 2015.

pain killer problems than do men in every age group. This trend may very well be different for other criteria (e.g., abuse problems for which individuals do not seek treatment), but it is born out by other studies of gender differences among prescription drug abusers. Large differences exist among racial and ethnic groups also, with prescription drug abuse occurring most commonly among individuals of American Indian or Alaska Native populations (4.7%), followed by whites (2.8%), Hispanics or Latinos (2.4%), African Americans (2.3%), Native Hawaiians or other Pacific Islanders (1.3%), and Asians (1.2%) ("Health, United States, 2013" 2014, Table 60, p. 203).

(It should be noted that statistical data about prescription drug abuse should be read with some caution. Various researchers provide data that sometimes seem contradictory or confusing because they conduct their studies in different way. For example, some studies inquire about so-called one-time use; that is, they ask respondents if they have *ever* used a prescription drug for nonmedical purposes. Other studies ask about drug use over the previous month or previous week, each time period providing a different perspective on prescription drug abuse. Researchers may also use different methodologies in carrying out their studies, such as by asking respondents directly versus studying hospital or law enforcement records. Even researchers who used direct questioning may phrase their queries differently, resulting in different statistical results (e.g., see "Results from the 2011 National Survey on Drug Use and Health: Summary of National Findings" 2012, Figure 8.6, with accompanying explanation). Different studies may also classify respondents in different ways, such as calling everyone from 12 to 24 years of age "young adults," while others reserve that term only for those between the ages of 18 and 25 or use some other system of categorization. The point is that different researchers can make different statements about the demographics of prescription drug abuse that may *seem* contradictory, but that must be interpreted in terms of the methods used in any given study. As an example, see the data collected from two different studies of "past year" nonmedical prescription drug use among two groups of young adults. The NSDUH and the Monitoring the Future studies collect data in two different ways and for two slightly different age groups, resulting in slightly different results (see "Results from the 2011 National Survey on Drug Use and Health: Summary of National Findings 2012, Figure 8.5).

The problem of prescription drug abuse among young adults is of special concern to many observers. (The definition of the term *young adults* varies from writer to writer and can mean males and females from almost any age from 12 to the mid-20s.) One recent publication of the National Institute on Drug Abuse states flatly, for example, that "[y]oung adults (age 18 to 25) are the biggest abusers of prescription (Rx) opioid pain relievers, ADHD stimulants, and anti-anxiety drugs." The publication says that 13 percent of all individuals between the ages of 18 and 25 used one or more prescription drugs for nonmedical purposes in the preceding year, compared to 7 percent of those between the ages of 12 and 17 and 4 percent of those over the age of 26 ("Abuse of Prescription [Rx] Drugs Affects Young Adults Most" 2013).

Studies indicate that the illicit use of prescription drugs is the second most prevalent form of drug abuse among young adults in the United States, after marijuana. Among boys and girls aged 12 to 17 in the 2013 NSDUH, for example, 2.2 percent reported using at least one psychotherapeutic drug in the month prior to the survey. The rate for those in the age group 12 to 13 was 1.3 percent; in the age group 14 to 15, 2.2 percent; and in the age group 16 to 17, 3.1 percent (the rate for marijuana, by comparison, was 7.1%; "Results from the 2013 National Survey on Drug Use and Health: Summary of National Findings" 2014, Figures 2.7 and 2.8). A similar pattern was observed for young adults in the age group 18 to 25, with 4.8 percent having reported using at least one prescription drug for nonmedical purposes in the month preceding the survey, compared to 19.1 percent having used marijuana during the same period ("Results from the 2013 National Survey on Drug Use and Health: Summary of National Findings" 2014, Figure 2.9).

Recent data may provide some cause of optimism in the battle against the prescription drug abuse epidemic. In its annual report on drug use in the United States, the Office of National Drug Control Policy noted that the rate of nonmedical use of prescription drugs in the United States dropped by 13 percent from 2010 to 2011 ("National Drug Control Strategy. Data Supplement 2013" n.d., I). As Table 2.3 shows, this decrease

Table 2.3   Estimated Numbers and Percentages Reporting Nonmedical Use of Prescription Drugs, Persons over the Age of 12, 2002–2011 (in thousands)

Year	Lifetime[a]		Past Year[b]		Past Month[c]	
2002	47,958	20.4	14,795	6.3	6,287	2.7
2003	49,001	20.6	15,163	6.4	6,451	2.7
2004	49,157	20.4	14,849	6.2	6,110	2.5

(continued)

Table 2.3 *(continued)*

Year	Lifetime[a]		Past Year[b]		Past Month[c]	
2005	49,571	20.4	15,346	6.3	6,491	2.7
2006	50,983	20.7	16,482	6.7	7,098	2.9
2007	50,541	20.4	16,334	6.6	6,907	2.8
2008	52,154	20.9	15,190	6.1	6,210	2.5
2009	51,991	20.6	16,064	6.4	6,980	2.8
2010	51,832	20.4	16,051	6.3	6,957	2.7
2011	51,243	19.9	14,657	5.7	6,119	2.4

[a] Used at least one drug at least once in one's lifetime.

[b] Used at least one drug at least once in the year preceding the survey.

[c] Used at least one drug at least once in the month preceding the survey.

Source: "Estimated Numbers and Percentages Reporting Nonmedical Use of Psychotherapeutic Drugs, 2002–2011." National Drug Control Strategy. Data Supplement 2013." n.d. n.p., Table 3, p. 23. https://www.whitehouse.gov/sites/default/files/ondcp/policy-and-research/2013_data_supplement_final2.pdf. Accessed on April 26, 2015.

may be significant or it may be only a one-year variation in what otherwise appears to be a relatively steady trend in prescription drug misuse.

Nonmedical Use of Prescription Drugs: Mortality and Morbidity Data

Asking individuals about their nonmedical use or nonuse of prescription drugs is only one way of collecting data on the extent of the current prescription drug abuse epidemic. One can also use other criteria, such as rates of death (mortality) and morbidity (diseases and other disorders). The most recent data on deaths resulting from overdose of opioid analgesics (the most common of misused prescription drugs) are shown in Table 2.4. Note that the death rate from this source has increased from 4,030, or 1.4 per 100,000 persons in 1999 to 16,007, or 5.1 per 100,000 in 2012, an increase of 264 percent

Table 2.4 Deaths from Opioid Analgesics in the United States, 1999–2012
(Rates per 100,000 Population)

Year	All Drugs*		Opioid Analgesics		Heroin*	
1999	16,849	6.1	4,030	1.4	1,960	0.7
2000	17,415	6.2	4,400	1.5	1,842	0.7
2001	19,394	6.8	5,528	1.9	1,779	0.6
2002	23,518	8.2	7,456	2.6	2,089	0.7
2003	25,785	8.9	8,517	2.9	2,080	0.7
2004	27,424	9.4	9,857	3.4	1,878	0.6
2005	29,813	10.1	10,928	3.7	2,009	0.7
2006	34,425	11.5	13,723	4.6	2,088	0.7
2007	36,010	11.9	14,408	4.8	2,399	0.8
2008	36,450	11.9	14,800	4.8	3,041	1
2009	37,004	11.9	15,597	5	3,278	1.1
2010	38,329	12.3	16,651	5.4	3,036	1
2011	41,340	13.2	16,917	5.4	4,397	1.4
2012	41,502	13.1	16,007	5.1	5,925	1.9

* For comparison.

Source: "Number and Age-Adjusted Rate of Drug-poisoning Deaths Involving *Opioid Analgesics and Heroin*: United States, 1999–2012." Warner, Margaret, Holly Hedegaard, and Li-Hui Chen. 2014. "Trends in Drug-poisoning Deaths Involving Opioid Analgesics and Heroin: United States, 1999–2012." Health E-Stats. Table, p. 5. http://www.cdc.gov/nchs/data/hestat/drug_poisoning/drug_poisoning_deaths_1999-2012.pdf. Accessed on April 26, 2015.

(Warner, Hedegaard, and Chen 2014, Table). These data differed significantly among various age groups, racial and ethnic populations, and between genders. As Table 2.5 shows, death rates from opioid analgesic misuse was much higher among individuals in the mid-age range (25 to 65), among men more than women, and among whites and American Indian populations, compared to other groups.

One way of measuring morbidity associated with prescription drug abuse is to count the number of emergency department (ED) visits that can be attributed to the misuse of a prescription drug. Good data on this measure are now available. Among

Table 2.5   Drug Poisoning Deaths Involving Opioid Analgesics in the United States among Various Age, Gender, Racial, and Ethnic Groups, 1999–2000 through 2009–2010 (Rates per 100,000 Population)

	Total					
	1999–2000	2001–2002	2003–2004	2005–2006	2007–2008	2009–2010
All Groups	1.9	2.9	4.0	5.2	6.1	6.6
Age						
15–24	0.7	1.5	2.4	3.2	3.8	3.7
25–34	1.9	2.8	4.1	6.1	7.2	8.1
35–54	3.4	4.9	6.6	8.2	9.2	9.9
54–64	1.0	1.6	2.4	3.5	4.8	6.0
>64	0.3	0.5	0.6	0.9	1.0	1.2
Gender						
Male	2.6	3.7	5.0	6.6	7.5	8.1
Female	1.3	2.1	3.0	3.9	4.6	5.1
Racial/Ethnic Group						
White, not Hispanic	2.2	3.5	5.1	6.7	8.0	8.9
Black, not Hispanic	1.1	1.5	1.7	2.8	2.4	2.7
Hispanic or Latino	1.8	1.7	2.0	2.3	2.6	2.4
American Indian or Alaska Native	1.7	2.6	4.2	5.4	6.1	7.1
Asian or Pacific Islander	0.2	0.3	0.3	0.6	0.5	0.7

Source: "Drug Poisoning Deaths Involving Opioid Analgesics among Persons Aged 15 and Over, by Race and Hispanic Origin, Sex, and Age: United States, 1999–2000 through 2009–2010." "Health, United States, 2013." Centers for Disease Control. National Center for Health Statistics. Data Table for Figure 28, p. 38. http://www.cdc.gov/nchs/data/hus/hus13.pdf. Accessed on April 24, 2015.

the best are those that come from a report by the Drug Abuse Warning Network (DAWN) of the Substance Abuse and Mental Health Services Administration. In its 2013 report on this topic, DAWN noted that 1,428,415 ED visits in 2011 could be

Table 2.6   Emergency Department Visits for Prescription Drug Abuse and Illicit Drug Use, 2004 to 2011

Year	Prescription Drug Abuse	Illicit Drug Use
2004	626,470	991,640
2005	765,314	922,018
2006	859,136	958,866
2007	984,749	974,852
2008	1,126,403	994,583
2009	1,243,606	974,392
2010	1,344,393	1,172,276
2011	1,428,145	1,252,500

Source: "Reasons for Drug-Related Emergency Department (ED) Visits, by Year: 2004 to 2011." Highlights of the 2011 Drug Abuse Warning Network (DAWN) Findings on Drug-Related Emergency Department Visits." 2013. Center for Behavioral Health Statistics and Quality. Substance Abuse and Mental Health Services Administration. Figure 1. http://archive.samhsa.gov/data/2k13/DAWN127/sr127-DAWN-highlights.htm. Accessed on April 25, 2015.

attributed to misuse of a pharmaceutical drug, 28 percent of all ED visits for the year. This number of visits was slightly greater than the number of ED visits because of reactions to illicit drugs, such as marijuana, cocaine, and heroin (1,252,500 visits, or 25% of all ED visits). Of this number, 87 percent of all visits involved a patient over the age of 20, half were male and half female, and about a quarter (27%) resulted in a hospital admission ("Highlights of the 2011 Drug Abuse Warning Network [DAWN] Findings on Drug-Related Emergency Department Visits" 2013). As Table 2.6 shows, the number of ED visits because of prescription drug abuse has been rising steadily over the period from 2004 to 2011, from 626,470 in the former year to 1,428,415 in the latter year. Prescription drug abuse cases have gradually overtaken and surpassed cases associated with illicit drugs, with the crossover point being 2007.

Nonmedical Use of Prescription Drugs: First-Time Use

One of the measures used by public health experts in following the nonmedical use of prescription drugs is called *first-time use*, a

Table 2.7   **First-Time Abusers of Prescription Drugs in the United States, 2002–2011 (in Thousands)**

Year	First-Time Users
2002	2,552
2003	2,583
2004	2,836
2005	2,526
2006	2,576
2007	2,532
2008	2,512
2009	2,567
2010	2,428
2011	2,346

Source: "Number of Past-Year Initiates among Persons Aged 12 or Older, 2002–2011 (Thousands)." National Drug Control Strategy. Data Supplement 2013. n.d. n.p., Table 5, p. 25. https://www.whitehouse.gov/sites/default/files/ondcp/policy-and-research/2013_data_supplement_final2.pdf. Accessed on April 26, 2015.

count of the number of individuals who have used prescription drugs illegally for the first time in the year preceding a study. This measure allows a determination as to whether interest in and use of an illegal substance has begun to drop off, or if it is still popular in the general population. As Table 2.7 shows, the number of first-time abusers of prescription drugs has remained relatively constant until the last two years of the survey on this question.

The International Scene

Estimating the worldwide abuse of prescription drugs is a challenging task for a number of reasons. For one thing, some types of drugs, such as opioids or stimulants, are more popular in some parts of the world, but not others. Also, researchers sometimes fail to clarify precisely what they mean by a particular term, such as *opioids*, in collecting and reporting demographic data. Or, they may classify all types of opioids into one category, so that the data they provide include a wide range of drugs, such as both opiates (like heroin) and synthetic opioids. In addition, many regions and individual countries do not have an interest in or a capability of collecting data on drug misuse.

In general, the best single source of information about the data that are available about all kinds of drug problems worldwide is the *World Drug Report* (WDR), published annually by the United Nations Office on Drugs and Crime. Each year, the WDR provides up-to-date, but slightly different data, about all kinds of drug use and abuse. In 2011, the WDR estimated that about 40 percent of all prescription drug abusers were located in North America, primarily the United States and Canada. In the United States, the rate of nonmedical use of prescriptions was 6.4 percent, compared with 0.5 percent (2009 data) for Canada. The rate in Mexico was significantly less, estimated to be about 0.06 percent (2008 data) (United Nations Office on Drugs and Crime 2011, 36). The WDR opined that a major reason for the high rate of prescription drug abuse in the United States and some other developed nations was the ready availability of opioid drugs, stimulants, tranquilizers, and sedatives.

The rate of opioid misuse in South and Central America is also quite low, estimated by WDR 2011 at 0.4 percent, with the highest rates found in Brazil, Chile, and Costa Rica. The report also claimed that prescription drug abuse was not yet seen as a major drug problem in most of Europe, although rates tended to be somewhat higher in some countries such as Denmark, Estonia, and Finland, especially, with Northern Ireland having the highest rate of any European country. The report cautioned, however, that these data were somewhat suspect since some countries are more aggressive about collecting and reporting these data than are others (United Nations Office on Drugs and Crime 2011, 39).

Nonmedical use of prescription drugs has also been high in some parts of Asia, although for reasons other than those in North America. In nations like Afghanistan, Bangladesh, India, and Nepal, the smoking of mind-altering drugs such as opium has a long history, and some users have recently been choosing to use opioids in place of opiates to maintain their habits because of the lower cost of the synthetic products over the natural substances (United Nations Office on Drugs and Crime 2011, 43). In countries were modernization has occurred or is well under way—such as South Korea, the Philippines, Jordan, Qatar, and the United Arab Emirates—prescription drugs have also become the drug of choice among many users. In Kuwait, for example, about 16 percent of all drug abusers who appear at treatment centers are there because of nonmedical use of prescription drugs (United Nations Office on Drugs and Crime 2011, 43).

The issue of nonmedical use of prescription drugs in Australia and New Zealand is also a matter of growing concern. Data from 2009 placed the rate of opioid misuse in Australia at about 0.2 percent, with about one in six young adults between the ages of 12 and 17 having reported that they misused prescription drugs at least once in their lifetime. A report out of New Zealand also found the misuse of prescription drugs widespread in the country (United Nations Office on Drugs and Crime 2011, 44). The report concluded that about 27 million people around the world (about 0.6% of the world's population) had misused at least one prescription drug in the year preceding the report (United Nations Office on Drugs and Crime 2014, 1). In 2012, an additional resource became available with the publication of an extensive and comprehensive study of illicit drug use and dependence and its effect on the global burden of disease in the highly regarded medical journal, *Lancet* (Degenhardt and Hall 2012). That report estimated that there are between 1.166 and 20,660 abusers of prescription opioids around the world, between 0.3 and 0.5 percent of the world's population (Degenhardt and Hall 2012, 58).

Misused Prescription Drugs

Many authorities identify three categories of prescription drugs as being those used for nonmedical purposes: opioid analgesics (pain relievers), stimulants, and central nervous system (CNS) depressants. Some experts also recognize a fourth category of misused prescription drugs, tranquilizers, which can also be considered as sedatives. Finally, a small number of over-the-counter (OTC) drugs are also used for nonmedical purposes, primarily cough and cold remedies that include the medication dextromethorpan. Depending on the particular research study or other circumstance, some researchers also list other substances or classes of compounds as abused prescription medicines. Amphetamines are an example of such substances.

The most common type of prescription drug used for nonmedical purposes is the opioid analgesics, followed by all types of sedatives (including tranquilizers), and stimulants. As shown in Table 2.8, just over half of all prescription drug misusers (59.5%) used opioid analgesics for nonmedical purposes,

Table 2.8   Estimated Number of Respondents Reporting Nonmedical Use of Four Categories of Prescription Drugs, 2002–2011 (in Thousands)

Year	Pain Relievers	Tranquilizers	Stimulants	Sedatives
2002	4,377	1,804	1,303	436
2003	4,693	1,830	1,310	294
2004	4,404	1,616	1,312	265
2005	4,658	1,817	1,188	272
2006	5,226	1,761	1,385	385
2007	5,188	1,838	1,051	345
2008	4,732	1,796	908	237
2009	5,282	2,030	1,299	367
2010	5,093	2,159	1,082	375
2011	4,471	1,840	970	231

Source: "Estimated Numbers and Percentages Reporting Nonmedical Use of Psychotherapeutic Drugs, 2002–2011." n.d. National Drug Control Strategy. Data Supplement 2013. Table 3, p. 23. https://www.whitehouse.gov/sites/default/files/ondcp/policy-and-research/2013_data_supplement_final2.pdf. Accessed on April 26, 2015.

followed by about half that number (24.5%) who used tranquilizers, 12.9 percent who used stimulants, and 3.1 percent who used other sedatives. This distribution has remained relatively constant for more than a decade.

Other data on the mortality and morbidity rates for various classes of abused prescription drugs are also available and of considerable interest. They tend to use different methods of classification, however, and are not, therefore, easily summarized here (see, e.g., deaths from opioid analgesic overdoses at Warner, Hedegaard, and Chen, 2014, Table and "Drug Abuse Warning Network, 2011: National Estimates of Drug-Related Emergency Department Visits, 2011," 2013 Table 18, p. 49; "Drug Abuse Warning Network, 2011: National Estimates of Drug-Related Emergency Department Visits" 2013).

Opioids

Opioids are opium-like drugs most commonly prescribed for the treatment of pain. They are not used for low or moderate levels of pain, which can normally be treated by OTC medications such as aspirin, acetaminophen, and ibuprofen. They are usually prescribed for more serious pain episodes, such as those that occur after a surgical procedure or in conjunction with a variety of diseases and injuries. Some common types of opioid drugs are codeine, diphenoxylate (trade name: Lomotil), fentanyl (Duragesic), hydrocodone (Vicodin, Lortab, Lorcet), hydromorphone (Dilaudid), meperidine (Demerol), methadone, morphine (Kadian, Avinza, MS Contin), propoxyphene (Darvon), and oxycodone (OxyContin, Percodan, Percocet). Opioid drugs are also known by street names such as happy pills, hillbilly, OC, oxy, percs, or vikes.

Opioids work in the body by attaching to proteins known as *opioid receptors* that occur in the brain, the spinal cord, the gut, and other organs. Opioid receptors have evolved for the interaction with a number of naturally occurring opium-like substances in the body known as *endogenous opioids* (*endogenous* means "originating within the body"). Three of the best known and most thoroughly studied groups of endogenous opioids are the endorphins, enkephalins, and dynorphins. When an endogenous opioid attaches to an opioid receptor, it causes the release of a neurotransmitter (a chemical that carries nerve messages between cells) that travels to a second nearby cell. When the neurotransmitter reaches the second cell, it enters that cell and causes the release of a second neurotransmitter known as dopamine. Dopamine then travels to surrounding cells where it produces a variety of effects, such as a sense of well-being, a reduction in pain, an increase in attentiveness, and other positive sensations (for more detail on this complex process, see "Brain and Addiction" 2015; "How Drugs Affect Neurotransmitters" 2015; "The Neurobiology of Drug Addiction" 2015; "What Are Opioids?" 2015).

Exogenous opioids work in essentially the same way as do endogenous opioids. Exogenous opioids are opioids that originate from *outside* the human body. In many cases, they have been synthesized by human chemists. They are the same substances as those that have been referred to simply as *opioids* to this point. That is, if one were to add (swallow, inhale, receive intravenously) an exogenous opioid such as oxycodone, it would be attracted to and attach to opioid receptors in the same way as do natural endogenous opioids, such as an endorphin. It would stimulate the release of dopamine that would produce essentially the same effects as would an endorphin.

And that is the reason that some individuals choose to take synthetic opioids as recreational drugs rather than medicines. They are hoping to experience the "high" that comes from ingesting the drug, producing a warm, happy, pleasant feeling of relaxation and peacefulness. People who take opioids for medical reasons may also experience similar feelings, but seldom with the intensity of those felt by the person who is using the drug for recreational purposes.

So, if the pathway by which opioids act in the body is the same for endogenous and exogenous opioids, how does the therapeutic use of prescription drugs differ from those of recreational drugs? Why is one "good" and reasonably safe, while the other is "bad" and potentially extremely harmful? Officials at the National Institute on Drug Abuse have developed an explanatory scheme that explains this difference. In the first place, the amount of a substance ingested (the dose) and the frequency of dosing are very different for therapeutic and recreational purposes. In the former case, the amount and timing over which a drug is administered to a patient are carefully controlled to ensure that he or she will get enough of the drug to help with his or her medical problem (e.g., pain), but not enough to cause harmful side effects. The recreational user, by contrast, *intends* to exceed the medically minimal level of dosage and ingest enough of the substance to experience some of the drug's side effects.

Recreational users also employ forms of administration that are seldom if ever used in a medical setting; they generally smoke or inject the drug rather than taking it orally. The reason for using a different method of administration is that they want to get the drug into their body as quickly as possible and experience its desired effects as soon as possible. One can achieve that result by inhaling a substance or injecting it directly into the bloodstream, but not by swallowing a pill. By contrast, patients receive a prescription drug in very controlled quantities either by means of a pill or by intravenous ("drip") injection so that they receive only the precise amount needed for therapeutic purposes, and no more than that.

Another key difference between therapeutic and recreational use of a drug is also based on the expectation that one had in taking the drug in the first place. Of course, in the case of therapeutic use, the purpose of taking the drug is to overcome pain or relieve some other symptom. For recreational users, the whole point of taking a prescription drug is *not* to deal with a medical problem, but to take advantage of pleasant side effects. Finally, the setting in which a substance is ingested is a critical factor in determining whether its use is therapeutic or recreational. Someone who takes a prescription drug at a party, in the privacy of his or her own home, or at a bar is almost certainly not doing so for some therapeutic reason, but in order to "get high" or experience some other pleasant reaction in the process (Compton 2015; "Use, Abuse, Misuse & Disposal of Prescription Pain Medication Clinical Reference" 2011).

A number of short- and long-term side effects are associated with the nonmedical use of opioids. These side effects come about because the normal biochemical reactions that occur in the body, described earlier, continue to occur with uncontrolled doses and frequency of opioid ingestion. For example, activation of opioid receptors does tend to slow down or block some biochemical reactions in the body (desirable results in pain control), it may also go beyond a stage that is critical for normal body function. It is hardly surprising, then, that drowsiness, sedation, and dizziness may be typical short-term side effects of nonmedical use of opioids. Other side effects may include nausea, vomiting, respiratory distress, and constipation. Less common side effects of opioid use included delayed gastric emptying, hyperalgesia (increased sensitivity to pain), immunologic and hormonal dysfunction, muscle rigidity, and myoclonus (muscle spasms) (Benyamin 2008). These effects may be relatively easy to control, usually by discontinuing the use of the opioid in question, although carrying out this treatment is very much simpler for patients who are taking an opioid under medical direction than for an individual who is taking the same drug recreationally.

If these conditions are not treated, however, they can result in far more serious medical conditions that may require immediate medical attention at an ED and may, in the most severe cases, result in death from respiratory distress or cardiac insufficiency. Both conditions may develop when the presence of opioids in the body depresses the CNS, which controls both the rate of respiration and the heart rate.

The two most serious long-term effects of nonmedical opioid use are dependence and addiction. The two terms are sometimes used together, but they describe two very different medical conditions. Dependence is the condition in which one's body becomes used to receiving exogenous opioids. In many cases, the body may develop a *tolerance* to the opioid, meaning that it requires a greater and greater amount of the substance in order to achieve the same physiological response. If the body does not receive these ever-increasing amounts of exogenous opioid, it may go into *withdrawal*, which includes symptoms such as agitation, anxiety, increased tearing, insomnia, muscle aches, runny nose, sweating, and yawning. Left untreated, additional symptoms that may develop include abdominal cramping, diarrhea, dilation of the pupils, "goose bumps," nausea, and vomiting. These symptoms are unpleasant, but they are not generally life-threatening and they can be treated rather easily by drugs and maintenance programs ("Opiate Withdrawal" 2015).

Opioid dependence may or may not be associated with the medical use of a substance. It may then be followed by *addiction*, which may have many of the symptoms of dependence, but also is characterized by controllable cravings for the drug that may soon take over a person's life. A person who becomes addicted to an opioid, or any other drug, may become so obsessed with the substance that it becomes the dominant theme in his or her life. A person's waking hours may be spent in thinking about the drug and finding ways of obtaining enough of the drug to satisfy his or her needs and desires for it. At this point, the problem is no longer one of physical dependence on the substance, but on a complete psychological agenda of building one's life around the need to obtain and use the drug in question ("Physical Dependence and Addiction" 2014).

Stimulants

As their name suggests, stimulants are drugs that increase the rate of any bodily function, primarily the brain and the CNS. Some of the prescription stimulants that are most commonly used for nonmedical purposes are dextroamphetamine (Dexedrine), methylphenidate (Ritalin and Concerta), and amphetamines (Adderall, a mixture of amphetamine and dextroamphetamine). Some street names for these drugs include bennies, black beauties, crosses, hearts, jif, LA turnaround, R-ball, skippy, the smart drug, vitamin R, kibbles and bits, speed, truck drivers, and uppers. These drugs have become increasingly popular over the past two decades for the treatment of attention deficit hyperactivity disorder (ADHD), primarily for children under the age of 18. The fraction of children in the United States receiving prescriptions of one of these drugs increased from 4.2 to 5.1 percent among those in the 6 to 12 age range and from 2.3 to 4.0 percent in the 13 to 18 age range (Lakhan and Kirchgessner 2012). Stimulants are also used for other medical conditions, including narcolepsy and asthma and depression that do not respond to other treatments.

The characteristic symptoms of ADHD include difficulty in paying attention to details, easy distraction from tasks, inability to sustain attention on tasks, frequent shift of attention from one task to another, procrastination, disorganized work habits, forgetfulness, and inability to complete assigned tasks. Researchers have learned that a primary cause of ADHD is an imbalance in neurotransmitters in the brain, especially the balance between serotonin versus dopamine and norepinephrine. The ingestion of stimulants appears to increase the level of these neurotransmitters and relieve the symptoms of ADHD. This effect has long puzzled researchers because one would expect that administering a stimulant such as Ritalin or Concerta to a person with ADHD would *increase* his or her level of activity (after all, they are *stimulants*). In fact, this is not the case. Taking a stimulant such as Ritalin or Concerta actually decreases the hyperactivity associated with ADHD, seeming to "smooth out" a person's level of activity (Fenichel 2012).

The use of stimulants for the treatment of ADHD has always had its critics who often base at least some of their criticism on the fact that the disorder was not well known or characterized until the point at which drugs for its treatment had been invented, developed, and widely advertised to the medical profession (Lakhan and Kirchgessner 2012). However, evidence seems to indicate that stimulants are effective in about 80 percent of the cases where they have been prescribed, although the effects produced are not necessarily long-lasting ("Attention Deficit Hyperactivity Disorder: Stimulant Therapy" 2013; Lakhan and Kirchgessner 2012).

Although the nonmedical use of prescription stimulants is relatively modest in the general population (about 2%), it is especially high in some specialized groups, including college students, premedical students, and professional athletes, although prevalence rates within these groups also tend to vary quite significantly. A variety of studies have found prevalence rates ranging from about 6 percent to as high as 35 percent among different groups of college students (Lakhan and Kirchgessner 2012).

Most studies of the nonmedical use of prescription stimulants have focused on college students, who report three main reasons for using these drugs. First, drugs provide the kind of "high" that drug abusers often seek from their substance of choice. This effect is a result, as in the case of opioids, of increased levels of dopamine in the brain produced by the ingestion of a stimulant. Second, stimulants also improve a person's ability to concentrate on studying over longer periods of time without becoming tired or distracted. One widely acknowledged fact about stimulant use in colleges is that the use of such products increases dramatically at the end of a school term when many students find it necessary to "cram" for an examination, which may require staying awake and studying for long periods of time that may include "overnighters."

The third reason that college students take prescription stimulants is that they believe that the drugs will actually improve their intellectual level, making them "smarter." While the first two results of taking stimulants are at least biologically valid, the third is not: There is very little evidence that taking stimulants has any effect on a person's cognitive abilities (Lakhan and Kirchgessner 2012, Table 1).

As with all medications, some side effects are associated with even the carefully controlled use of prescription stimulants. These effects may include headache, nausea, increased blood pressure, dizziness, dry mouth, decreased appetite, weight loss, nervousness, insomnia, tics, reduction in growth, visual problems, and allergic reactions ("Attention Deficit Hyperactivity Disorder: Stimulant Therapy" 2013). Most of these problems can be resolved fairly easily by changing dosage, adjusting the medication schedule, or switching to a different stimulant.

More serious side effects are also possible, especially when an individual ingests a quantity of stimulant greater than that normally recommended for medical treatment. Among the side effects that have been observed under such circumstances include hypertension, tachycardia (rapid heartbeat), and other cardiovascular disorders; depression, hallucinations, mania, and other psychotic effects; and sudden death (for a good general summary of this topic, see "Nonmedical Use of Prescription Stimulants" 2015.)

A relatively new concern about the misuse of stimulants normally used for the treatment of ADHD has arisen in the past few years. Evidence suggests that some mostly young adults are turning to such pills as a way of dealing with the increasing pressures of the workplace. Young men and women who work in high-pressure law firms, financial markets, high-tech businesses, and similar organizations are finding it difficult to keep up with the pace of activity expected of them, and some of them are turning to prescription stimulants to find ways of working longer hours with less sleep. As one might expect, experts in the field are concerned about the potential health effects of this practice, as data begin to suggest that increasing number of workers are experiencing the harmful side effects of overuse of stimulant drugs (Schwarz 2015).

CNS Depressants

The term *CNS depressants* usually refers to subclasses of drugs, tranquilizers, and sedatives. Three classes of drugs make up the majority of CNS depressants used medically and nonmedically: barbiturates, benzodiazepines, and sleep medications. Some familiar examples of drugs belonging to each category are barbiturates: mephobarbital (Mebaral) and sodium pentobarbital (Nembutal); benzodiazepines: diazepam (Valium), alprazolam (Xanax), estazolam (ProSom), clonazepam (Klonopin), and lorazepam (Ativan); and soporifics (sleep medications): zolpidem (Ambien), zaleplon (Sonata), and eszopiclone (Lunesta) (more complete lists of the drugs in these categories can be found at "Barbiturates" 2015 and "Benzodiazepine Equivalence Table" 2007). Some of the street names by which these drugs are known include A-minus, barbs, candy, downers, phennies, reds or red birds, tooies, yellows or yellow jackets, and zombie pills.

As their name suggests, CNS depressants have an effect on animal bodies just the reverse of stimulants. Rather than increasing the rate of bodily functions, they tend to slow the pace at which those functions occur. They achieve this result because, once ingested, they begin to increase the rate of a neurotransmitter known as gamma aminobutyric acid (GABA). In the brain and the CNS, GABA molecules have a tendency to bind to nerve cell receptors and inhibit the flow of nerve messages from one neuron to another neuron. This reduction in nerve transmission also reduces the stimulation of muscles, causing the reduction in bodily activity characteristics of CNS depressants.

CNS depressants have a number of important medical applications, such as reducing stress, tension, and anxiety and preventing convulsions, seizure disorders, and panic attacks. They are also used in treating sleep disorders. A number of trade names of CNS depressants have become familiar terms in everyday life because the drugs are so widely used in dealing with the physical and psychological problems created by the hectic life that many people lead today.

Individuals cite a number of reasons for using CNS depressants for nonmedical reasons. As with all drugs, some people just want to experiment with drugs to see what results they will experience. Other people start out using a CNS depressant for a legitimate medical reason, but find that they have become addicted to the drug and have problems giving it up. Still others experience the same symptoms for which CNS depressants are legitimately prescribed—for example, stress and anxiety in everyday life—but decide to try to deal with the problem on their own rather than seeking professional help. As an example, one of the CNS depressants that gained wide popularity among illicit drug users at the beginning of the 21st century was gamma hydroxybutyrate (or gamma hydroxybutyric acid), better known as GHB. The drug has very few legitimate medical applications (no legal applications in the United States), but became popular among prescription drug abusers because it helped people overcome social inhibitions, providing them a modest "high" and sense of euphoria and a feeling of relaxation in social settings (Teter and Guthrie 2001).

The immediate side effects of taking a CNS depressant are those one would expect from someone whose bodily reactions have begun to slow down: slurred speech, shallow breathing, sleepiness, disorientation, and lack of coordination, for example. If too much of a CNS depressant is consumed, one's body functions may slow down to the point where life-maintaining functions begin to fail, and coma and/or death may occur. In 2011, about 30 percent of all deaths caused by misuse of prescription drugs (6,800 deaths out of 22,810) involved the use of benzodiazepines ("Prescription Depressant Medications" 2015).

Two additional warnings are often provided regarding the use of CNS depressants. First, one should never combine a CNS depressant with another drug because the second drug might also cause the same bodily effects as the CNS depressant. In such a case, respiration and heart rate may be reduced to a level where the respiratory and/or cardiovascular system may stop working, resulting in death. The second warning is that one should never try to discontinue the use of a CNS depressant drug without medical advice. In such a case, the body may begin functioning normally, but at a greater rate than the one to which it had become accustomed, resulting in a seizure ("Central Nervous System (CNS) Depressants and Stimulants" 2012).

Over-the-Counter Medications

Most of the discussion about prescription drug abuse tends to focus on drugs that are available only by prescription. This fact means that one of the important issues in this area has to do with how people are able to get a hold of such drugs, other than through the normal process of having a legitimate prescription filled. (More on this topic later.) But some drugs that are readily available without prescription (so-called *OTC* drugs) are also being used for recreational purposes. Probably the most commonly abused of these drugs are cough and cold medicines, which typically include the compound dextrometho-rphan (DXM) as an active ingredient. DXM is an ingredient in more than two dozen popular OTC medications including Alka Seltzer Plus; Cheracol; Contac; Coricidin; Diabetic Tussin; Kids Eeze; Mucinex DM & Cough Products; Robitusin; Sineoff; Sudafed; Triaminic; Tylenol Cough, Cold, & Flu Products; and a variety of Vicks products. Products containing DXM are also available on the street under names such as candy, drank, dex, robo, skittles, triple c, tussin, and velvet. The practice of using such products is also commonly known as robotripping.

According to the most recent data available (2014), 2.0 percent of all 8th graders, 3.70 percent of all 10th graders, and 4.10 percent of all 12th graders in the United States reported using a cough medicine product for nonmedical purposes in the year preceding the study. At all three grade levels, these percentages represented significant decreases from data collected in 2011, 2012, and 2013 ("Monitoring the Future Study: Trends in Prevalence of Various Drugs 2015").

DXM has an inhibitory effect on neuroreceptors in the brain. That is, it tends to bind to those receptors and interrupt the flow of normal neural messages through the brain. In this respect, DXM acts in the brain in much the same way as do hallucinogens. This process has the general effect of slowing down mental processes in such a way as to produce a sense that one is removed from his or her body, a *dissociative* effect. DXM abusers often say that they feel completely relaxed and at ease, with a sense that they are floating through the air, released from their bodies. It is these feelings of euphoria and escape for which abusers are searching when they take DXM products ("Cough and Cold Medicine (DXM and Codeine Syrup)" 2015; "Stop Medicine Abuse" 2015).

But the nonmedical use of DXM may also have a number of other side effects that are not as pleasurable as those a user is hoping for. These side effects include nausea, numbness, slurred speech, dizziness, sweating, insomnia, and lethargy. At more advanced stages, a user may also experience more serious effects, such as delusions, hallucinations, hyperexcitability, and hypertension. With prolonged use, liver and brain damage may result, and physical dependence and addiction may occur.

Another OTC product that is sometimes misused or abused, especially by teenagers, is called *bath salts*. The term has only the most tenuous relationship with the legitimate commercial product that many people add to their bath water for the soothing and relaxing feeling it can produce. The "bath salts" described here contain one or more synthetic analogues of cathinone, an alkaloid found in the leaves of the *Catha edulis* (khat) plant. It has physiological effects on the brain similar to those produced by amphetamine and its analogues. The product is sold under a variety of names, of which *bath salts* is only one. It is also marketed as plant food, a jewelry cleaner, or cleaner for a cell phone screen. The package in which the product comes is usually labeled "Not for Human Consumption" to avoid having to deal with regulations for legitimate drugs ("DrugFacts: Synthetic Cathinones ('Bath Salts')" 2012; Prosser and Nelson

2012). When sold on the Internet, the product may carry trade names such as Bloom, Cloud Nine, Ivory Wave, Lunar Wave, Scarface, Vanilla Sky, or White Lightning.

Bath salt products are typically ingested in a variety of ways, including by inhalation, by injection, or orally. Individuals take bath salts because of the sense of euphoria they provide, along with feelings of greater sociability, increased sex drive, and higher energy levels. These feelings may be accompanied, however, by other side effects that are not as pleasant, such as shortness of breath, abdominal pain, abnormal vision, anxiety, confusion, fever, rash, drowsiness, and dizziness. More serious side effects include abnormal renal function and renal failure, paranoia, psychosis, abnormal liver function and liver failure, and cardiovascular disorders (Prosser and Nelson 2012, Table 4).

Concerns about the use of bath salts to obtain a "legal high" began to grow rapidly both in the United States and in Europe after 2010. The rate of bath salt use by high school students increased from essentially 0 percent for 8th graders in 2011 to 0.50 percent in 2014 and from 0 to 0.90 percent in the same period for both 10th and 12th graders surveyed for the Monitoring the Future study of drug behavior in the United States ("Monitoring the Future Study: Trends in Prevalence of Various Drugs" 2015). In response to this increase in use, a number of new laws were passed and regulations imposed with the goal of reducing access to bath salt products by young adults ("DrugFacts: Synthetic Cathinones ('Bath Salts')" 2012). Evidence for the success of these regulations is not yet available.

Yet another OTC medication that is sometimes used for recreational purposes is motion sickness pills. This medication has some useful legitimate applications, such as preventing a person's becoming seasick on an ocean cruise. But motion sickness pills also have other side effects. They may produces feelings of euphoria and relaxation, a sense of getting "high." They may also cause hallucinations such as those produced by taking illegal drugs such as LSD. These feelings are caused by one of the main ingredients in motion sickness pills, compounds called dimenhydrinate (Dramamine) or diphenhydramine (Benadryl). Instances have been recorded in which a person took a whole package of motion sickness pills at the same time in order to achieve these feelings. As with other drugs, however, dimenhydrinate and diphenhydramine can have more or less serious side effects, such as drowsiness, headache, blurred vision, ringing in the ears, nausea, dizziness, irregular heartbeat, coma, heart attacks, and death. When taken over a long period of time, additional side effects may include itchy skin, abdominal pain, eye pain, liver and kidney damage, memory loss, and depression ("Dimenhydrinate" 2015; "Diphenhydramine" 2015).

Prevention

For individuals and organizations interested in the problem of prescription drug abuse, the most important issues are likely to be prevention and treatment. That is, what can society do to help men and women and boys and girls who have become abusers of prescription and OTC drugs in the first place? And then, how can such individuals be helped in dealing with their problems of abuse, dependence, and/or addiction if and when that problem gets out of control?

Many medical and health specialists now agree that the most efficacious way of dealing with personal and public health problems is to prevent a problem from developing, rather than waiting until it has occurred and must be treated. In the field of cancer, for example, experts are now convinced that the best way to "treat" lung cancer caused by smoking is not radiation therapy, chemotherapy, surgery, or some other method of treatment. It is, instead, to convince people that they should not start smoking to begin with or, at the very least, to quit smoking as soon as possible. Using that same line of thinking, authorities in the field of prescription drug abuse are now looking for ways to convince individuals of all ages that they should avoid become abusers of prescription drugs, rather than trying to treat those individuals later in their lives.

The Etiology of Prescription Drug Abuse

That approach for dealing with prescription drug abuse means, of course, that health care specialists need to know *why* people start using prescription drugs for nonmedical purposes and *how* they gain access to those drugs. Perhaps the most important point to be made at the outset of this discussion is that experts today simply do not know what it is that causes one person to become a drug abuser, physically dependent on a drug, and/ or addicted to the drug, while another person is uninterested in drug use. Any number of reasons for this inclination have been suggested, including a person's genetic makeup, the specific way in which one person reacts to a drug and another person does not, a person's individual "metabolic system, peer pressure, emotional distress, anxiety, depression, and environmental stress" (Converse 2015).

Addiction Following Legitimate Use of Prescribed Drugs

In spite of this uncertainty about the etiology of prescription drug abuse, a number of working hypotheses have been suggested about the problem. One pattern that might seem to explain at least some cases of prescription drug dependence and addiction involves individuals who were prescribed pain killers or other prescription drugs for legitimate medical reasons, such as dealing with postoperative pain, pain associated with a dental procedure, chronic pain caused by a disease such as cancer, or pain caused by an accident. Once a person begins to use such drugs for legitimate reasons it might seem reasonable that he or she might enjoy the side effects provided by the drug and continue using it after the medical justification no longer existed. Data as to the validity of this hypothesis are very uncertain, however, with estimates of the number of patients who follow this pathway ranging anywhere from 3 to 40 percent ("Prescription Drug Abuse" 2014, 13).

In a recent study conducted by the Partnership for Drug-Free Kids, about 10 percent of respondents (7% of chronic pain patients and 13% of acute pain patients) reported that they had continued to use prescription pain medicines after their legitimate medical reason for use had ended. A somewhat larger fraction (13% of chronic pain patients and 15% of acute pain patients) said that they continued using prescription pain killers provided by someone else after their pain had been relieved ("Report: Prescribers, Patients and Pain" 2015, 6–7; one of the best summaries of this issue is Frakt 2014).

The debate over the possible addictive effects of using prescribed pain medications has become a major issue in the health care and drug enforcement communities today. On the one hand, some authorities argue that the rate at which pain patients abuse or become addicted to pain medications is very low. On the other hand, other experts say that the prescription drug epidemic is so serious that every step possible must be taken to reduce the illegitimate use of pain medications.

This issue took on a new reality in late 2014 when the Drug Enforcement Administration (DEA) rescheduled the drug hydrocodone from Schedule III to Schedule II in the national Schedules of Controlled Substance ("Schedules of Controlled Substances: Rescheduling of Hydrocodone Combination Products from Schedule III to Schedule II" 2014). Drugs containing hydrocodone, such as Vicodin, Lorcet, and Norco, are the most commonly used of all narcotic painkillers in the United States. The rescheduling means that a person using a hydrocodone product will have to get a new prescription every 90 days, rather than simply having an older prescription refilled, as was previously the case. The two views about this type of action were expressed by DEA administrator Michele Leonhart and David Belian, a spokesperson for the maker of generic hydrocodone. Leonhart justified the DEA action by saying that "these products are some of the most addictive and potentially dangerous prescription medications available." Belian responded to this view by suggesting that the DEA's action "will place a significant burden on patients, the vast majority of whom use them in a legitimate manner" (Radnofsky and Walker 2014; for more useful resources on the interaction of pain treatment and drug abuse, see "Pain and Addiction" 2015).

Initiation to Prescription Drug Abuse among Young Adults

As with individuals of other ages, it is often difficult for researchers to determine which of many possible factors is or are responsible for a young person's decision to start using prescription drugs for recreational purposes (for summary of a recent study on this question, see "2012 Partnership Attitude Tracking Study" 2013). In many cases, teenagers and even younger children may start to use prescription drugs for the same psychological or emotional reasons that older adults do, that is, as a way of dealing with personal anxiety, depression, feelings of hopelessness, anger, or stress. In some cases, young people grow up in homes where their parents, other relatives, and/or their friends use drugs as a way of dealing with problems such as these, and drugs become the only coping mechanism they understand ("Prescription Drug Abuse & Addiction Causes, Signs, Side Effects & Symptoms" 2015). In instances such as these, drugs—both illegal and prescription—may also be readily available for the taking and use by younger members of such a household.

In other cases, young adult abusers may simply want to "get high," to experience the euphoria, release, and out-of-body experiences that some drugs can offer. It is fairly clear that the desire to experiment with life in a variety of ways is a typical characteristic of adolescence, and it is hardly surprising that young people want to try out some of the experiences that drugs can offer. And the fact that such behaviors are regarded as unacceptable by adults may only make such experimentation even more attractive. In such cases, young adults often seem to prefer using prescription drugs over illegal drugs such as marijuana, cocaine, and heroin because, after all, they have been tested and approved by the government. So they are safer than street drugs that some teenagers prefer to use. Or so their thinking may go. Some young prescription drug abusers may even believe that prescription drugs are not really harmful (since they are used to cure disease and help people get over medical problems), so there should be little harm in using them recreationally. The 2012 Partnership Attitude Tracking Study sponsored by the MetLife Foundation and the Partnership at DrugFree.org found that one in four teenagers (and one in six of their parents) agreed with this assumption. The same fraction of teenagers agreed with the statement that "there is little or no risk in using prescription pain relievers without a prescription," and nearly that fraction (about 20%) said they thought that prescription pain relievers are "not addictive" ("2012 Partnership Attitude Tracking Study" 2013, 10). All of these presumptions are, of course, false.

Another factor that many researchers have pointed to as a motivation for prescription drug abuse is so-called *peer pressure*, that is, a feeling that, since all of one's friends are doing some activity, he or she ought to be following their lead. Recent studies have suggested that this issue is somewhat more complicated than once thought. Researchers at Purdue University found that college students who were using prescription drugs for recreational purposes did not necessarily feel "pressure" from their peers to do so. Instead, they learned that drug use was just part of their "social scene." It was part of going to parties or clubs, "hanging out" with friends, or just socializing with one's peers. The researchers suggested that this apparently modest difference of explanations might have significance for developing prevention programs and treatment for prescription drug abuse (Neubert 2014).

Sources of Prescription Drugs

A question of some interest in dealing with the nonmedical use of prescription drugs is how individuals obtain these drugs. The more authorities know about this question, the better they may be able to interrupt the supply of legal drugs to those who wish to use them for illegal purposes. A 2014 booklet published by the Centers for Medicare and Medicaid Services of the U.S. Department of Health and Human Services provides a summary of the most likely methods of diversion of prescription drugs to nonmedical uses ("Partners in Integrity" 2014; the term *diversion* means the illegal distribution of a prescription drug for purposes for which it is not intended). Those methods include the following:

- Selling prescription drugs. Patients who obtain prescription drugs legally may then offer them for sale to other individuals.

- Doctor shopping. This term refers to the practice used by some individuals of visiting more than one doctor, describing false symptoms that may allow them to obtain a number of prescriptions for legal drugs, which they can then sell to other individuals.

- Illegal Internet pharmacies. Individuals and companies may create websites through which they offer controlled substances to individuals without prescriptions, thus avoiding state licensing requirements and standards by operating across state and international borders.

- Drug theft. Some individuals may simply break in and steal prescription drugs from a variety of sources, including manufacturers, doctors' offices, hospital supply cabinets, pharmacies, or patients themselves.

- Prescription pad theft and forgery. Other individuals may print or steal prescription pads, making it possible for them to write fraudulent prescriptions or to alter a prescription for a prescribed drug.

- Illicit prescribing. Health care workers may write or fill unnecessary prescriptions or they may prescribe larger quantities of tablets or capsules than what is medically necessary. Locations that follow such a practice are sometimes known as *pill mills*. ("Partners in Integrity" 2014, 6)

Without question, all of these practices are used for the diversion of prescription drugs to illegal use. However, they are not all equally popular. The most recent data on the methods used by individuals for the diversion of prescription drugs come from the 2013 National Survey on Drug Use and Health, conducted by the Substance Abuse and Mental Health Administration of the U.S. Department of Health and Human Services. According to that study, by far the most common source from which individuals receive the prescription drugs that they use for nonmedical purposes are friends and relatives, from whom they obtain the drugs at no cost. Just over half (53.0%) of all respondents said that they obtained their drugs in this way. The next most common source was by prescription from a single doctor (21.2% of all respondents), followed by purchase from a friend or relative (14.6%), from a drug dealer or stranger (4.3%), from more than one doctor by prescription (2.6%), by purchase through the Internet (0.1%), and from some other source (4.3%). The term other included three subcategories: by writing a false prescription; by theft from a doctor's office, clinic, or pharmacy; or in some other way ("Results from the 2013 National Survey on Drug Use and Health: Summary of National Findings" 2014, Figure 2.16).

Researchers for the NSDUH study further analyzed the largest of these categories, "friends and relatives" to learn the source of the prescription drug for these suppliers. They found that more than four out of five "friends and relatives" (83.8%) had obtained these drugs from a single doctor by way of a legal prescription. Thus, the legal drugs that were eventually used for nonmedical purposes were obtained ultimately by means of legal prescriptions to the abuser (about one time out of five) or to the supplier ("friend or relative"; about four times out of five) in the very large majority of cases. This information makes it clear that prevention programs need to focus primarily on controlling the flow of legal prescriptions from physicians and other health care workers to individuals who receive those prescriptions (the "friends and relatives" who obtained prescription drugs from sources other than a single physician cited other sources such as friends and relatives at the next level up the chain, by purchase [4.9%], or for free [5.1%]; more than one doctor [3.3%]; a drug dealer or stranger [1.4%]; through the Internet [0.3%)] or from some other source [1.2%]; results from the "2013 National Survey on Drug Use and Health: Summary of National Findings" 2014, Figure 2.16).

Somewhat more extensive and complete data about the diversion of prescription drugs by young adults are available from the annual Monitoring the Future study conducted by the University of Michigan Institute for Social Research for the National Institute on Drug Abuse. Table 2.9 summarizes trends in drug diversion practices among 12th-grade students between 2007 and 2013. These data differ somewhat from the general data provided in the previous paragraph because many respondents reported using more than one source for prescription drugs, so totals add to more than 100 percent in all cases. Notice that "friends and relatives" are still the most common source for diverted prescription drugs, although purchases from "friends and relatives" and "my own prescription" are much higher in popularity than for adults in general data noted in the previous paragraph (Johnson, et al. 2014, Table 10–5, 527).

Prevention Programs

Recommendations for controlling the nonmedical use of prescription drugs have come from a wide variety of sources, including governmental agencies at the federal, state, and local levels; many professional organizations; nongovernmental associations; academic organizations and institutions; and concerned professionals and laypersons from every part of society. Some common themes appear in these recommendations, themes that are reflected, for example, in a report issued by the Obama administration in 2011, "Epidemic: Responding to

Table 2.9 Sources of Prescription Drugs Used for Nonmedical Purposes by 12th Graders, 2007–2013

Category	Amphetamines		Tranquilizers		Opioids Other Than Heroin	
	2007–2008	2009–2013	2007–2008	2009–2013	2007–2008	2009–2013
Bought on Internet	4.6	6.0	2.4	4.1	2.3	1.4
Took from friend/relative without asking	19.6	9.8	21.1	19.2	24.2	19.5
Took from friend	*	4.2	*	5.1	*	4.1
Took from relative	*	7.9	*	17.1	*	18.0
Given for free by friend/relative	58.2	59.4	59.8	65.6	50.5	57.2
Given by friend	*	56.1	*	55.1	*	50.7
Given by relative	*	9.2	*	20.9	*	15.4
Bought from friend/relative	45.0	43.6	44.1	40.4	37.1	33.6
Bought from friend	*	43.1	*	39.4	*	33.1
Bought from relative	*	2.2	*	5.4	*	3.9
From my prescription	15.1	15.0	18.4	14.9	40.2	36.7
Bought from dealer/stranger	26.7	20.3	24.2	24.1	18.6	17.5
Other method	17.8	13.2	7.5	9.5	8.5	10.3

* No date; question not asked.

Source: "Source of Prescription Drugs among Those Who Used Last Year, Grade 12, 2007–2013." Johnston, Lloyd D., et al. 2014. "Monitoring the Future National Survey Results on Drug Use, 1975–2013. Vol. I, Secondary School Students." Table 10–5, p. 527. Ann Arbor, MI: Institute for Social Research. The University of Michigan. http://www.monitoringthefuture.org//pubs/monographs/mtf-vol1_2013.pdf. Accessed on May 2, 2015.

America's Prescription Drug Abuse Crisis." That report lists four areas in which prevention programs could be developed: education, tracking and monitoring, proper medication disposal, and enforcement.

Education

Education is a field of emphasis for nearly every organization or individual who has suggestions about the prevention of prescription drug abuse. That education is directed primarily at three targets: health care workers, patients, and pharmacists. Health care workers are of critical importance in reducing the spread of prescription drug abuse because physicians and other health care personnel are responsible for writing the prescriptions for drugs that may later be used for other than medical purposes. One of the critical steps that health care workers can take to help deal with the problem of nonmedical use of prescription drugs is self-education, improving their own understanding of the issue. A number of commentators have pointed out the limited exposure that physicians, nurses, and other health care providers may have had to issues related to prescription drug abuse in their professional training. The 2011 Obama review of the prescription drug abuse epidemic noted that

> prescribers and dispensers, including physicians, physician assistants, nurse practitioners, pharmacists, nurses, prescribing psychologists, and dentists, all have a role to play in reducing prescription drug misuse and abuse. Most receive little training on the importance of appropriate prescribing and dispensing of opioids to prevent adverse effects, diversion, and addiction. Outside of specialty addiction treatment programs, most healthcare providers have received minimal training in how to recognize substance abuse in their patients. Most medical, dental, pharmacy, and other health professional schools do not provide in-depth training on substance abuse;

often, substance abuse education is limited to classroom or clinical electives. Moreover, students in these schools may only receive limited training on treating pain. ("Epidemic: Responding to America's Prescription Drug Abuse Crisis" 2011, 2–3)

Under the circumstances, it is incumbent upon health care providers to take responsibility for staying up-to-date on recent developments in issues relating to prescription drug abuse. Among the recommendations with regard to this issue made by various boards, committees, review groups, and other organizations is one offered by the Center for Lawful Access and Abuse Deterrence in its National Prescription Drug Abuse Prevention Strategy position paper, published in 2010. That paper recommended that health care providers "[c]omplete continuing education [programs] on prescription drug abuse-related issues, including recognition of abuse, safe prescribing methods, use of PMP [prescription monitoring programs] data, and use of abuse-deterrent medications" ("National Prescription Drug Abuse Prevention Strategy" 2010, 55). Some examples of the courses that have been designed to meet this recommendation include:

• "Clinical Challenges in Prescribing Controlled Drugs: Prescribing Opioids for Chronic Pain." Substance Abuse and Mental Health Services Administration. http://www.dpt .samhsa.gov/providers/prescribingcourses.aspx.

• Protecting Your Practice and Patients from Prescription Drug Abuse. PharmCon. http://www.freece.com/freece/ CECatalog_Details.aspx?ID=d13bc174-55a8-48bd-be5f-9 549c971d551.

• Prescriber's Summit on Prescription Drug Abuse/Misuse. Ohio Pharmacists Association. http://www.ohiopharmacists.org/aws/ OPA/pt/sd/calendar/38758/_PARENT/layout_interior_details/ true.

- Drug Diversion Training and Best Practice Prescribing. Wild Iris Medical Education, Inc. http://www.nursingceu .com/courses/486/index_nceu.html.
- Various topics: PCSS-O Training. http://pcss-o.org/modules.

A number of states have now adopted or are considering legislation that would require some categories of health care providers to complete approved continuing education courses dealing with prescription drug abuse ("Prevention of Prescription Drug Overdose and Abuse" 2014).

Prescriptions providers can take a number of other concrete actions to help prevent the misuse of prescription drugs, such as:

- Educate their own patients about the hazards involved in the nonmedical use of prescription drugs.
- Take part in more general educational programs to provide this information to the general public.
- Take all precautions necessary to store prescription drugs to prevent access to prospective misusers of those substances.
- Maintain careful control over prescription pads used in the office.
- Be aware of the signs and symptoms of potential or actual prescription drug abuse by patients and prospective patients.
- Institute screening programs for possible prescription drug abuse among patients. Screening programs are relatively simple questionnaires about patients' thoughts about prescription drugs that may provide hints as to individuals who may be at risk for misusing such drugs.
- Be aware of the symptoms of prescription drug abuse and, where possible, institute brief intervention programs to reduce or eliminate such behaviors in patients. Among the signs and symptoms that are characteristic of prescription drug abuse are:
  - Memory problems after taking medicine
  - Loss of coordination (walking unsteadily, frequent falls)

- ○ Changes in sleeping habits
- ○ Unexplained bruises
- ○ Being unsure of oneself
- ○ Irritability, sadness, depression
- ○ Unexplained chronic pain
- ○ Changes in eating habits
- ○ Wanting to stay alone a lot of the time
- ○ Failing to bathe or keep clean
- ○ Having trouble finishing sentences
- ○ Having trouble concentrating
- ○ Difficulty staying in touch with family or friends
- ○ Lack of interest in usual activities ("Pharmacists and Physicians" 2015)

Another aspect of education for physicians, nurses, dentists, and other prescribers of medication is the recently promulgated Risk Evaluation and Mitigation Strategy (REMS) program announced by the U.S. Food and Drug Administration (FDA). This program was recommended by the 2011 White House Prescription Drug Abuse Prevention Plan as a way of reducing deaths resulting from the misuse of opioid painkillers. The REMS program, announced in July 2012, encourages manufacturers of long-acting (LA) and extended-release (ER) opioid products to offer short (three-hour) courses on the safe prescribing of LA and ER drugs for more than 320,000 individuals who routinely prescribe such drugs for their patients (Bryson and Tanzi 2015; details of the REMS proposal are available at "Extended-release (ER) and Long-acting (LA) Opioid Analgesics Risk Evaluation and Mitigation Strategy (REMS)" 2014.)

Tracking and Monitoring

One of the most popular approaches to the prevention of prescription drug abuse has been tracking and monitoring of prescription drug sales. This approach is used by individual states rather than the federal government. It had its origin in the creation of the California Triplicate Prescription Program (TPP) in 1939. In that program, every prescription for Schedule II drugs had to be written in triplicate, one copy of which went to a central state recording office (the office of the state attorney general), a second copy remained with the prescriber, and a third copy stayed with the dispensing pharmacy. Over time, the California TPP developed more efficient methods of carrying out this program, changing from written prescriptions to electronic transmissions. Also, additional states adopted programs similar to the California TPP, all with a similar philosophy and similar goals, but with a variety of details as to how they operate. Today, such programs are called *prescription drug monitoring programs* (PDMPs). They exist in 49 of 50 states and the District of Columbia. (As of August 2015, Missouri is the only state without a PDMP; Clark, et al. 2012; "Prescription Drug Monitoring Program Frequently Asked Questions [FAQ]" 2015).

PDMPs have a number of benefits. Most importantly, they allow governmental agencies ranging from public health offices to law enforcement agencies to keep track of prescriptions that are being written for drugs that have the potential for nonmedical use, such as opioids, stimulants, and depressants. They alert these agencies to the possibility that specific prescribers, dispensers, and/or users may be involved in the nonmedical use of these drugs. PDMPs also make possible a variety of educational programs for prospective abusers of prescription drugs as well as for the general public. They also provide the data and statistics on which such educational programs can be based ("CURES/PDMP" 2015; "State Prescription Drug Monitoring Programs" 2011).

Although the federal government has no part in the administration, operation, or other activity of state PDMPs, it does provide financial assistance to states for the development and enhancement of those programs. The primary source of funding for this activity is the Harold Rogers Prescription Drug

Monitoring Grant Funding Program, named for Representative Harold Rogers (R-KY). Rogers introduced legislation in 2001 to the U.S. Congress that was eventually adopted the following year, creating the program that now carries his name. States that receive grants from the program are free to use them for any one of a variety of purposes, such as collecting and using data to determine drug abuse trends in a state, developing and carrying out the evaluation of existing drug prevention programs, contributing to the development of prescription drug abuse prevention programs, and enabling Native American communities to create and operate prescription drug abuse prevention programs and coordinating their efforts with those of the state in which they are located ("Harold Rogers Prescription Drug Monitoring Program. FY 2015 Competitive Grant Announcement" 2015).

Proper Medication Disposal

The importance of proper systems for disposing of unused or unwanted prescription drugs is illustrated by the number of individuals who obtain prescription drugs illegally from that source. In many studies, nearly three quarters of people who use prescription drugs for nonmedical purposes say they got those drugs from friends or relatives ("Epidemic: Responding to America's Prescription Drug Abuse Crisis" 2011, 7). The inference is that many individuals who had received those drugs legitimately for medical purposes then failed to take them all and stored them in a medicine cabinet or some other location in their homes, from which they gave them to an unauthorized user. The solution to such a pattern, many experts say, is to develop and put into use simple, accessible systems through which a person can dispose of unwanted or unneeded medications.

Prior to 2014, the only legal methods for disposing of unused or unwanted prescription drugs was to flush them down the toilet, dispose of them in the trash, surrender them to law enforcement agencies, or seek some other method of disposal from the DEA. Many people decided, by intent or not, simply to store these drugs in their homes, often in locations that were readily available to other family members and friends. In September 2014, the DEA announced a new rule concerning the secure disposal of prescription drugs. The rule established a variety of disposal techniques for such drugs, ranging from mail-back programs, in which drugs could be sent back at no cost to manufacturers; take-back events, community-based occasions at which individuals could turn in unused drugs; and specially designed and situated disposal centers, where drugs could be dropped off. The new rule provided detailed instructions for the development and implementation of these systems of drug disposal ("Disposal of Controlled Substances" 2014; "Drug Disposal Information" 2015).

Enforcement

A fourth focus of the 2011 Obama administration program for dealing with prescription drug abuse was improved and enhanced law enforcement efforts. The "Epidemic" document emphasized in particular two specific issues related to the tracking and prosecution of illegal use of prescription drugs: so-called pill mills and the process known as doctor shopping ("Epidemic: Responding to America's Prescription Drug Abuse Crisis" 2011, 8–9). According to one definition, a pill mill is a doctor's office, pharmacy, clinic, or other facility that "sell[s] prescription drugs to those who have no medical need of them, or in excessive amounts" ("What Are Pill Mills?" 2015) The term *doctor shopping* refers to the practice of a person's "obtaining controlled substances from multiple healthcare practitioners without the prescribers' knowledge of the other prescriptions" ("Doctor Shopping Laws" 2012). The practice allows a person to obtain large quantities of a prescription drug for which he or she has no medical use.

The impetus provided by documents like the one outlined in "Epidemic" has led a number of states to adopt more aggressive programs for combating the nonmedical use of prescription drugs. A particularly instructive example comes from the state of Florida, which, in 2010, had the nation's highest rate of diversion of prescription drugs for illegal use. One consequence of that dubious record is that an estimated seven Floridians were dying every day in the state as a result of this problem ("Pill Mill Initiative" 2011). In 2011, the state legislature adopted a so-called anti-pill mill bill whose provisions included increasing administrative and criminal penalties for doctors and clinics convicted of prescription drug trafficking, establishing new standards for doctors who prescribe narcotic drugs, adding requirements for the registration of such drugs, banning doctors from prescribing certain drugs especially likely to be used for nonmedical purposes, increasing the monitoring of pharmacies and companies that dispense prescription drugs, and improving the system for monitoring prescription drug dispensing ("Pill Mill Initiative" 2011; a copy of the bill is available online at http://www.flsenate.gov/Session/Bill/2011/7095/BillText/er/ PDF. Accessed on May 6, 2015).

As of early 2013, nine states had adopted some form of legislation designed to identify and, monitor, and (usually) close pill mills: Florida, Georgia, Kentucky, Louisiana, Mississippi, Ohio, Tennessee, Texas, and West Virginia ("Prescription Drug Abuse, Addiction and Diversion: Overview of State Legislative and Policy Initiatives" 2014). Other states continue to consider similar types of pill mill legislation.

Some observers have pointed out that anti-pill mill bills are not without their undesirable and sometimes unexpected consequences. On the one hand, some patients who have legitimate needs for certain opioids or other prescription drugs, usually for the control of pain, are unable to get their prescriptions filled. On the other hand, pharmacists may feel so pressured by the pill mill laws that they refuse to fill such prescriptions for fear of running afoul of the law (Friedman 2014).

Another unintended consequence of pill mill and similar prescription drug laws is that people who have become dependent upon or addicted to prescription drugs may switch to other drugs, at least as dangerous as the prescription drugs to which they no longer have access. In many cases, the drug of choice is an old, familiar, and illegal substance: heroin. A number of studies have now shown that pill mill laws may produce decreases—often rapid and large—in the number of facilities where prescription drugs may be illegally obtained, but that such successes are countered by comparable rapid and large increases in the use of illegal drugs such as heroin (Huecker and Shoff 2014).

All 50 states and the District of Columbia also have some type of legislation dealing with doctor shopping. Those laws differ from state to state and can be classified as "general" doctor shopping laws or "specific" doctor shopping laws. General doctor shopping laws tend to adopt language from the federal Uniform Controlled Substances Act ("Uniform Controlled Substances Act (1994)" 1994) or the much older Uniform Narcotic Drug Act (which it supplanted) that restrict the sale and purchase of all and any kind of drug. The relevant Delaware law, for example, is based on the former statute and the California law, on the latter statute. Other states, such as Rhode Island, have two general doctor shopping laws, one based on each of the two federal statutes ("Doctor Shopping Laws" 2012). General doctor shopping laws tend to use phrases such as "[i]t is unlawful for any person knowingly or intentionally . . . [t]o acquire or obtain or attempt to acquire or obtain, possession of a controlled substance or prescription drug by misrepresentation, fraud, forgery, deception or subterfuge" ("Miscellaneous Drug Crimes; Class B, C and F Felony" 2015).

Other states have more specific and more rigorous laws that make it clear that they refer specifically to the practice of doctor shopping. These laws generally describe and prohibit the practices used by individuals in doctor shopping, as in the Montana law that makes it illegal for a person to

> knowingly or purposefully failing to disclose to a practitioner, . . . that the person has received the same or a similar dangerous drug or prescription for a dangerous

drug from another source within the prior 30 days; or . . . knowingly or purposefully communicating false or incomplete information to a practitioner with the intent to procure the administration of or a prescription for a dangerous drug. ("45-9-104. Fraudulently obtaining dangerous drugs" 2014)

While many public health and law enforcement agencies are generally enthusiastic about the potential for doctor shopping laws as a way of reducing the illegal use of prescription drugs, some legal and civil rights specialists have expressed concerns about the possible intrusion of such laws on an individual privacy. They argue that a person's medical records should be sacrosanct and developing databases that can be shared among doctors, pharmacists, law enforcement officers, and others is a substantial threat to anyone's privacy ("ACLU Asks Court to Protect Confidentiality of Rush Limbaugh's Medical Records" 2004; also see "Your Prescriptions and Your Privacy" 2015; for a very interesting exchange among individuals involved in doctor shopping, see "I've Been Caught Doctor Shopping . . . What Next?" 2015).

Treatment

Two categories of treatment are available for dealing with prescription drug dependence and addiction: behavioral counseling and medication. The term *behavioral counseling* refers to any form of treatment in which a patient works individually or in a group with a trained counselor to modify one's behavior with regard to some problem behavior, such as prescription drug use. The counselor introduces a variety of techniques for helping a patient avoid contact with drugs entirely, stay away from situations in which he or she may come into contact with those drugs, learn to live a normal life without depending on prescription drugs, become familiar with resources that are available to assist a patient with drug cravings, and develop strategies for avoiding or dealing with relapses that may lead to further involvement with prescription drugs.

A second approach involves the use of some medication that will help a person overcome dependence on drugs. The most common of the medications used for this purpose are methadone, naloxone, naltrexone, and buprenorphine. The treatment chosen for any particular individual depends to a large extent on the type of prescription drug on which one is dependent or to which one has become addicted.

Opioids

The treatment of choice for abuse of opioids is one of the medications listed in the previous paragraph. These medications are helpful because they act chemically on opioid receptors in the brain to counteract the effect of opioids themselves. Naloxone and naltrexone are opioid *antagonists*, chemicals that bind to opioid receptors in the brain, making them unavailable for access to opioids themselves. When these receptors become blocked, the introduction of an opioid to the brain can have none of the effects on which a user expects from the drug because the opioid receptors are already blocked and unavailable to react with the introduced opioid. (For a video that shows how naloxone and naltrexone work in the brain, see http://www.vivitrol.com/About/HowVIVWorksOPD.) Naloxone acts more quickly and over a shorter period of time (a few hours), so is most commonly used for the treatment of opioid overdoses. Since naltrexone works more slowly and over longer periods of time (a few days), it is generally recommended for long-term therapeutic treatment of people who have become dependent upon or addicted to opioids ("Opioid Antagonists: Naloxone and Naltrexone" 2013; Preda 2014).

Methadone works in the brain in a very different way. It is an *agonist*, that is, a substance that binds to a receptor and initiates a biochemical reaction. In that regard, it is similar to heroin and other opioids. When one ingests methadone, it goes to the brain and binds to opioid receptors in the same way as do heroin and other opioids. The difference between methadone and other opioids, however, is that its stimulating effects are more moderate than are those of heroin and other opioids. Receptors to which methadone are attached release dopamine, as they do with heroin. But the "high" produced is less intense and smoother than that from heroin. A person on methadone therapy needs to take a methadone dose only once a day, during which time he or she no longer feels the intense desire for heroin or other opioids. Methadone therapy has been in use for nearly half a century and generally works very well with the majority of patients, provided it is accompanied by regular supportive counseling and therapy sessions ("Overview of Methadone Maintenance Treatment" 2009; for more information on the biochemical action of methadone in the brain, see "Brain Scans Confirm Hunch about Methadone's Effect" 2000).

A third medication used for the treatment of opioid dependence and addiction is buprenorphine. Buprenorphine is a *partial opioid agonist*, meaning that it attaches to opioid receptors in the brain and produces effects similar to those produced by heroin and other opioids, but to a significantly reduced extent. It is a semisynthetic opioid derived from thebaine, a constituent of the poppy seed. A person who ingests buprenorphine experiences euphoria like that produced by heroin, but to a lesser extent with a significantly reduced risk of dependence and addiction. Substituting buprenorphine for heroin or other opioids, thus, can help wean a person away from more dangerous opioid drugs ("Clinical Guidelines for the Use of Buprenorphine in the Treatment of Opioid Addiction" 2004, 11–13).

The format in which medications are available and the way in which they are used may have to be adjusted for specific situations. For example, the FDA has approved the use of a combination product consisting of buprenorphine and naxolone for treatment of individuals thought to be at risk for continued illegal drug use. The combination is safe and efficacious when taken orally, but produces severe withdrawal symptoms when dissolved and injected, thus greatly reducing the risk that users will switch to buprenorphine alone for recreational purposes ("Clinical Guidelines for the Use of Buprenorphine in the Treatment of Opioid Addiction" 2004, 23).

Stimulants and Depressants

There are currently no FDA-approved medications for use in treating dependence on or addiction to stimulants and CNS depressants. The systems of treatment that can be used, then, are those behavioral methods that have been developed for other forms of drug abuse, such as those involving cocaine. The essential approach in such cases is *not* to allow a patient to quit using drugs "cold turkey," but to develop a program of gradual withdrawal that allows the body to lose its physical dependence on a substance, while providing the patient with assistance and support through the process of giving up the drug ("Prescription Drug Abuse" 2014).

Summary and Conclusion

Over the past two decades, the nonmedical use of prescription drugs has become a public health problem of major concern in the United States. Drugs that have been developed to bring relief from a variety of difficult medical conditions have begun to attract attention as substances that can also be used for recreational purposes, often with serious or even devastating side effects. A number of policies and practices have been developed to deal with this problem, including the use of new types of medication, improved programs of prevention, and more aggressive approaches to the control of prescription medications. And those policies and practices appear to be having some effects in bringing down the rate of use, morbidity, and mortality association with prescription drug abuse. The problem is not, however, completely solved. Further diligence in helping people understand the deleterious effects of using prescription drugs for recreational purposes is needed if the problem can ultimately and fully be brought under control.

References

"Abuse of Prescription (Rx) Drugs Affects Young Adults Most." 2013. http://www.drugabuse .gov/related-topics/trends-statistics/infographics/ abuse-prescription-rx-drugs-affects-young-adults-most. Accessed on April 24, 2015.

"ACLU Asks Court to Protect Confidentiality of Rush Limbaugh's Medical Records." 2004. American Civil Liberties Union. https://www.aclu.org/news/ aclu-asks-court-protect-confidentiality-rush-limbaughs- medical-records. Accessed on May 7, 2015.

"Addressing Prescription Drug Abuse in the United States: Current Activities and Future Opportunities." 2013. Behavioral Health Coordinating Committee. Prescription Drug Abuse Subcommittee. U.S. Department of Health and Human Services. http://www.cdc.gov/ HomeandRecreationalSafety/pdf/HHS_Prescription_ Drug_Abuse_Report_09.2013.pdf. Accessed on April 23, 2015.

"Attention Deficit Hyperactivity Disorder: Stimulant Therapy." 2013. Cleveland Clinic. http:// my.clevelandclinic.org/health/diseases_conditions/ hic_Attention-Deficit-Hyperactivity_Disorder/hic_ Attention-Deficit-Hyperactivity_Disorder_Stimulant_ Therapy. Accessed on April 28, 2015.

"Barbiturates." 2015. Drugs.com. http://www.drugs.com/ drug-class/barbiturates.html. Accessed on April 28, 2015.

Benyamin, Ramsin, et al. 2008. "Opioid Complications and Side Effects." *Pain Physician* 11 (2 Suppl): S105–20.

"Benzodiazepine Equivalence Table." 2007. http://www .benzo.org.uk/bzequiv.htm. Accessed on April 28, 2015.

"Brain and Addiction." 2015. NIDA for Teens. http://teens. drugabuse.gov/drug-facts/brain-and-addiction. Accessed on April 27, 2015.

"Brain Scans Confirm Hunch about Methadone's Effect." 2000. News and Notes. The Rockefeller University. http://www.rockefeller.edu/pubinfo/news_notes/121500e.html. Accessed on May 7, 2015.

Bryson, Michelle, and Maria Tanzi. 2015. "Risk Evaluation and Mitigation Strategy Compliance." Practical Pain Management. http://www.practicalpainmanagement.com/treatments/pharmacological/opioids/risk-evaluation-mitigation-strategy- compliance. Accessed on May 4, 2015.

"Central Nervous System (CNS) Depressants and Stimulants." 2012. Spine Universe. http://www.spineuniverse.com/treatments/medication/central-nervous-system-cns-depressants-stimulants. Accessed on April 28, 2015.

Clark, Thomas, John Eadie, Peter Kreiner, and Gail Strickler. 2012. "Prescription Drug Monitoring Programs: An Assessment of the Evidence for Best Practices." The Prescription Drug Monitoring Program Center of Excellence. Brandeis University. http://www.pdmpexcellence.org/sites/all/pdfs/Brandeis_PDMP_Report_final.pdf. Accessed on May 4, 2015.

"Clinical Guidelines for the Use of Buprenorphine in the Treatment of Opioid Addiction." 2004. Substance Abuse and Mental Health Services Administration. http://www.ncbi.nlm.nih.gov/books/NBK64245/pdf/TOC.pdf. Accessed on May 8, 2015.

Compton, Wilson M. 2014. "The Science of Addiction: Prescription Drug Abuse." American Osteopathic College of Occupational and Preventative Medicine. http://www.aocopm.org/assets/documents/AM14/d-omed%20rx%20addiction%20science.pdf. Accessed on April 27, 2015.

Converse, Deborah. 2015. "Prescription Drug Abuse: Etiology, Prevention and Treatment. https://s3.amazonaws.com/EliteCME_WebSite_2013/f/pdf/SWUS06PDI15.pdf. Accessed on April 30, 2015.

"Cough and Cold Medicine (DXM and Codeine Syrup).
2015. NIDA for Teens. http://teens.drugabuse.gov/drug-
facts/cough-and-cold-medicine-dxm-and-codeine-syrup.
Accessed on April 29, 2015.

"CURES/PDMP." 2015. Office of the Attorney General.
California Department of Justice. http://oag.ca.gov/sites/
all/files/agweb/pdfs/pdmp/brochure.pdf. Accessed on
May 4, 2015.

Degenhardt, Louisa, and Wayne Hall. 2012. "Extent of Illicit
Drug Use and Dependence, and Their Contribution to
the Global Burden of Disease." *Lancet* 379 (9810): 55–70.
http://www.thelancet.com/pdfs/journals/lancet/PIIS0140-
6736(11)61138-0.pdf. Accessed on April 26, 2015.

"Dimenhydrinate." 2015. Medline Plus. http://www.nlm.nih
.gov/medlineplus/druginfo/meds/a607046.html. Accessed
on May 8, 2015.

"Diphenhydramine." 2015. Medline Plus. http://www
.nlm.nih.gov/medlineplus/druginfo/meds/a682539.html.
Accessed on May 8, 2015.

"Disposal of Controlled Substances." 2014. Federal Register 79
(174): 53520–70. http://www.deadiversion.usdoj.gov/fed_
regs/rules/2014/2014-20926.pdf. Accessed on May 4, 2015.

"Doctor Shopping Laws." 2012. Centers for Disease Control
and Prevention. http://www.cdc.gov/phlp/docs/menu-
shoppinglaws.pdf. Accessed on May 6, 2015.

"Drug Abuse Warning Network, 2011: National Estimates
of Drug-Related Emergency Department Visits."
2013. Center for Behavioral Health Statistics and
Quality. Substance Abuse and Mental Health Services
Administration. http://www.samhsa.gov/data/sites/default/
files/DAWN2k11ED/DAWN2k11ED/DAWN2k11ED
.pdf. Accessed on April 27, 2015.

"Drug Disposal Information." 2015. Drug Enforcement
Administration. http://www.deadiversion.usdoj.gov/drug_
disposal/index.html. Accessed on May 4, 2015.

"DrugFacts: Synthetic Cathinones ("Bath Salts")." 2012. National Institute on Drug Abuse. http://www.drugabuse.gov/publications/drugfacts/synthetic-cathinones-bath-salts. Accessed on April 29, 2015.

"Effects of Prescription Drug Abuse." 2015. Narconon International. http://www.narconon.org/drug-abuse/effects-of-prescription-drugs.html. Accessed on April 22, 2015.

"Epidemic: Responding to America's Prescription Drug Abuse Crisis." 2011. Washington, DC: The White House. https://www.whitehouse.gov/sites/default/files/ondcp/issues-content/prescription-drugs/rx_abuse_plan.pdf. Accessed on May 3, 2015.

"Extended-release (ER) and Long-acting (LA) Opioid Analgesics Risk Evaluation and Mitigation Strategy (REMS)." 2014. U.S. Food and Drug Administration. http://www.fda.gov/downloads/Drugs/DrugSafety/PostmarketDrugSafetyInformationforPatientsandProviders/UCM311290.pdf. Accessed on May 4, 2015.

Fenichel, Marilyn. 2012. "Brain Chemical Transporters: Solving the Ritalin Paradox." BrainFacts.org. http://www.brainfacts.org/brain-basics/cell-communication/articles/2012/brain-chemical-transporters-solving-the-ritalin-paradox/. Accessed on April 28, 2015.

45-9-104. Fraudulently obtaining dangerous drugs. 2014. Montana Code Annotated 2014. http://leg.mt.gov/bills/mca/45/9/45-9-104.htm. Accessed on May 7, 2015.

Frakt, Austin. 2014. "Painkiller Abuse, a Cyclical Challenge." New York Times. http://www.nytimes.com/2014/12/23/upshot/painkiller-abuse-a-cyclical-challenge.html?_r=0&abt=0002&abg=1. Accessed on April 30, 2015.

Friedman, Emily. 2014. "Stopping Dr. Feelgood: The Challenge of Overprescribing." H&HN Daily. http://www.hhnmag.com/display/HHN-news-article.dhtml?dcrPath=/

templatedata/HF_Common/NewsArticle/data/HHN/
Daily/2014/Feb/020414-article-Emily-Friedman-precription-
drugs. Accessed on May 6, 2015.

"Harold Rogers Prescription Drug Monitoring Program. FY 2015
Competitive Grant Announcement." 2015. Bureau of Justice
Assistance. U.S. Department of Justice. https://www.bja.gov/
Funding/15PDMPsol.pdf. Accessed on May 4, 2015.

"Health, United States, 2013." Centers for Disease Control and
Prevention. National Center for Health Statistics. http://www
.cdc.gov/nchs/data/hus/hus13.pdf. Accessed on April 24, 2015.

"Highlights of the 2011 Drug Abuse Warning Network (DAWN)
Findings on Drug-Related Emergency Department Visits."
2013. Center for Behavioral Health Statistics and Quality.
Substance Abuse and Mental Health Services Administration.
http://archive.samhsa.gov/data/2k13/DAWN127/sr127-
DAWN-highlights.htm. Accessed on April 25, 2015.

"How Drugs Affect Neurotransmitters." 2015. The Brain from
Top to Bottom. http://thebrain.mcgill.ca/flash/i/i_03/i_03_m/
i_03_m_par/i_03_m_par_heroine.html#drogues. Accessed on
April 27, 2015.

Huecker, Martin R., and Hugh W. Shoff. 2014. "The Law
of Unintended Consequences: Illicit for Licit Narcotic
Substitution." *Western Journal of Emergency Medicine* 15
(4): 561–63. http://www.ncbi.nlm.nih.gov/pmc/articles/
PMC4100869/. Accessed on May 6, 2015.

"I've Been Caught Doctor Shopping . . . What Next?" 2015.
Drugs.com. http://www.drugs.com/forum/featured-conditions/
Ive-been-caught-doctor-shopping-what-next-34036.html.
Accessed on May 7, 2015.

Johnston, Lloyd D., Patrick M. O'Malley, Jerald G. Bachman,
John E. Schulenberg, and Richard A. Miech. 2014.
"Monitoring the Future National Survey Results on Drug Use,
1975–2013." Vol. I, Secondary School Students. Ann Arbor:
Institute for Social Research, The University of Michigan.

http://www.monitoringthefuture.org//pubs/monographs/
mtf-vol1_2013.pdf. Accessed on May 2, 2015.

Lakhan, Shaheen E., and Annette Kirchgessner. 2012.
"Prescription Stimulants in Individuals with and without
Attention Deficit Hyperactivity Disorder: Misuse,
Cognitive Impact, and Adverse Effects." *Brain and Behavior*
2 (5): 661–77. http://www.ncbi.nlm.nih.gov/pmc/articles/
PMC3489818/. Accessed on April 28, 2015.

"Medicine Use and Shifting Costs of Healthcare." 2014. IMS
Institute for Healthcare Informatics. http://www.imshealth
.com/deployedfiles/imshealth/Global/Content/Corporate/
IMS%20Health%20Institute/Reports/Secure/IIHI_US_
Use_of_Meds_for_2013.pdf. Accessed on April 22, 2015.

"Miscellaneous Drug Crimes; Class B, C and F Felony."
2015. Delaware Code Online. Title 16. Chapter 47. http://
www.delcode.delaware.gov/title16/c047/sc04/index.shtml.
Accessed on May 7, 2015.

"Monitoring the Future Study: Trends in Prevalence of
Various Drugs." 2015. National Institute on Drug Abuse.
http://www.drugabuse.gov/trends-statistics/monitoring-
future/monitoring-future-study-trends-in-prevalence-
various-drugs. Accessed on April 29, 2015.

"National Drug Control Strategy. Data Supplement 2013."
n.d. n.p. https://www.whitehouse.gov/sites/default/files/
ondcp/policy-and-research/2013_data_supplement_final2
.pdf. Accessed on April 26, 2015.

"National Prescription Drug Abuse Prevention Strategy."
2010. Center for Lawful Access and Abuse Deterrence.
http://claad.org/wp-content/uploads/2013/10/2010_
National_Strategy.pdf. Accessed on May 4, 2015.

Neubert, Amy Patterson. 2014. "Study: Peers, but Not
Peer Pressure, Key to Prescription Drug Misuse among
Young Adults." Purdue University News. http://
www.purdue.edu/newsroom/releases/2014/Q3/

study-peers,-but-not-peer-pressure,-key-to-prescription-drug-misuse-among-young-adults.html. Accessed on April 30, 2015.

"The Neurobiology of Drug Addiction." 2015. National Institute of Drug Abuse. http://www.drugabuse.gov/publications/teaching-packets/neurobiology-drug-addiction. Accessed on April 27, 2015.

"Nonmedical Use of Prescription Stimulants." 2015. Center on Young Adult Health and Development. University of Maryland School of Public Health. http://medicineabuseproject.org/assets/documents/NPSFactSheet.pdf. Accessed on April 28, 2015.

"Opiate Withdrawal." 2015. Medline Plus. http://www.nlm.nih.gov/medlineplus/ency/article/000949.htm. Accessed on April 27, 2015.

"Opioid Antagonists: Naloxone and Naltrexone." 2013. Opiophilia. http://opiophilia.blogspot.com/2013/07/opioid-antagonists-naloxone-and.html. Accessed on May 8, 2015.

"Overview of Methadone Maintenance Treatment." 2009. Centre for Addiction and Mental Health. http://knowledgex.camh.net/amhspecialists/specialized_treatment/methadone_maintenance/Pages/default.aspx. Accessed on May 7, 2015.

"Pain and Addiction." 2015. American Society of Addiction Medicine. http://www.asam.org/for-the-public/pain-and-addiction. Accessed on April 30, 2015.

"Partners in Integrity." 2014. Centers for Medicare and Medicaid Services. U.S. Department of Health and Human Services. http://www.cms.gov/medicare-medicaid-coordination/fraud-prevention/medicaid-integrity-education/provider-education-toolkits/downloads/prescriber-role-drugdiversion.pdf. Accessed on May 2, 2015.

"Pharmacists and Physicians." 2015. Preventing Prescription Drug Misuse. http://www.prescriptiondrugmisuse.org/index.php?page=pharmacists_and_physicians. Accessed on May 4, 2015.

"Physical Dependence and Addiction." 2014. The National Alliance of Advocates for Buprenorphine Treatment. http://www.naabt.org/addiction_physical-dependence.cfm. Accessed on April 27, 2015.

"Pill Mill Initiative." 2011. Office of the Attorney General of Florida. http://myfloridalegal.com/pages.nsf/Main/AA7AAF5CAA22638D8525791B006A30C8. Accessed on May 6, 2015.

"Popping Pill: Prescription Drug Abuse in America." 2014. National Institute on Drug Abuse. http://www.drugabuse.gov/related-topics/trends-statistics/infographics/popping-pills-prescription-drug-abuse-in-america. Accessed on April 24, 2015.

Preda, Adrian. 2014. "Opioid Abuse Treatment & Management." Medscape. http://emedicine.medscape.com/article/287790-treatment. Accessed on May 8, 2015.

"Prescription Depressant Medications." 2015. NIDA for Teens. http://teens.drugabuse.gov/drug-facts/prescription-depressant-medications. Accessed on April 28, 2015.

"Prescription Drug Abuse." 2014. National Institute on Drug Abuse. https://d14rmgtrwzf5a.cloudfront.net/sites/default/files/prescriptiondrugrrs_11_14.pdf. Accessed on April 30, 3015.

"Prescription Drug Abuse, Addiction and Diversion: Overview of State Legislative and Policy Initiatives." 2014. The National Alliance for Model State Drug Laws and the National Safety Council. http://www.namsdl.org/NAMSDL%20Part%202%20Revised%20April%204%202014.pdf. Accessed on May 6, 2015.

"Prescription Drug Abuse & Addiction Causes, Signs, Side Effects & Symptoms." 2015. Abilene Behavioral Health.

http://www.abilenebehavioralhealth.com/addiction/
prescription-drugs/signs-symptoms-effects#Causes.
Accessed on April 30, 2015.

"Prescription Drug Monitoring Frequently Asked Questions
(FAQ)." 2015. Prescription Drug Monitoring Program
Training and Technical Assistance Center. http://www
.pdmpassist.org/content/prescription-drug-monitoring-
frequently-asked-questions-faq. Accessed on May 4, 2015.

"Prevention of Prescription Drug Overdose and Abuse."
2014. National Conference of State Legislatures. http://
www.ncsl.org/research/health/prevention-of-prescription-
drug-overdose-and-abuse.aspx. Accessed on May 4, 2015.

Prosser, Jane M., and Lewis S. Nelson. 2012. "The Toxicology
of Bath Salts: A Review of Synthetic Cathinones." *Journal
of Medical Toxicology* 8 (1): 33–42. http://www.ncbi
.nlm.nih.gov/pmc/articles/PMC3550219/. Accessed on
April 29, 2015.

Radnofsky, Louise, and Joseph Walker. 2014. "DEA Restricts
Narcotic Pain Drug Prescriptions." Wall Street Journal.
http://www.wsj.com/articles/dea-restricts-narcotic-pain-drug-
prescriptions-1408647617. Accessed on April 30, 2015.

"Report: Prescribers, Patients and Pain" 2015. Partnership
for Drug-Free Kids. http://www.drugfree.org/wp-content/
uploads/2015/04/FULL-REPORT-FINAL-Prescribers-
Patients-and-Pain-Research.pdf. Accessed on April 30,
2015.

"Results from the 2011 National Survey on Drug Use and
Health: Summary of National Findings." 2012. Center
for Behavioral Health Statistics and Quality. Substance
Abuse and Mental Health Services Administration.
U.S. Department of Health and Human Services.
http://archive.samhsa.gov/data/NSDUH/2k11Results/
NSDUHresults2011.htm. Accessed on April 24, 2015.

"Results from the 2013 National Survey on Drug
Use and Health: Summary of National Findings."

2014. Center for Behavioral Health Statistics and Quality. Substance Abuse and Mental Health Services Administration. U.S. Department of Health and Human Services. http://www.samhsa.gov/data/sites/default/files/NSDUHresultsPDFWHTML2013/Web/NSDUHresults2013.pdf. Accessed on April 24, 2015.

"Schedules of Controlled Substances: Rescheduling of Hydrocodone Combination Products from Schedule III to Schedule II." 2014. Drug Enforcement Administration. http://www.deadiversion.usdoj.gov/fed_regs/rules/2014/fr0822.htm. Accessed on April 30, 2015.Schwarz, Alan. 2015. "Workers Seeking Productivity in a Pill Are Abusing A.D.H.D. Drugs." New York Times, April 18, 2015, A1–17. http://www.nytimes.com/2015/04/19/us/workers-seeking-productivity-in-a-pill-are-abusing-adhd-drugs.html?_r=0. Accessed on May 7, 2015 (Subscription required).

"State Prescription Drug Monitoring Programs." 2011. Office of Diversion Control. Drug Enforcement Administration. http://www.deadiversion.usdoj.gov/faq/rx_monitor.htm#4. Accessed on May 4, 2015.

"Stop Medicine Abuse." 2015. http://stopmedicineabuse.org/. Accessed on April 29, 2015.

Teter, Christian J., and Sally K. Guthrie. 2001. "A Comprehensive Review of MDMA and GHB: Two Common Club Drugs." *Pharmacotherapy* 21 (12): 1486–513.

"2012 Partnership Attitude Tracking Study." 2013. MetLife Foundation and the Partnership at DrugFree.org. http://www.drugfree.org/wp-content/uploads/2013/04/PATS-2012-FULL-REPORT2.pdf. Accessed on April 30, 2015.

"Uniform Controlled Substances Act (1994)." 1994. National Conference of Commissioners on Uniform State Laws. http://www.uniformlaws.org/shared/docs/controlled%20substances/UCSA_final%20_94%20with%2095amends.pdf. Accessed on May 7, 2015.

United Nations Office on Drugs and Crime. 2011. "World Drug Report 2011." Vienna: United Nations. http://www .unodc.org/documents/data-and-analysis/WDR2011/ World_Drug_Report_2011_ebook.pdf. Accessed on April 26, 2015.

United Nations Office on Drugs and Crime. 2014. "World Drug Report 2014." Vienna: United Nations. http:// www.unodc.org/documents/wdr2014/World_Drug_ Report_2014_web.pdf. Accessed on April 26, 2015.

"Use, Abuse, Misuse & Disposal of Prescription Pain Medication Clinical Reference." 2011. American College of Preventive Medicine. http://www.acpm .org/?UseAbuseRxClinRef. Accessed on April 27, 2015.

Volkow, Nora D. 2014. "Prescription Drug Abuse." National Institute on Drug Abuse. http://www.drugabuse.gov/ publications/research-reports/prescription-drugs/director. Accessed on April 24, 2015.

Warner, Margaret, Holly Hedegaard, and Li-Hui Chen. 2014. "Trends in Drug-Poisoning Deaths Involving Opioid Analgesics and Heroin: United States, 1999–2012." Health E-Stats. http://www.cdc.gov/nchs/data/hestat/ drug_poisoning/drug_poisoning_deaths_1999-2012.pdf. Accessed on April 26, 2015.

"What Are Opioids?" 2015. NIDA for Teens. http://teens. drugabuse.gov/node/1271. Accessed on August 11, 2015.

"What Are Pill Mills?" 2015. Pain.com. http://pain.com/ archives/2013/09/12-pill-mills/. Accessed on May 6, 2015.

"Your Prescriptions and Your Privacy." 2015. Privacy Rights Clearinghouse. https://www.privacyrights.org/fs/fsC4/CA-medical-prescription-privacy. Accessed on May 7, 2015.

3 Perspectives

Introduction

The issue of prescription drug abuse affects many people in a variety of different ways. This chapter provides essays of individuals and representatives of organizations concerned about that problem with an opportunity to express their individual viewpoints on some specific aspect of the topic.

State Efforts to Curb the Prescription Drug Abuse Epidemic
Carmen A. Catizone

Faced with sobering statistics indicating that millions of Americans continue to misuse prescription drugs, state and federal regulators have taken several steps since the early 2000s to reduce overdose and abuse rates and protect the public health. These efforts include increasing awareness about the dangers of abusing prescription drugs, educating consumers about proper drug storage and disposal of drugs to prevent abusers from obtaining them, and implementing laws that help keep prescription drugs out of the wrong hands. Nevertheless, prescription drug abuse rates remain at epidemic proportions, and new issues, including a potential link between prescription painkiller abuse and growing rates of heroin use, have kept this

---

Pharmacists understand that they must routinely double- and even triple-check the medications that they supply to customers. (sjlockeview/iStock-Photo.com)

public health crisis a subject of national concern. State boards of pharmacy, the Substance Abuse and Mental Health Services Administration, and the Centers for Disease Control and Prevention (CDC) are among the state and federal agencies that continue to analyze the situation and implement programs to address this complex issue.

According to the most recent National Survey on Drug Use and Health, an estimated 6.5 million persons over the age of 12 are currently misusing psychotherapeutic drugs, including painkillers, tranquilizers, stimulants, and sedatives. A common misconception about prescription drugs is that they are safer to abuse than illicit "street" drugs such as heroin. In reality, people who abuse prescription medications are taking a big risk. In 2009, the federal government estimated that more than 1.2 million annual visits to hospital emergency departments involved the nonmedical use of pharmaceuticals (Substance Abuse and Mental Health Services Administration 2010). Further, more than 22,000 people died from drug overdoses involving pharmaceuticals in 2010—representing nearly 60 percent of all drug overdose deaths that year. Opioid painkillers were involved in three out of four of those deaths (Centers for Disease Control and Prevention 2013).

Following over a decade of educational and legislative efforts to curb prescription drug abuse, rates appear to be relatively flat, though still high compared to rates in the 1990s. Unfortunately, this good news has been dampened by evidence that heroin use rates are growing rapidly. In fact, some groups have speculated that as prescription painkillers become harder to access, some users may switch to heroin when it becomes easier to obtain. One study found that while the vast number of prescription painkiller abusers did not turn to heroin, those who did start using heroin were much more likely to have abused prescription painkillers first (Muhuri, Gfoerer, and Davies 2013).

The relationship between misuse of prescription painkillers and heroin use is still being determined; however, there is enough evidence to warrant concern. Medically, opioid pain killers and heroin act on the same receptors in the brain, and "[non-medical pain reliever] use may precondition one to engage in heroin use" (Muhuri, Gfoerer, and Davies 2013).

Although some people may be switching to heroin as a replacement for misusing prescription painkillers, it does not appear that heroin overdose rate increases have any significant association with decreases in prescription drug overdoses. In October 2014, CDC indicated that in 18 states increases in heroin overdose rates correlated with increases in prescription overdose rates (Rudd et al. 2014).

In response to this alarming trend, many states have taken steps to increase access to naloxone, a prescription medication that can help to reverse effects of an opioid overdose and save lives. In October 2014, the National Association of Boards of Pharmacy (NABP) issued a policy statement promoting an active role for pharmacists in expanding access to naloxone.

Nonmedical use of Adderall and other stimulants prescribed for people with attention deficit hyperactivity disorder is another area of concern. It has been estimated that 17 percent of college students have misused or abused prescription stimulants (Benson et al. 2015, 50). Many of these students abuse and misuse stimulants because they believe the drugs will help them study or lose weight. In addition, many students believe that nonmedical use of stimulants poses the same level of risk as consuming an energy drink. In reality, abuse of Adderall and similar medications may lead to adverse effects such as sleep disorders, restlessness, headaches, irritability, and depression as well as the potential for psychological and physiological dependence.

In addition to raising public awareness, tools such as prescription drug monitoring programs (PDMPs), have been shown to prevent abuse and diversion of prescription drugs. PDMPs work by requiring pharmacists to submit relevant dispensed prescriptions (as determined by state law) to a state-run database. Prescribers and dispensers can consult these records to make the most appropriate prescribing and dispensing decisions. PDMP records can also help health care providers identify "doctor shopping," that is, patients visiting multiple prescribers in a short period of time to receive multiple prescriptions. By identifying patients at risk for dependence or addiction, prescribers or dispensers may be able to assist by offering medication counseling or determining if other care is needed.

PDMPs may also be effective in changing prescribing behavior, thereby reducing doctor shopping and reducing prescription drug abuse (Finklea, Sacco, and Bagalman 2014). For example, a number of policy and law enforcement measures in Florida, including the implementation of a PDMP, have been credited in helping to reduce the prescription drug overdose rate by 23 percent from 2010 to 2012, according to the CDC. New York and Tennessee saw 75 percent and 36 percent drops in doctor shopping, respectively, following 2012 requirements that prescribers check their states' PDMPs before prescribing painkillers. To date, 49 states and the District of Columbia have either established or passed legislation allowing some form of PDMP.

With the immense scope and complexity of the prescription drug abuse issue, relevant agencies must take a multipronged approach to addressing the problem. For example, NABP and its member boards of pharmacy developed a program to enhance the effectiveness of PDMPs by allowing for the secure sharing of PDMP data across state borders through the PDMP InterConnect program. Additionally, through its AWAR$_x$E Prescription Drug Safety Program, NABP educates pharmacists and consumers about prescription drug abuse and the importance of prevention efforts. Interested pharmacists and consumers can also download tools to help spread these important messages to their family, friends, and community. Going forward, preventing and reducing prescription drug abuse will continue to be a major area of focus for NABP and other stakeholders.

References

Benson, Kari, Kate Flory, Kathryn L. Humphreys, and Steve S. Lee. 2015. "Misuse of Stimulant Medication among College Students: A Comprehensive Review and Meta-analysis." *Clinical Child and Family Psychology Review* 18 (1): 50–76.

Centers for Disease Control and Prevention. 2013. "Opioids Drive Continued Increase in Drug Overdose Deaths." http://www.cdc.gov/media/releases/2013/p0220_drug_ overdose_deaths.html. Accessed on June 16, 2015.

Finklea, Kristin, Lisa Sacco, and Erin Bagalman. 2014. "Prescription Drug Monitoring Programs." Congressional Research Service. https://www.fas.org/sgp/crs/misc/ R42593.pdf. Accessed on June 16, 2015.

Muhuri, Pradip, Joseph Gfoerer, and M. Christine Davies. 2013. "Associations of Nonmedical Pain Reliever Use and Initiation of Heroin Use in the United States." CBHSQ Data Review. http://www.samhsa.gov/data/sites/default/ files/DR006/DR006/nonmedical-pain-reliever-use-2013. htm. Accessed on June 16, 2015.

Rudd, Rose A., et al. 2014. "Increases in Heroin Overdose Deaths—28 States, 2010 to 2012." *Morbidity and Mortality Weekly Report (MMWR)* 63 (39): 849–54. http://www.cdc .gov/mmwr/preview/mmwrhtml/mm6339a1.htm. Accessed on June 16, 2015.

Substance Abuse and Mental Health Services Administration, Center for Behavioral Health Statistics and Quality. 2010. "The DAWN Report: Highlights of the 2009 Drug Abuse Warning Network (DAWN) Findings on Drug-Related Emergency Department Visits." http://www.oas.samhsa.gov/2k10/ DAWN034/EDHighlights.htm. Accessed on June 16, 2015.

Carmen A. Catizone, MS, RPh, DPh, is the executive director of the National Association of Boards of Pharmacy (NABP) and the secretary of the Association's Executive Committee. NABP is the independent, international, and impartial association that assists its member boards and jurisdictions for the purpose of protecting the public health.

Communicative Behavior
Nicholas E. Hagemeier

Data from the National Survey on Drug Use and Health indicate that nearly 90 percent of nonmedical users of prescription pain relievers obtained medications from friends, family, or one prescriber. Moreover, 84 percent of friends and family from whom pain relievers were freely obtained got the drugs from one prescriber (Substance Abuse and Mental Health Services Administration 2014). Considering these data and the number of drugs with abuse potential dispensed in community pharmacies annually (IMS Institute 2014), it is logical to assert that prescribers and pharmacists are intimately, and perhaps unwittingly, involved in the initial distribution of a large majority of prescription drugs that are eventually abused or misused. As a health professional and researcher, I find this assertion is simultaneously saddening, angering, convicting, and perplexing.

I transitioned from nine years of community pharmacy practice to an academic position in 2011, initiated prescription drug abuse research, and only then genuinely paused to reflect on my practice experiences. I was sad that I often had not provided the level of care I had been trained to provide. I was angry with myself for often focusing more so on my comfort (i.e., making choices that made my life easier) than on choices that considered my patients' needs first and foremost. I was convinced that I had enabled prescription drug abuse. I was perplexed because I did not understand the underpinnings of my practice-based decision making. While decision making is influenced by many internal and external factors, a foundational skillset I lacked in practice was communication know-how.

Interpersonal communication—oral, written, verbal, and nonverbal—is ubiquitous. It is ubiquitous in the events of daily living and it is ubiquitous in health care. Regardless of how they are conceptualized, interpersonal communication processes are complex, especially when considering perceivably uncomfortable situations such as those that commonly present specific to prescription drug, or engaging in any other health behavior change conversation for that matter. Interactions between patients and health care providers, and interactions among health care providers commonly rely on interpersonal communication; yet, interpersonal communication skills are seldom direct targets of interventions to address health crises such as prescription drug abuse and the ramifications thereof. Effective dyadic health care provider-patient interpersonal communication requires rapport building, information management, active listening, and addressing feelings. Few health care providers, and really few individuals in general, are naturally fully equipped with a communication skillset that promotes healthy behavior change. These skills have to be honed.

Characteristics of communication among providers and between providers and patients are understudied, especially as they pertain to prescription drug abuse. In fact, communication attributes have not yet been identified directly as essential in the prevention of prescription drug abuse despite a general perception that health care providers "feel uncomfortable asking" patients about prescription drug abuse (Pittman 2012).

Policy implications in the United States have been realized as a result of prescriber and pharmacist roles in prescription drug abuse, including an Office of National Drug Control Policy call for increased prescription drug abuse-specific provider education and training, increased controlled substance monitoring via prescription drug monitoring programs (PDMPs), and increased attention to illegitimate prescribing and dispensing by the Drug Enforcement Administration and other law enforcement agencies. Researchers have also examined the efficacy of Screening, Brief Intervention, and Referral to Treatment

(SBIRT) models specific to opioid drug abuse (Humeniuk, Dennington, and Ali 2008). While results of the WHO study are encouraging, drug abuse SBIRT studies in general have noted variable efficacy across situational factors (e.g., provider, setting, and patient characteristics) (Substance Abuse and Mental Health Services Administration 2011). The variability is not surprising given individual health care professional communication styles and approaches. Moreover, health behavior change communication resembles a tennis match. The content of each communication event should be adapted to the content of the patient's communication event. Given wide variation in patient responses, including responses to prescription drug abuse inquiries, one-size-fits-all approaches to communication seldom reap widespread positive patient outcomes.

Research that my colleagues and I have conducted with prescribers and pharmacists supports the need for increased knowledge of and skills required to engage patients in effective, patient-centered, prescription drug abuse communication. For example, prescribers and pharmacists in our focus groups commonly employ individually developed internal policies that help them avoid difficult communication situations. One prescriber approached investigating prescription drug abuse in this manner: "I think the first thing you do is you pull the database [the prescription drug monitoring database report] and do a drug screen [a urine drug screen] . . . I mean pull the drug screen, do a drug screen and see if they fall out because a lot of times they'll fall out then that takes care of your problem." The patient who "falls out" is subsequently fired by the prescriber. One pharmacist approached a difficult conversation in this way, "As a drug seeker . . . my behavior is, I just tell them I don't have them [the medications being sought]." The health care professionals described in both of these scenarios have passed up opportunities to engage patients in patient-centered communication that has the potential to improve patient outcomes. Obviously there are health care providers who do a marvelous job of providing patient-centered care, but these folks are the exception. Patient-centered communication is difficult, but foundationally necessary, in my opinion, to turn down prescription drug abuse.

As a reader, what can you do to foster patient-centered communication and prescription drug abuse prevention? I offer you a few starting points:

- Become acquainted with the concept of motivational interviewing. www.motivationalinterviewing.org is a great place to start. MI skills can positively change the way you communicate with those around you, regardless of the situation.
- Engage the health care providers with whom you interact in rapport building communication, even if you have to initiate the conversation.
- Kindly and constructively provide feedback to your health care providers about their communication skills. A large majority of prescribers and pharmacists we've spoken with indicated they would be grateful for such feedback.

There is a need for an increased understanding of health care provider communication specific to prescription drug abuse. Simply put, we know provider communication is necessary, yet we know little about it. George Bernard Shaw once said, "The single biggest problem in communication is the illusion that is has taken place." Prescription drug abuse prevention and treatment necessitate that it takes place.

References

Humeniuk, Rachel, Victoria Dennington, and Robert Ali. 2008. "The Effectiveness of a Brief Intervention for Illicit Drugs Linked to the Alcohol Smoking and Substance Involvement Screening Test (ASSIST) in Primary Health Care Settings: A Technical Report of Phase III Findings of the WHO ASSIST Randomized Control Trial." WHO ASSIST Phase III Study Group. http://www.who.int/

substance_abuse/activities/assist_technicalreport_phase3_final.pdf. Accessed June 15, 2015.

Pittman, David. 2012. "Drug Abuse Office Offers Videos for Docs." *Medpage Today.* http://www.medpagetoday.com/PainManagement/PainManagement/35055. Accessed June 15, 2015.

Substance Abuse and Mental Health Services Administration. 2011. "Screening, Brief Intervention and Referral to Treatment (SBIRT) in Behavioral Healthcare." United States Department of Health and Human Services. Rockville, MD. http://www.samhsa.gov/sites/default/files/sbirtwhitepaper_0.pdf. Accessed on June 16, 2015.

Substance Abuse and Mental Health Services Administration. 2014. "Results from the 2013 National Survey on Drug Use and Health: Summary of National Findings." NSDUH Series H-48, HHS Publication No. (SMA) 14-4863. United States Department of Health and Human Services. Rockville, MD. http://www.samhsa.gov/data/sites/default/files/NSDUHresultsPDFWHTML2013/Web/NSDUHresults2013.pdf. Accessed on June 16, 2015.

Nicholas E. Hagemeier, PharmD, PhD, is an assistant professor of pharmacy practice in the East Tennessee State University (ETSU) Gatton College of Pharmacy. He also holds an adjunct faculty position in the ETSU College of Public Health, Department of Community and Behavioral Health. He conducts research at the intersection of health communication, health behaviors, and prescription drug abuse prevention and treatment.

A Perfect Storm for Prescription Drug Misuse
Kenneth M. Hale

Six to seven million Americans have misused a prescription pain medication, sedative or stimulant in the past month (SAMHSA 2014, 16), and approximately 5,500 do so for the first time every day (SAMHSA 2014, 64). This phenomenon has resulted in myriad social, financial, legal, and health problems, with drug overdose accounting for nearly 44,000 deaths in 2013 (CDC 2015, 32)—the leading cause of accidental death in the United States. The Centers for Disease Control and Prevention has labeled this problem an *epidemic* (CDC 2014, 1), and community, state, and national strategies have emerged to combat this epidemic. How did we get to the point where prescription medications have become the gateway to drug misuse? Why are medications, which have been developed to help us, among our most misused substances? I believe that Americans have a "perfect storm" for prescription drug misuse in the United States, and the first factor contributing to this disaster may lie in the drug-taking culture in which they live.

The United States generated more than 4.3 billion prescriptions in 2014 (IMS 2015, 39), and Americans spend far more on these medications per capita than any other nation (OECD 2012). They have a "quick fix" culture, often preferring to medicate as opposed to changing their behaviors to correct a health concern, and the United States is one of only two developed countries that allow direct-to-consumer advertisements for prescription medications (WHO 2009, 576-77). America has normalized the use of drugs through marketing, social acceptability, and the pervasive use of prescription medications in its medical system. Americans have the world's trove of health care information at their fingertips, and it is very easy to forget that there is a reason for the prescription, as they sometimes use this information for inappropriate self-care. Medical writer Greg Critser calls this "pharmaceutical populism"—a growing culture of self-diagnosis and self-prescription (Critser 2005, 149). So, taking someone else's prescription drugs or sharing their medications with others starts to feel like a cultural norm. It's just what Americans do, and perhaps they lose sight of the risks of doing so.

As a result, nearly 70 percent of those who misuse medications get them from family members or friends, most often for free (SAMHSA 2014, 31-33). We sometimes practice "sympathetic diversion" by giving medications to others who can't afford them or simply sharing medications with acquaintances who may be experiencing symptoms similar to our own or use someone else's medication for the same reason. In some cases, others may be taking our medications without our knowledge, because we typically store prescription drugs in unsecured locations and are prone to keeping them when they are no longer needed—just in case we, or someone we know, might need them later on. These substances can become easy prey for those wishing to misuse them. Perhaps it is someone living in your home, a visitor, a worker, or even a drug seeker who uses opportunities such as an open house to search through the family medicine cabinet. The supply of medications is abundant in the United States, providing relatively easy access through normal health care channels or from friends, relatives, or others who have a legitimate prescription.

Is it safer to misuse prescription medications than illicit "street" drugs? Is it legal to do so? Can prescription medications lead to addiction? These questions, and the misperceptions which often surround them, contribute to our misuse of prescription drugs as well. According to the 2013 Partnership Attitude Tracking Study (Partnership for Drug-Free Kids 2013, 14-18), 23 percent of American teens report misusing a prescription drug at least once in their lifetime. A telling factor that may underlie this phenomenon is perception of risk. While 50 percent of teens report that concerns about overdosing would prevent them from using medications without a prescription, only 30 percent feel similarly about the possibility of endangering their health or becoming addicted. And only 21 percent report concerns about getting into legal troubles. Perhaps more disturbing is the fact that 16 percent of parents believed that using prescription drugs to get high is much safer than using illicit drugs. Actually, some of the most misused medications are not that different from illicit "street" drugs. For example, opioid pain relievers are similar to the opiate heroin in terms of chemical structure and pharmacology (or effects on the body). These medications can lead to addiction, they are not inherently safer, and possessing them without a prescription is felonious.

It is easy to assume that medications that are approved by the Food and Drug Administration (FDA), manufactured in the legitimate pharmaceutical industry, and prescribed and dispensed by licensed health professionals must be safe. Prescription drugs can certainly help us live longer and healthier lives, but only when used under the supervision of a health care provider. Think about the drug-use process in the United States. Billions of dollars are spent to systematically develop the medications that end up in the local pharmacy, subsequent to elaborate testing for safety and efficacy. Panels of experts working with the FDA ultimately determine that a prescription must be required for the use of many medications because of the inherent risks that accompany the expected benefits for the patient. After all, when we take a medication, we introduce a foreign substance into our body, which always has the potential to do harm. Some pharmaceuticals (many pain medications, sedatives, and stimulants) are, furthermore, classified as "controlled substances" by the Drug Enforcement Administration due to the substantial risk of misuse or dependence. When we misuse these powerful pharmaceuticals, when we take medications that are not prescribed for us or in ways that our health care providers did not intend, it can be a prescription for disaster.

So, Americans have a "perfect storm" for medication misuse in the United States resulting from the pharmaceuticalization of their society, easy access to medications, and misperceptions of safety and legality. The result can be deadly. This storm will pass only when they return to safe medication-taking practices, learn to store their medications securely and properly dispose of prescription drugs they no longer need, and educate people of all ages about the myths of safety and legality that help fuel this calamity.

References

CDC (Centers for Disease Control and Prevention). 2014. "Examining the Growing Problems of Prescription Drug and Heroin Abuse." http://www.cdc.gov/washington/testimony/2014/t20140429.htm. Accessed on May 29, 2015.

CDC (Centers for Disease Control and Prevention). 2015. "Rates of Deaths from Drug Poisoning and Drug Poisoning Involving Opioid Analgesics—United States, 1999–2013." *Morbidity and Mortality Weekly Report* 64(1): 32.

Critser, Greg. 2005. *Generation Rx: How Prescription Drugs Are Altering American Lives, Minds, and Bodies.* New York: Houghton Mifflin Company.

OECD (Organisation for Economic Co-operation and Development) 2012. "Health Resources—Pharmaceutical Spending." https://data.oecd.org/healthres/pharmaceutical-spending.htm. Accessed June 3, 2015.

Partnership for Drug-Free Kids 2013. "The Partnership Attitude Tracking Study: Teens & Parents 2013." http://www.drugfree.org/wp-content/uploads/2014/07/PATS-2013-FULL-REPORT.pdf. Accessed on June 12, 2015.

SAMHSA 2014. "Results from the 2013 National Survey on Drug Use and Health: Summary of National Findings." NSDUH Series H-48, HHS Publication No. (SMA) 14-4863. Rockville, MD: Substance Abuse and Mental Health Services Administration.

WHO 2009. "Direct-to-Consumer Advertising under Fire." *Bulletin of the World Health Organization* 87: 576–77.

Dr. Hale is a clinical professor in the College of Pharmacy and associate director of the Higher Education Center for Alcohol and Drug Misuse Prevention and Recovery (HECAOD.osu.edu) at the Ohio State University. He founded the Generation Rx Initiative (go.osu.edu/generationrx) in 2007 to develop resources for prescription drug misuse prevention.

Prescription Drug Abuse
Ginger Katz

Prescription drug abuse is a significant problem in the United States, especially among youth. According to the National Institute on Drug Abuse, prescription and over-the-counter (OTC) medications account for most of the commonly abused drugs among high school seniors, and 70 percent of these 12th graders said they were given to them by a friend or relative. Many assume they are safe because a physician prescribes these medications or they are legal and easily available in any convenience store. Misuse and abuse of these medications can lead to addiction and overdose, just like the illicit drugs sold on the street.

The disease of addiction has been growing in the suburbs since 1995 due to the allure, access, and availability of prescription medication. According to the Centers for Disease Control and Prevention, drug overdoses kill more Americans than car crashes, and Director Thomas Frieden stated, "Emergency department visits involving non-medical use of these prescription drugs are now as common as emergency-department visits for use of illicit drugs" ("Study Shows 111 Percent Increase in Emergency Department Visits" 2015).

Consider what is in your medicine cabinet—pain relievers such as aspirin or Tylenol, cold and flu tablets, cough syrup, and prescription medications. Children as young as 12 are trying prescription drugs to get high, which are often easily available to them because the drugs can be taken from their home medicine cabinet or that of a relative or friend. An added danger of abusing prescription drugs is that teens consider them safer than street drugs because they are manufactured by a pharmaceutical company. Younger teens most commonly abuse sedatives for anxiety and sleep disorders "to relieve stress," as well as abuse pain relievers such as Vicodin and Oxycontin. Older teens are known to abuse prescription medications for attention deficit/hyperactivity disorder such as Adderall and Ritalin in order to "concentrate" or "stay awake to study."

The mixing of two or more drugs, also known as polydrug use, carries a higher risk due to increased side effects and increased risk of overdose. The most serious reactions to polydrug use are synergistic, instances in which the combined drugs enhance each other. Polydrug combinations include alcohol and/ or perfectly legal energy drinks and OTC medications. Cold and cough medications are most commonly abused and contain the drug dextromethorphan, known to have hallucinogenic effects in large amounts. Polydrug use—whether intentional to achieve a desired effect or the user merely lacks knowledge of the consequences—is a dangerous and growing trend.

In 1996, I founded the Courage to Speak Foundation shortly after my 20-year-old son Ian, died of an accidental drug overdose. The toxicology report indicated that Ian died of a Valium and heroin combination. I made a promise to Ian that I would do everything in my power to prevent this tragedy from happening to another family.

For the past 19 years I've shared Ian's story with hundreds of thousands of people in over a thousand presentations across the nation, providing insight into his journey into addiction that began in eighth grade with cigarettes, beer, and marijuana to his death from a heroin and Valium overdose. Ian's story connects educators, parents, and students to the urgent need to obtain knowledge and skills to address youth drug abuse and provides resources, programs, and strategies for healthy solutions in schools/communities.

Working with prevention experts, the Courage to Speak Foundation developed distinctive drug prevention programs for elementary, middle, and high school and Courageous Parenting 101 for parents in English and Spanish. This multicomponent prevention model recommended by Yale University engages home, school, and community to address youth drug abuse, facilitates social and emotional development for students, and builds capacity for them to utilize supportive resources. These programs provide prevention strategies, teacher training, and student skill and asset building that foster open communication with trusted adults about the dangers of drugs and other risky behaviors.

Prevention education, beginning at an early age, is key to ending this public health issue. According to researchers at Penn State and Iowa State Universities and an article published in a 2013 issue of the *American Journal of Public Health*, young adults reduce their overall prescription drug misuse up to 65 percent if they are part of a community-based prevention effort while still in middle school (Spoth et al. 2013).

Parents need to know what their children are being exposed to and must be given knowledge and tools to talk openly and honestly with their children about the dangers of drugs. Many communities have set up medicine disposal sites to educate and raise awareness about securing medications in your home and the safe disposal of unused and expired medicine.

For more information about the Courage to Speak Foundation programs visit www.couragetospeak.org.

References

Spoth, Richard, et al. "Longitudinal Effects of Universal Preventive Intervention on Prescription Drug Misuse: Three Randomized Controlled Trials with Late Adolescents and Young Adults." *American Journal of Public Health* 103 (4): 665–72.

"Study Shows 111 Percent Increase in Emergency Department Visits Involving Nonmedical Use of Prescription Opioid Pain Relievers in Five-Year Period." Substance Abuse and Mental Health Services Administration. http://www.samhsa.gov/newsroom/press-announcements/201006170145. Accessed on June 9. 2015.

Ginger Katz, a nationally recognized figure in youth drug prevention, is CEO and founder of the Courage to Speak Foundation, and author of Sunny's Story, *a drug prevention book told from the perspective of the family pet. She founded the organization after her son Ian lost his battle with addiction. Ginger has shared Ian's story in over 1,000 presentations in schools, communities, and state and national conferences. With a team of experts, she led the development of the Courage to Speak Drug Prevention Education Programs for elementary, middle, and high schools and Courageous Parenting 101—a multicomponent prevention model evaluated and recommended by Yale University. Her numerous honors include the Connecticut Association of Schools, Distinguished Friend of Education Award, and Prevention Works Award from the U.S. Substance Abuse & Mental Health Services Administration. To know more, visit www .couragetospeak.org.*

The Dangers of Smart Drugs: College Students' Prescription Drug Addiction
Troy Keslar

Prescription stimulants such as Adderall and Ritalin have helped thousands of students diagnosed with attention deficit hyperactivity disorder (ADHD) or attention deficit disorder (ADD) acquire the focus they need to reach their full potential. Unfortunately, individuals who don't qualify for an ADHD/ ADD diagnosis, but who still crave the focus and high grades often provided by these drugs, have begun taking them illegally. These drugs are commonly referred to as *smart drugs*. The illegal consumption of these smart drugs has led to a growing prescription drug abuse epidemic that is highly dangerous for young adults.

Smart drugs, sometimes referred to as *neuro enhancers* or nootropics, improve brain function in attention-impaired individuals. *Nootropics* is a broad term that includes everything from prescription smart drugs such as Ritalin to caffeine, nicotine, and omega-3 fish oil. Individuals with impaired focus, memory, or motivation often benefit from adding a smart drug to their daily regimen. In addition to ADHD/ADD patients, individuals who have other neurological problems such as Alzheimer's disease, Parkinson's disease, and Huntington's disease also benefit from nootropics ("Smart Drugs and Should We Take Them" 2015). Although nonprescription nootropics may benefit the ADD/ADHD-diagnosed student, a prescription drug such as Adderall is usually the most effective pharmacological remedy, especially when accompanied by behavior modification.

Symptoms of individuals who suffer from certain neurological impairments clearly improve when given prescription smart drugs or nootropics—and especially when they take nootropics precisely as directed while under the care of a qualified physician. Unfortunately, these drugs often fail to produce the same results for individuals who don't have ADD or ADHD. In addition, the effects of prescription smart drugs on a "normal"-functioning brain are incredibly dangerous. Prescription stimulants are addictive, and they can even cause overdose.

In addition to Adderall and Ritalin, there are other dangerous smart drugs (CNN Money 2015). Other common nootropics include dextroamphetamine and lisdexamfetamine. These drugs, in therapeutic doses, benefit attention, memory, and inhibition problems. Methylphenidate is another drug that improves the user's ability to focus on a boring job that requires significant work. Armodafinil and modafinil help sleep-deprived people stay awake, and they are most frequently prescribed for conditions such as sleep apnea and narcolepsy. Omega-3 fish oil supplements benefit brain power and more. Found in fatty fish such as salmon, omega-3 fish oil also comes in the form of supplements. Caffeine and nicotine improve alertness and performance, especially in higher doses. Unfortunately, these substances are also highly addictive. In the case of nicotine, these substances can lead to cancer, heart disease, and more.

Although taking a supplement of omega-3 fish oil and drinking a cup of coffee are unlikely to cause lasting harm, the same cannot be said of prescription smart drugs under certain circumstances. Although decades of research clearly demonstrate that individuals with ADD/ADHD who take prescription stimulants in therapeutic doses suffer little to no harm, individuals without an ADD/ADHD diagnosis can hurt themselves significantly.

Smart drugs are also illegal, and taking them is cheating (NPR.com 2009). A recent investigative report in *The Guardian* noted that college students who consumed smart drugs such as modafinil, a narcolepsy drug, avoided sleep and focused on work for hours—even to the point of skipping meals (*The Guardian* 2015). Modafinil makes it possible for students to increase their advantage over students who avoid stimulants for health reasons. Students interviewed in *The Guardian* report stated that intense competition, as well as paying back large student loans following graduation, played important roles in their decisions to use drugs such as modafinil, Dexedrine, and Adderall. However, the negative side effects of anxiety, depression, dependency, and addiction show that there is a darker side to these smart drugs than students might be willing to acknowledge.

In America, *The Guardian* reports that one-third of all students have a prescription for a mind-altering substance, including antidepressants, antianxiety drugs, and stimulants. These drugs are everywhere (MedShadow.org 2014) and are often sold by students. In many cases, the drugs aren't even coming from the local pharmacy—they're coming from Internet dispensaries from as far overseas as Thailand. After only a few months, one of the subjects interviewed realized he had developed dependency and was continuing to take the smart drug, even though he had no school deadlines to worry about.

Students aren't the only ones taking drugs for added concentration and wakefulness. *The Guardian* reports that everyone from academic scholars and writers to surgeons and tech enthusiasts take drugs off-label to increase their ability to focus on unpleasant or challenging tasks. Individuals with addictions to other substances, such as alcohol and cocaine, are also likely to take smart drugs. The side effects, which include physical ailments, emotional discomfort, and dependency, downplay the positives of the perceived increase in productivity. After all, science has yet to conclude definitively that smart drugs are effective in individuals without ADD/ADHD or narcolepsy.

There are also plenty of ethical considerations presented by using these drugs if they aren't prescribed to a student for a legitimate purpose. In fact, Duke University recently decided to consider cheating and the use of unprescribed smart drugs as the same act (*The Guardian* 2015). Aside from the ethical considerations, smart drugs also cause serious side effects, including addiction and overdose, without careful medical supervision. Although smart drugs may one day find themselves gaining legal acceptance much like marijuana, the illegal abuse of smart drugs is ultimately a huge risk for students and young adults—taking these drugs can cause academic, ethical, mental, and bodily harm.

References

"Smart Drugs and Should We Take Them." DNA Learning Center Blog. http://blogs.dnalc.org/2009/09/21/smart-drugs-and-should-we-take-them/. Accessed on June 10, 2015.

Troy Keslar is the vice president and director of admissions for 12 Keys Rehab, a private, dual-diagnosis, and residential-style drug and alcohol treatment center nestled on 10 waterfront acres Jensen Beach, FL. To know more, visit www.12keysrehab.com.

Fighting Prescription Opioid Abuse Shouldn't Increase Pain for Patients
Srinivas Nalamachu

Doris Fisher's[1] pain made it difficult for her to stand or even sit. To climb stairs, she had to hang onto the hand rail. Only when sleeping could she escape the pain, which finally forced her to retire early from a successful executive career with a reputable nonprofit organization.

---

[1] Name changed to protect patient privacy.

I treated Doris for piriformis syndrome, the source of her pain, with prescription opioid pain medications and a neuro-stimulator implanted in her lower back. With treatment, Doris now has her pain reduced enough to resume some day-to-day activities.

Like Doris, patients sometimes require prescription medication because their pain exceeds what over-the-counter medications such as Tylenol or Advil can treat. For example, prescription pain medications may treat a cancer patient who is suffering through chemotherapy, a person who survived a car accident and has broken bones or painful injuries, or a patient who recently had his wisdom teeth extracted.

Yet not all patients use these medications properly, and not all users are proper patients. Many people obtain these medications illegally or use them unwisely. As a result, the United States faces a prescription drug abuse epidemic. The Centers for Disease Control and Prevention estimates that 44 people in the United States die every day because of prescription opioid overdose (Centers for Disease Control and Prevention 2015).

Policy makers must deal with prescription pain pill abuse, but they must also consider the needs of patients living with debilitating pain. A fair, successful solution is one that ad-dresses both sides of the issue—patients need these medications to continue their everyday lives and abusers must be prevented from getting medications they don't need.

Let us consider two popular policy solutions, their intended effects, and the consequences they may unintentionally pose for patients.

Prescription Monitoring Programs. One way that states try to limit prescription drug abuse is through prescription monitoring programs (PDMPs). These programs track and analyze which prescription pain medications are prescribed to which patients—and by which doctors. As of 2015, 49 states have monitoring programs in place or have passed bills to cre-ate such programs (National Association of State Controlled Substances Authorities 2014).

Intended Effect. Monitoring programs could help to decrease what's known as "doctor shopping," patients visiting multiple doctors to get multiple prescriptions for pain medications (Centers for Disease Control and Prevention 2012). But to keep these programs from hurting patients who legitimately need pain medication, the programs must be feasible for doctors to implement in their clinics without undue burden.

Unintended Effect. Staff in the hospitals and clinics are already burdened with administrative responsibilities because of new technologies and constantly changing mandates related to accountable care organizations and the Affordable Care Act. When prescription monitoring programs introduce more administrative duties, some doctors may decide that prescribing pain medication is not worth the added workload. Other doctors may stop prescribing these medications due to fear of the penalties for doctors who don't comply fully with program rules. Because monitoring is done electronically, these penalties may unintentionally target older and less technologically savvy doctors (Pain Therapy Access Physicians Working Group 2013, 5).

When doctors stop prescribing opioid pain medications, patients may be forced to find the medications they need from another source. The sources may be illegal. Or, they may require patients to travel long distances to see a new doctor. For elderly patients who depend on others for transportation or cancer patients who may be struggling for their very lives, the added burden may lead patients to forego treatment altogether.

Balanced Solution. To avoid unintended consequences, monitoring programs must be streamlined and easy to use, not burdening the doctors and staff who implement them. Instead of implementing a penalty system that may intimidate doctors and unfairly target older health care providers, policy makers should consider incentive systems that positively reinforce compliance.

Shutting Down Pain Management Centers. Another way that law enforcement is trying to reduce prescription pain pill overdose is by shutting down so-called pill mills. These are clinics where misguided health care providers profit financially by prescribing more opioid pain medications than might be necessary.

Intended Effect. Pill mill prescriptions may go on to be misused or diverted, perhaps sold on the black market. Shutting down these clinics can curb over-prescribing of opioid pain medications and limit the amount of pain medications in circulation.

Unintended Effect. Though pill mills do unfortunately exist, most pain management clinics have responsible physicians treat patients appropriately for pain that would otherwise disrupt their everyday lives. Efforts to shut down pill mills may inadvertently shut down legitimate pain management centers. Overregulation may include undue burden of excessive documentation, record keeping and administrative requirements; costly annual inspections; and a requirement that the clinic's medical director be board certified. Faced with increased administrative burdens and public stigma, some well-intentioned centers may close, leaving limited options for patients with legitimate pain.

Balanced Solution. Rather than restricting access, policy makers should consider positive approaches such as prevention. For example, new technology allows pain medications to be made in a form that's difficult to crush or dissolve for snorting or recreational drug use. Research already suggests that these "abuse-deterrent" forms are helping to reduce prescription pain pill overdoses (Larochelle et al. 2015, 1).

Prevention through education is also important. The Food and Drug Administration has several programs that encourage education for both patients and prescribing doctors about the risks and proper uses of prescription pain medication (Pain Therapy Access Physicians Working Group 2013, 7).

Patients with pain make up a sizeable group. The U.S. Pain Foundation reports that 100 million Americans battle pain every day. The annual cost of these patients' lost productivity, medical treatments, and disability payment totals $635 billion

("About U.S. Pain Foundation" 2015). Leaving these patients untreated is not a feasible solution.

The best approach, therefore, is a balanced one. Where prescription drug monitoring programs exist, they should be streamlined and easy to implement, using positive reinforcement techniques wherever possible. When lawmakers seek to shut down pill mills, they must consider the effect on legitimate pain management centers and the patients who need medical care from pain specialists. Finally, education and prevention should be used as positive strategies for curbing abuse whenever possible.

Policy makers must tackle abuse. But they should also allow responsible physicians to continue treating patients with pain appropriately.

References

"About U.S. Pain Foundation." 2015. U.S. Pain Foundation. http://www.uspainfoundation.org/about-us.html. Accessed on June 15, 2015.

Centers for Disease Control and Prevention. 2012. "Public Health Law: Doctor Shopping Laws." http://www.cdc .gov/phlp/docs/menu-shoppinglaws.pdf. Accessed on June 9, 2015.

Centers for Disease Control and Prevention. 2015. "Deaths from Prescription Opioid Overdose." http://www.cdc .gov/drugoverdose/data/overdose.html. Accessed on June 9, 2015.

Larochelle, Marc R., et al. 2015. "Rates of Opioid Dispensing and Overdose after Introduction of Abuse-Deterrent Extended-Release Oxycodone and Withdrawal of Propoxyphene." http://archinte.jamanetwork.com/article .aspx?articleid=2276923&resultClick=3. Accessed on June 11, 2015.

National Association of State Controlled Substances Authorities. 2014. "Prescription Drug Monitoring

Programs." http://www.nascsa.org/nascsaPDMP/
NationalPDMPmap1.26.14.pdf. Accessed on June 8, 2015.

Pain Therapy Access Physicians Working Group. 2013.
    "Prescription Pain Medication: Preserving Patient Access
    While Curbing Abuse." http://1yh21u3cjptv3xjder
    1dco9mx5s.wpengine.netdna-cdn.com/wp-content/
    uploads/2013/12/PT_White-Paper_Finala.pdf. Accessed
    on June 4, 2015.

*Srinivas Nalamachu, MD, is the president and medical director
of the International Clinical Research Institute in Overland Park,
Kansas, and a member of the Alliance for Patient Access.*

Prescription Drugs and the Brain
Maia Pujara

The Human Brain

Every day, your brain pumps out its very own concoction of
drugs, or chemicals. These chemicals control everything, from
making you fall asleep to making you fall in love.

Just like how the skin is made up of skin cells, the brain is
made up of tiny cells called neurons. Neurons are special because, unlike skin cells, they talk to each other very fast using
electrical and chemical signals. The chemicals that your brain
makes are called *neurotransmitters*. The neurotransmitters attach themselves to special places on the neuron called *receptors*
to get their message across.

Think of a neurotransmitter as a text message that one neuron sends to another neuron and the receptor as the cell phone.
And let's say our friend Katie is sleepy. In Katie's brain, Neuron #1 sends a "text"—a neurotransmitter molecule—from its
cell phone to Neuron #2's cell phone saying: "Hey, Neuron
#2, you might want to tell Katie to turn off her phone so she

can close her eyes and fall asleep." And then, thousands upon thousands of Katie's other neurons send each other neurotransmitter "texts" back and forth on their cell phones, so she can shut off her phone, close her eyes, and finally, fall asleep.

Your brain is made up of about 100 billion neurons. This means a **lot** of neurotransmitter "text messages" are happening at once to keep things running smoothly.

Prescription Drugs: How Exactly Are They Working in the Brain?

Prescription drugs are chemicals designed to work with the brain's natural chemistry—in fact, they look and act very similar to the chemicals in the brain. Though these drugs can help people feel better, they're not perfect. There is no "miracle" drug. There can be surprising side effects because of how they work in the brain, and addiction can happen if someone takes a drug for longer than needed.

Sleep Drugs: GABA

When you fall asleep, your brain activity decreases because of a neurotransmitter called gamma-aminobutyric acid, or GABA, for short. Now let's say Katie has been having problems falling asleep no matter what she tries. Her doctor prescribes a drug for a sleep disorder called *insomnia,* an inability to fall asleep. Because this drug helps neurons release more GABA, Katie is able to fall asleep very well at night. Sadly, she also starts getting headaches, muscle aches, sleepier during the day, scatter-brained, and dizzy (National Institute on Drug Abuse 2015). Katie's doctor also warned her that, because the drug is so strong, it could be deadly when combined with other drugs such as cold medicine, alcohol, or painkillers. All of those drugs also work on GABA receptors and slow down brain activity, heart rate, and breathing.

Painkillers: Opioids

Let's say Katie oversleeps and is late to class. Panicking and rushing out of bed, she trips, falls, and breaks her ankle. In Katie's brain, neurons are talking—no, yelling and screaming—to each other about how painful a broken bone feels. There are natural neurotransmitters called opioids attaching themselves to opioid receptors on neurons to dial down the pain, but this is not enough. So Katie's doctor prescribes her painkillers, which are stronger opioids. Although opioids are good at bringing down moderate-to-severe pain, they can make a person feel drowsy, confused, nauseous, constipated, and short of breath (National Institute on Drug Abuse 2014).

Stimulants: Dopamine and Norepinephrine

With everything Katie has been dealing with, she can no longer pay attention in class. She goes to a doctor who prescribes her a drug that will help her focus her attention. This type of drug, called a stimulant, helps neurons release natural neurotransmitters called *dopamine* and *norepinephrine*. Dopamine is important for motivating movements and for feeling good, while norepinephrine helps us pay attention and focus. Just like the other drugs, stimulants help improve attention and focus but can come with some nasty side effects including chest pains, stomachaches, and feelings of fear or anger. If they are taken for too long, they can cause deadly seizures and irregular heartbeats (National Institute on Drug Abuse 2015).

Long-Term Effects on the Brain and Addiction

The brain is wired such that, if it comes across something that feels good, it will continue to look for that special something, to bring that feeling back again (Bragdon and Gamon 2000, 28). Prescription drugs, especially painkillers and stimulants, can be addictive because they can make a person feel very good.

Although all of the different prescription drugs release different neurotransmitters, scientists think that they all work on the brain in the same exact way: by releasing the "feel good" neurotransmitter dopamine first (Bragdon and Gamon 2000, 30). Increased levels of dopamine cause the person to feel very good—much lighter and happier. An addicted brain eventually changes, or rewires, and wants only one thing: the drug.

There are many ways that scientists are tackling the problem of prescription drug addiction, and addiction overall: (1) by creating new drugs that are less addictive but just as helpful for treating problems with pain, sleeping, and attention/focus; (2) by discovering the genes that put some people at a greater risk for becoming addicted to drugs in the first place; (3) by figuring out the long-term effects these drugs have on the brain, potentially reversing the damage that has already been done.

References

Bragdon, Allen D., and David Gamon. 2000. "Alcoholism, Etc: Triggering Transmitters." *Brains That Work a Little Bit Differently*. South Yarmouth, MA: Allen D. Bragdon Publishers, Inc., 21-33.

National Institute on Drug Abuse (NIDA). November 2014. "Prescription Drug Abuse: Research Report Series." http://www.drugabuse.gov/publications/research-reports/prescription-drugs/. Accessed on June 6, 2015.

National Institute on Drug Abuse (NIDA). 2015. "Mind over Matter—Prescription Drug Abuse." http://teens.drugabuse.gov/educators/nida-teaching-guides/mind-over-matter/prescription-drug-abuse. Accessed on June 6, 2015.

Maia Pujara looks at how peoples' brains "light up" to things like food, money, and drugs. She is currently learning about science journalism at Voice of America, an international news organization in Washington, D.C., and is studying for her PhD in neuroscience.

Can Information Technology Help Curb Prescription Drug Abuse?
Jeremy Summers

Just a few decades ago, Americans dreamed of a future with scientific advancements that improved every facet of their daily lives—better living through science. Along with fantasies of flying cars, robotic maids, and powdered meals, many Americans believed that one day, science would progress to the point that all a person would need to do to cure an illness or improve their health is take a pill.

Trying to fulfill these fantasies, scientists used advances in chemistry and biomedical research to start producing these types of pills. For many, these pills were a godsend—people with attention deficit hyperactivity disorder, for example, could now receive the extra chemical boost they needed, as could people with anxiety, sleep disorders, and many other illnesses.

But perhaps the makers of these pills were too successful in their mission. As the popularity and prevalence of prescription drugs rose, people began wholeheartedly subscribing to this complicated future of medicine. Capitalizing on this trend, big pharmaceutical companies began coming out with pills for every type of disorder, no matter how small or what other methods existed for treating the disorder.

In recent years, prescription drugs have become so effective and widespread that nearly 70 percent of Americans are on at least one prescription drug and more than 50 percent take two or more ("Nearly 7 in 10 Americans Take Prescription Drugs" 2013) Technological innovation had not only ushered in a new era of medicine but also introduced a new kind of scourge on the American people.

A 2013 report from the Trust for America's Health found that approximately 6.1 million Americans abuse or misuse prescription drugs. Overdose deaths from prescription drugs have at least doubled in more than 29 states, where they now exceed vehicle-related deaths. Rates have tripled in 10 of these states and even quadrupled in 4 of them. These increases mean that more Americans now overdose from prescription drugs than from heroin, methamphetamine, and cocaine combined ("What Is a Public Health Approach to Reducing Prescription Drug Abuse?" 2013). But if advances in technology helped create this problem, can technology also help to solve it?

The same study found that the most commonly misused prescription drugs are painkillers, including some of the most popular, OxyContin, Percocet, and Vicodin. According to the study, men between the ages of 25 and 54 are most likely to abuse these drugs, though rates of female abusers are rapidly accelerating ("What Is a Public Health Approach to Reducing Prescription Drug Abuse?" 2013).

The statistics make it clear that this has moved beyond a law enforcement problem and has become a national health care crisis. Approximately 50 Americans die from prescription painkiller overdoses each day, leading to more than 16,000 deaths and nearly half a million emergency room visits per year. Additionally, more than 70,000 children go to the emergency room every year for "medication poisoning," or when a child takes medicine prescribed for an adult ("What Is a Public Health Approach to Reducing Prescription Drug Abuse?" 2013).

So what role can technology play in this solution?

Many experts agree that digitizing medical records and "e-prescription" tools can help curb prescription drug abuse. By utilizing electronic records, doctors can limit drug diversion and doctor shopping and crack down on physicians who overprescribe or recommend drugs for nonmedical purposes. Implementation of information technology can address this problem immediately. More specifically, they can address the failures of current systems.

Currently, 49 states in the country have monitoring programs for prescription drugs. The problem is that the strategies in place are often too broad in scope, are woefully underfunded, and can even work against other systems fighting the same problem. Much of this, unfortunately, is due to a long history of inefficient bureaucracy, long paper trails, and lack of interconnectivity between different offices.

Much as it has done in countless other fields, information technology can address these failures. Perhaps the biggest improvement that can be yielded from implementation of information technology is the integration and connectivity of different public health systems networks so that all healthcare providers have access to these records and programs.

Information technology is not only the perfect tool to make these improvements and address perhaps the most serious health issue of the United States but it is also one that will help improve its economy.

This crisis extends beyond just health care. A recent study estimated that nearly every year, nonmedical use of prescription painkillers costs the U.S. economy roughly $53.4 billion–$42 billion lost in productivity, $8.2 billion in increased court costs, $2.2 billion for publicly funded drug abuse treatment programs, and $944 million in medical complications (Hansen et al. 2011).

Unfortunately, despite the fact that many of these systems are already in place to varying degrees, due to underfunding and lack of awareness, many states don't have access to them. For example, many state providers don't have access to prescription drug monitoring programs (PDMPs)—electronic databases that fight against doctor shopping, one of the most common methods people have for abusing prescription drugs. These programs track prescriptions by patients and automatically flag possible misuse by recognizing when multiple prescriptions of the same or similar drugs have been prescribed by different doctors.

Additionally, many states have access to PDMPs but are not fully utilizing them. Many states also vary the requirements for reporting and determining who can access and report data. While all states except Missouri currently have PDMPs, only 16 of those 49 require health care providers to use them ("Prescription Drug Abuse Now More Deadly than Heroin, Cocaine Combined" 2013).

Furthermore, only a mere 2 percent of health care providers nationwide have adopted PDMPs or other electronic monitoring systems. Pharmacies adopt these methods at a far higher rate, at nearly 78 percent, but the sad fact still remains in this day of technological innovation: only 2 percent of all controlled substances are prescribed electronically in the United States. These staggering numbers make it clearer than ever that most Americans are at risk for prescription drug abuse.

While it is clear that information technology can help curb prescription drug abuse, the biggest challenge to the implementation of these methods is not staunch opposition to them, but rather a lack or organization or combined effort by the many different facets of the health care industry.

The real challenge in the coming years will be to involve prescribers, pharmacies, law enforcement agencies, insurance executives, and policy makers to work together to be part of the solution to this very real problem. Beyond expanding access to PDMPs, however, improved training for doctors and other health care providers is also key to curbing prescription drug abuse. Along these same lines, it is imperative that private and public insurance programs expand to cover a full range of substance abuse treatment programs to help cure patients of their addictions.

While there are still some very large hurdles to overcome in addressing this national health care crisis, society can take some comfort in the fact that information technology can clearly help curb prescription drug misuse and abuse. It seems, then, that it is just a matter of when, not if, we will utilize the benefits of technology to help us solve this problem.

References

Hansen, Ryan N., Gerry Oster, John Edelsberg, George E. Woody, and Sean D. Sullivan. 2011. "Economic Costs of Nonmedical Use of Prescription Opioids." *Clinical Journal of Pain* 27 (3): 194–202.

"Nearly 7 in 10 Americans Take Prescription Drugs."
    2013. Mayo Clinic. http://newsnetwork.mayoclinic.
    org/discussion/nearly-7-in-10-americans-take-presc
    ription-drugs-mayo-clinic-olmsted-medical-center-find/.
    Accessed June 2, 2015.

"Prescription Drug Abuse Now More Deadly than Heroin,
    Cocaine Combined." 2013. The Christian Science Monitor.
    http://m.csmonitor.com/USA/Society/2013/1007/
    Prescription-drug-abuse-now-more-deadly-than-heroin-
    cocaine-combined. Accessed May 14, 2015.

Jeremy Summers is a freelance science writer whose work has appeared in Forbes, RealClearScience, *and* Truth About Trade, *among others. He lives and works in North Carolina and is a graduate of Appalachian State University.*

PILL PUSHER
C2-10-0056

ELLERS

REGIONAL CELL HEAD
TITLE-III

MICHAEL E. MCCALL
716-578-4434

ERS

RBAN
HEAD
E-III

SOS

WHOLESALE DISTRIBUTORS

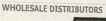

OYLE
6320

PARTNER

PARTNERS

RETAIL CUSTOMERS

ES

STREET LE

Introduction

The issue of prescription drug abuse and misuse has been, and continues to be, one of significant importance to a wide variety of organizations and individuals. This chapter provides an annotated listing of some of the most important of those organizations and individuals.

Alliance for Safe Online Pharmacies

The Alliance for Safe Online Pharmacies (ASOP) was established in 2009 in response to the increasing number of online suppliers of prescription drugs who did not meet minimum standards for safety and efficacy of their products. The organization points out that there are anywhere from 35,000 to 50,000 active online sellers of drugs and medications, of which 97 percent do not comply with relevant national and international laws and regulations dealing with patient safety. Without guidance from some reliable source, such as the ASOP, the average consumer has virtually no way of knowing which Internet sites are legitimate sources of safe drugs, and which are not.

The mission of ASOP, therefore, is to protect patient safety in the purchase of drugs online. The organization is an international association with headquarters in Washington, D.C. It is

Dale Kasprzyk, former head of the Drug Enforcement Administration in Buffalo, stands next to a compilation chart of suspects in a recent prescription drug ring arrest raid in Buffalo, New York. (AP Photo/Don Heupel)

classified as a 501(c)(4) social welfare organization that is supported financially by contributions from companies, nonprofit organizations, and trade associations, along with voluntary donations and contributions from interested individuals.

ASOP has two categories of participants, members and observers. Membership, in turn, is divided into two classes: board members and general members. Board members establish policy and carry out the organization's day-to-day operation. General members advise the board and participate equally in all policy decisions. Those decisions are not voted upon, but are made by consensus of all members participating in the discussion. Current members of the organization come from a variety of fields and include organizations such as the American Pharmacists Association, Amgen, Eli Lilly & Company, European Alliance for Safe Access to Medicines, Generic Pharmaceutical Association, Italian Medicines Agency, Johnson & Johnson, Partnership for Drug-Free Kids, Takeda Pharmaceuticals, and U.S. Pharmacopeial Convention.

The observers group consists of organizations to whom ASOP turns for specialized advice on specific topics or who provide information to the organization on a volunteer basis. Observers do not vote on ASOP policies or practices. Some organizations currently serving as observers are the American Association of Colleges of Pharmacy, Federation of State Medical Boards, National Health Council, Partnership for Safe Medicines, and Rx-360.

ASOP's activities focus on the collection of information about the sale of medications on the Internet, information that is then used to educate health care providers, policy makers, drug manufacturers and suppliers, and the general public. In collaboration with its members and observers, the organization develops policy solutions for issues related to online pharmaceutical marketing that it recommends to legislative and administrative agencies at all levels of government.

ASOP uses primarily two methods in its educational efforts: direct (usually video) presentations and electronic publications.

Examples of the former are presentations made by ASOP staff at the Asia-Pacific Economic Cooperation Life Sciences Innovation Forum Workshop on Medical Products Safety and Public Awareness and Establishing of a Single Point of Contact System in Seoul, Korea; at the Partnership for Safe Medicines' Interchange 2011; and at the PDA/FDA Pharmaceutical Supply Chain Conference: Patients Impacted by Supply Chain Dangers.

Some of the many electronic publications on Internet pharmacies available on the ASOP website are "How to Protect Yourself and Your Loved Ones Online," "Infographic about the Origin of Counterfeit Drugs in G8 Member Countries," "LegitScript's Legitimate Online Pharmacy List," Legitscript's Website Url Verification Tool," "Making the Internet Safe for Patients," "National Association of Boards of Pharmacy's VIPPS list," "Online Pharmacy 101: What You Need to Know," and the U.S. Food and Drug Administration's "Know Your Online Pharmacy" tool.

The ASOP website is also a valuable resource for reports, news items, and other documents about the availability of medications online. Some of these resources come from ASOP itself, others from government sources, others from academic sources, and still others from partner resources. The types of documents that one might find in this section of the website are articles on "Vaccine Shortages and Suspect Online Pharmacy Sellers," "ASOP One-Pager on the Online Pharmacy Safety Act," "Consumer Fact Sheet: FDA Online Medicine Buying Guide," "The Japanese Rogue Internet Pharmacy Market," "Assessing the Problem of Counterfeit Medications in the United Kingdom."

American Society of Addiction Medicine

The American Society of Addiction Medicine (ASAM) had its origins in the early 1950s, largely through the efforts of Dr. Ruth Fox, who initiated a series of meetings with fellow physicians interested in the research and clinical aspects of alcoholism and its treatment. In 1954, this group formalized its existence by creating the New York Medical Society on Alcoholism (NYMSA). The organization's work was funded primarily by the U.S. Alcohol, Drug Abuse, and Mental Health Administration, predecessor of today's Substance Abuse and Mental Health Services Administration (SAMHSA). In 1967, NYMSA decided to extend its work nationwide and changed its name to the American Medical Society on Alcoholism (AMSA).

As interest in medical aspects of drug abuse and addiction grew in the 1970s, a second organization began operation in California, the California Society for the Treatment of Alcoholism and Other Drug Dependencies (CSTAODD), expanding traditional alcohol treatment programs to include those dependent on or addicted to drugs. Over time, the two groups at opposite ends of the country, AMSA and CSTAODD, began to collaborate with each other, eventually leading to their union in 1983 under AMSA's name. In 1988, AMSA was accepted by the American Medical Association as a national medical specialty society and adopted its present name of the American Society of Addiction Medicine (ASAM). Today, the organization consists of more than 3,200 physicians and related health providers interested primarily in issues of substance abuse. It has state chapters in 36 states and the District of Columbia, along with regional chapters in northern New England and the Northwest that include states that do not have their own separate chapters.

The mission of ASAM consists of five major elements:

- to increase access to and improve the quality of addiction treatment;
- to educate physicians (including medical and osteopathic students), other health care providers, and the public;
- to support research and prevention;
- to promote the appropriate role of the physician in the care of patients with addiction;

- and to establish addiction medicine as a specialty recognized by professional organizations, governments, physicians, purchasers, and consumers of health care services, and the general public.

The work carried out by ASAM can be divided into four major categories: education, advocacy, research and treatment, and practice support. The organization's education component is designed to provide physicians and other health care workers with the most up-to-date information on basic issues in addiction treatment. In 2015, for example, ASAM offered a review course in addiction medicine and courses on buprenorphine treatment, state of the art in addiction medicine, and opioid risk evaluation and mitigation strategies. The advocacy element in ASAM's program is aimed at influencing state and federal policies involving substance abuse to reflect the organization's goals and objectives. Some examples of the types of action it has taken include pushing for insurance coverage of mental health and addiction disorders, working for the repeal of alcoholism exclusions in insurance policies, expanding treatment for substance abuse among veterans, and regulating the sale of tobacco and alcohol to minors.

The research and treatment feature of ASAM's work aims to provide health care providers with a wide range of informational materials on all aspects of addiction and substance abuse. Some of the materials it provides are a Common Threads Conference on Pain and Addiction; clinical updates from the International Association for the Study of Pain; a joint statement on pain and addiction from the American Pain Society, the American Academy of Pain Medicine, and the American Society of Addiction Medicine; and a variety of publications on prescription drug abuse from federal agencies. The area of practice support is designed to provide materials that will help addiction physicians and other providers with the best available information about best practices in the field of addiction medicine. These materials include guidelines and consensus documents, such as the National Practice Guideline for Medications for the Treatment of Opioid Use Disorder; "how to's" and practice resources, such as the Drug Enforcement Agency document, "How to Prepare for a DEA Office Inspection"; standards and performance measures, such as the ASAM Standards of Care for the Addiction Specialist Physician Document; and "ASAM Criteria," a comprehensive set of guidelines for placement, continued stay, and transfer/discharge of patients with addiction and co-occurring conditions.

ASAM produces and provides a wide variety of print and electronic publications for the addiction physician and health care worker, such as the books *Principle of Addiction Medicine* and *The ASAM Essentials of Addiction Medicine*; *Journal of Addiction Medicine*, the association's official peer-reviewed journal; *ASAMagazine*, a publication containing news and commentary; and *ASAM Weekly*, an online publication intended for both members and nonmembers who are interested in issues of addiction medicine.

Information about prescription drug abuse is available throughout the association's website in a number of different locations. It can best be found by using the site's search function by looking for "prescription drug abuse." One of the most useful publications is a position statement by the association on the issue, found at http://www.asam.org/docs/publicy-policy-statements/1-counteract-drug-diversion-1-12.pdf.

AWAR$_X$E

AWAR$_X$E is an organization whose mission it is to provide "authoritative resources about medication safety, prescription drug abuse, medication disposal, and safely buying medications on the Internet." The organization was founded in 2009 by the Minnesota Pharmacists Foundation (MPF) following the death of 24-year-old Justin Pearson from an overdose of a combination of prescription drugs that he had ordered from an illegal website. Pearson was a resident of St. Cloud, Minnesota, and his death struck members of MPF with special poignancy in asking themselves if there were not more that pharmacists could do to help deal with the epidemic of prescription drug abuse. The goals that MPF set for the AWAR$_x$E program were:

- informing parents and children of the risks involved in the use of prescription drugs for nonmedical purposes;
- informing the general public about safe and appropriate methods for disposing of unused prescription drugs;
- alerting parents and children of the dangers of using the Internet for the purchase of prescription drugs;
- helping consumers better understand the importance of developing an ongoing relationship with their pharmacist(s); and
- educating the general public about the role of prescription drugs in their health care and general lives.

In 2010, the AWAR$_x$E program came to the attention of the National Association of Boards of Pharmacy (NABP), which consists of representatives from boards of pharmacy in all 50 states, the District of Columbia, Guam, Puerto Rico, the Virgin Islands, Australia, 8 Canadian provinces, and New Zealand. NABP realized that the Minnesota program dealt with issues with which it, NABP, and individual pharmacists and pharmaceutical organizations around the country had been dealing with more and more frequently. It decided to work with the Minnesota Pharmacists Foundation to find ways of extending the AWAR$_x$E program to all parts of the nation.

In the transition from a state to national organization, the character of AWAR$_x$E has changed to some extent. In the former format, the organization focused on making presentations to students in middle schools about the risks of prescription drug abuse. In its first year of operation, it made about 100 such presentations to 2,582 students. The organization also produced billboard messages and radio spots on the topic of prescription drug abuse. It also developed a guide of the safe disposal of prescription drugs and cooperated with the Drug Enforcement Administration's National Prescription Drug Take Back Event on April 30, 2011, when they collected 376,593 pounds of surrendered prescription drugs.

The national AWAR$_X$E program focuses heavily on its website which has a plethora of information about prescription drugs, their use and misuse, and their availability on the Internet. The website consists of five major sections: Pharmacists, Corporations, Students, Resources, and Drug Disposal Sites. The first of these sections contains information for pharmacists as to their role in the campaign against prescription drug abuse. The second section provides resources that drug-related companies can use to educate their employees and to develop practices aimed at reducing abuse of prescription drugs. The Students section of the website provides basic information about the safe use of prescription drugs for middle school and high school students. The Resources section lists a number of publications providing basic information about prescription drug abuse. And the Drug Disposal Site section provides an interactive map, which one can use to find the drug disposal site nearest to a particular location.

The website also has four other sections, called Get Informed, Get Active, Get Local, and News. The first of these sections has a variety of resources dealing with the safe use of prescription drugs, which involves recording and understanding prescription information, safe acquisition of medications, appropriate use of those drugs, finding disposal information, and becoming educated on the abuse and misuse of prescription drugs. The Get Active section is a site that contains stories of individuals who have become involved in prescription drug abuse with the option for providing one's own story. Get Local discusses the important role that local communities can play in preventing prescription drug abuse, and provides an introduction to the locator tool available for finding drug disposal sites on the AWAR$_X$E website. And the News section is a collection of stories about all aspects of the prescription drug abuse issue in the United States that can be searched by the use of a number of filter topics, such as FDA, counterfeit prescriptions, painkillers, Internet pharmacies, medication disposal, and over-the-counter medications.

Hale Boggs (1914–1972/1973)

Boggs was a Democratic member of the U.S. House of Representative from Louisiana's Second Congressional District from 1947 to 1973. He was majority whip of the House from 1962 to 1971 and House Majority Leader from 1971 to 1973. In the years following the end of World War II, Boggs was one of the leading spokespersons for a more rigorous approach to sentencing for drug-related crimes. His position on the topic reflected that of many legislators, law enforcement officers, and members of the general public who believed that the use of illegal drugs had begun to skyrocket after the end of the war, and that some judges were treating the "drug epidemic" much too casually with overly generous fines and prison sentences. In 1951, Boggs submitted a bill to the Congress that dramatically increased the penalties for drug use and drug trafficking and, for the first time in U.S. history, applied those penalties equally to both narcotic drugs and marijuana. It also imposed mandatory sentencing for individuals convicted of drug-related crimes more than once. In 1956, Boggs also sponsored the Narcotic Control Act, which increased penalties even further.

Thomas Hale Boggs, Sr., was born on February 15, 1914, in Long Beach, Mississippi. He attended public and parochial schools in Jefferson Parish, Louisiana, before matriculating at Tulane University, in New Orleans, from which he received his bachelor's degree in journalism in 1934 and his law degree in 1937. He established his own law practice in New Orleans, but soon became interested in politics. He ran for the U.S. House of Representatives from the Second District of Louisiana in 1941 and was elected, but failed to receive his party's nomination for the same post a year later. He then returned to his law practice in New Orleans before enlisting in the U.S. Naval Reserve in November 1943, after which he was assigned to the Potomac River Naval Command. He was discharged from the service in January 1946, ran for Congress again, and was once more elected to the U.S. House of Representatives. He served in that body until October 16, 1972, when he was lost on a flight from Anchorage to Juneau, Alaska, working for the campaign of Representative Nick Begich. Neither the wreckage of the plane itself, nor any of its passengers were ever found, and Boggs was declared legally dead on January 3, 1973, to allow the election of his successor, who, it turned out, was his wife, Lindy Boggs. Mrs. Boggs was then reelected eight more times, serving in the House until 1991.

Mary Bono (1961–)

Bono served in the U.S. House of Representatives from 1998 to 2013 representing California's 45th Congressional District. While in the Congress, she was a particularly outspoken advocate for prevention and treatment programs in the field of prescription drug abuse. In 2010, she cofounded the Congressional Caucus on Prescription Drug Abuse with Representative Harold Rogers of Kentucky. Two years later, she also introduced the Stop the Tampering of Prescription Pills Act, which would have required drug companies to reformulate products that are especially subject to misuse and abuse or, alternatively, to withdraw those drugs from the market. The bill was not considered by the Congress. Bono's interest in the prescription drug abuse issue is said to have been based on a personal experience. Her son, Chesare, began taking the painkiller OxyContin after his father, performer Sonny Bono, was killed in a skiing accident. Chesare later enrolled in a rehabilitation program and has apparently recovered from his prescription drug problem. At the 2014 National Rx Drug Abuse Summit in Atlanta, Bono was presented with the Courage Award for her leadership in the battle against prescription drug abuse.

Mary Bono (née Whitaker) was born in Cleveland, Ohio, on October 24, 1961, to Karen Lee (née Taylor) and Clay Westerfield Whitaker. Her mother was a chemist and her father, a physician. When Mary was two years old, she moved with her family to South Pasadena, California, where she attended public schools, graduating from South Pasadena High School in 1979. She then enrolled at the University of Southern California, from which she received her bachelor of arts degree in art history in 1984.

In 1986, Bono married the performer Sonny Bono (perhaps best known for his singing partnership with Cher), who was later elected mayor of Palm Springs, California, and, in 1994, elected to the U.S. House of Representatives from California's 44th Congressional District. While still a member of Congress, Sonny Bono was killed in a skiing accident on January 5, 1998. Mary Bono was elected to replace her husband in a special election held three months after his death, and was then reelected seven more times before losing her seat to Democrat Raul Ruiz in 2012. She then accepted an offer to join the consulting firm of Faegre BD, in Washington, D.C. The company provides consulting services on a wide range of topics, including health and biosciences, energy and environment, economic development, financial services, food and agriculture, media and entertainment, and technology and privacy. At Faegre, Bono serves as senior vice president with responsibility for technology, media, entertainment, energy, health policy, and strategic communications.

Bono has been married three times, to Bono (1986–1998), Wyoming businessman Glenn Baxley (2001–2005), and fellow representative Connie Mack (2007–2013). During her marriage to Mack, she was known as Mary Bono Mack. The last of these marriages ended in 2013 when both Mack and Bono lost their bids for reelection to the U.S. House of Representatives. She continues to work on prescription drug abuse programs in a variety of venues. She serves on the board of directors of the Community Anti-Drug Coalitions of America, is honorary chair of Mothers Against Prescription Drug Abuse and of Rally2Recovery, and is a popular speaker on drug issues at meetings such as the Association of Recovery Schools Conference, America Honors Recovery, Recovery for Life Gala, and the Annual Drug-Free Kids Campaign Awards Dinner.

Center for Lawful Access and Abuse Deterrence

The Center for Lawful Access and Abuse Deterrence (CLAAD) was founded in 2009 "to prevent prescription drug fraud, diversion, misuse, and abuse while advancing consumer access to high-quality health care." Funding for the organization is provided by a coalition of about a dozen commercial members (pharmaceutical companies) such as Allergan, Mallinckrodt Pharmaceuticals, Millennium Laboratories, Purdue Pharmaceuticals, and Zogenix. In addition to its commercial members, the organization includes a number of governmental and nonprofit organizations, including the Alliance for Safe Online Pharmacies, Allies in Recovery, American Pharmacists Association, American Society for Pain Management Nursing, American Society of Addiction Medicine, American Society of Anesthesiologists, Community Anti-Drug Coalitions of America, Drug Free America Foundation, Healthcare Distribution Management Association, International Nurses Society on Addictions, Johns Hopkins Bloomberg School of Public Health, National Alliance for Model State Drug Laws, National Association of Attorneys General, National District Attorneys Association, National Family Partnership, National Governors Association, National Sheriffs' Association, Northeastern University, and the 15th Judicial Circuit of Florida.

CLAAD activities fall into three major categories: policy leadership, information and analysis, and coalition building. Policy leadership involves the development of laws, regulations, and other provisions that ensure that efforts to prevent the abuse and misuse of prescription drugs are effective without impeding the access of individuals to the medication they need for dealing with their own real medical problems. Some examples of actions taken within this context include the preparation of a document called "Abuse-Deterrent Formulations: Transitioning the Pharmaceutical Market to Improve Patient and Public Health and Safety," which discusses the pros and cons of various ways of developing alternative drug formulations to achieve both drug safety and efficacy; federal legislative recommendations, a form of draft legislation that, "if enacted, would effectively reduce prescription drug abuse," and that was presented to majority and minority staffs of the U.S. Senate Health, Labor, Education, and Pensions Committee in 2014; proposed draft legislation offered to the state of Florida as an aid for dealing with its prescription drug abuse problems; and letters to various federal and state legislators and agencies on specific bills under consideration at both levels for ways of preventing prescription drug abuse. CLAAD has also made presentations or attended dozens of meetings at which prescription drug abuse was being considered, such as the 25th annual meeting of the National Association of Drug Diversion Investigators, the U.S. Food and Drug Administration Public Meeting on the Development and Regulation of Abuse-Deterrent Opioid Medications, the Partnership for Safe Medicines Interchange, the Generation Rx University Conference, the National Rx Drug Abuse Summit, and the National Sheriffs' Association 2014 Winter Conference. All policy decisions and positions made by CLAAD are required to be approved by at least 80 percent of nonprofit members of the organization.

Coalition building has also been a field of active interest for CLAAD. In 2014 alone, for example, the organization reached out to form coalitions with a variety of nonprofit organizations, including Trust for America's Health, National Governors Association, U.S. Conference of Mayors, Pew Charitable Trusts, Clinton Foundation, Transforming Youth Recovery, Arthritis Foundation, NCAA, the Jed Foundation, Johns Hopkins Bloomberg School of Public Health, Legal Action Center, National Association of Counties, Network for Public Health Law, and State Association of Addiction Services. It also worked with a network of organizations in the state of Missouri in an attempt to assist in the adoption of prescription drug monitoring program legislature in that state, the last one in the country not to have such a program.

The area of information and analysis refers to the process of monitoring scientific research, legislation, policy recommendations and making, and other events related to the prescription drug abuse issue. Information obtained from such sources is then analyzed, and summaries and trends are made available to relevant stakeholders in the field through the organization's website, social media, mass media, and other sources. Probably the most important single document developed for this purpose was its "National Prescription Drug Abuse Prevention Strategy" document, first produced in 2008 and updated regularly ever since. All versions of the document are available online at http://claad.org/national-strategy/.

The CLAAD website is a goldmine of resources and general information on virtually every imaginable aspect of the prescription drug abuse issue. One section classifies news articles relating to six specific categories of topics: abuse-deterrent medication, access to quality care, counterfeit and black market drugs, prescriber education and standards, prescription monitoring programs, and prosecutions. Another section provides a wealth of resources on prescription drug abuse, including a summary of policy activities, prescription drug abuse statistics, medication safety A to Z, myths versus facts of drug abuse, a list of acronyms, and additional print and visual resources on the topic. A special section recently added to the website is entitled "2016 Presidential Campaign." It contains up-to-date news reports on statements made by and positions taken by announced and presumptive candidates for the 2016 presidential election.

Community Anti-Drug Coalitions of America

Community Anti-Drug Coalitions of America (CADCA) was founded in 1992 on the suggestion of Jim Burke, then chair of the President's Drug Advisory Council, as a possible mechanism for dealing with the growing problem of substance abuse throughout the United States. Today, CADCA claims to be "the premier membership organization representing those working to make their communities safe, healthy and drug-free." It works with more than 5,000 local communities to prevent tobacco use among youth, underage drinking of alcohol, and the use of illicit drugs. The coalition carries out its work in cooperation with about 30 partners from government, nonprofit organizations, the business world, and international associations and organizations. Some of those partners are the Centers for Disease Control and Prevention; Drug Enforcement Administration; and Departments of Education, Health and Human Services, Homeland Security, Justice, Labor, and State; National Institute on Drug Abuse; international drug prevention groups, such as FEBRAE (Brazil), MENTOR and SURGIR (Colombia), FUNDASALVA (El Salvador), SEC-CATID (Guatemala), ANCOD (Honduras), CEDRO and CRESER (Peru), and SANCA AND TASC (South Africa); the American College of Pediatrics; National Association of Counties; National Sheriffs Association; Students against Destructive Decisions; Consumer Healthcare Products Association; DIRECTV; Krispy Kreme; M&T Bank; the Robert Wood Johnson Foundation; and Xerox.

CADCA offers seven types of core services to communities: public policy and advocacy, training and technical assistance, research dissemination and evaluation, special events and conferences, communications, international programs, and youth programs. In the area of policy and advocacy, the group works with its partners to promote legislation and rulemaking that promotes drug prevention efforts that it supports. Recently, it has encouraged members and the general public to write letters to members of the U.S. Congress in support of four pieces of legislation, the Comprehensive Addiction and Recovery Act (CARA); Drug-Free Communities Program (DFC); Preventing Abuse of Cough Treatments (PACT) Act; and Sober Truth on Preventing (STOP) Underage Drinking Act. The CADCA training program has resulted in the training of more than 13,000 individuals from over 900 coalition members and over 150 coalition graduates from the organization's year-long National Coalition Academy. The coalition has also conducted more than 1,200 technical assistance sessions for its member coalitions. In addition to the National Coalition Academy, CADCA holds three other major training sessions, the Mid-Year Training Institute, National Leadership Forum, and National Youth Leadership Initiative.

Some of the organization's priority efforts are organized into ongoing events, programs, and campaigns on very specific topics. Some of the recent topics have been 17th Annual Drug-Free Kids Campaign Awards Dinner, Annual Survey of Coalitions, Drug-Free Kids Campaign, GOT OUTCOMES!, National Medicine Abuse Awareness Month, Tobacco Initiatives, and VetCorps. In connection with its efforts related to prescription drug abuse, CADCA has produced the "Prevent_Abuse" toolkit. The toolkit consists of four elements, the most basic of which is Prevention Strategies, seven methods of prevention that make use of access to information, enhancement of skills, provision of support, changes in access and barriers, changes in consequences, changes in physical design, and modification and change in policies. (Additional detailed information about the toolkit is available online at http://www.preventrxabuse.org/.)

The CADCA website is a rich source of reference materials on virtually every aspect of alcohol and drug prevention. These materials can be accessed by way of an interactive index at http://www.cadca.org/resources.

The primary element of the CADCA research function is the organization's Annual Survey of Coalitions, which attempts to identify coalitions around the country and learn more about what they are doing to address substance abuse problems in their communities. One result of the survey is the selection of a handful of local coalitions that have been most successful in achieving position outcomes in their communities. These results are published in a publication called GOT OUTCOMES!

In 2005, CADCA began to expand its work to others parts of the world and has since that date helped to establish 130 community anti-drug coalitions in 22 countries, including most of Central and South America, the Cape Verde Islands, Italy, Senegal, South Africa, Ghana, Kenya, Tanzania, Kyrgyzstan, Tajikistan, Iraq, and the Philippines. The organization offers essentially the same training, research, resource, and other services provided to domestic coalitions.

A useful overview of the structure and work of the coalition is available in its "Handbook for Community Anti-Drug Coalitions, which can be accessed online at http://www.cadca.org/sites/default/files/files/coalitionhandbook102013.pdf.

Thomas De Quincey (1785–1859)

De Quincey was an English author best known for his autobiographical work, *Confessions of an Opium Eater*. He also wrote a number of other works, including novels, essays, critical reviews, and additional autobiographical sketches. *Confessions* consists essentially of two parts, the first of which tells of De Quincey's early life as a homeless runaway in London in the early 1800s. The second part begins with a description of the author's introduction to opium and the feelings of joy the drug brought to him. It goes on, however, to outline his later experiences with the drug, that were characterized more by insomnia, nightmares, hallucinations, and an array of physical problems. The book was reprinted a number of times in succeeding years, and served to bring the problems of opium addiction before the general public as had few literary works before it. Although De Quincey eventually produced a number of other works, he will always be best known for his *Confessions*.

Thomas De Quincey was born on August 15, 1785, in Manchester, England. After his father died in 1796, De Quincey's mother moved the family to Bath, where he was enrolled in King Edward's School. He was an outstanding scholar, able to read Greek and compose poems in the language as a teenager. His home life was difficult, however, and he ran away to Wales at the age of 17, with the blessings and minimal financial support of his mother and uncle. Eventually he found his way to London, where he nearly died of starvation and survived only because of the kindness of a 15-year-old prostitute whom we now know of only as "Anne of Oxford Street."

In 1804, he was found by friends in London and returned to his family, who arranged for him to enroll at Worcester College, Oxford. It was at Oxford that he first took opium, in the form of laudanum, for a painful and persistent toothache. He soon became addicted to the drug, an addiction that persisted to a greater or lesser degree for the rest of his life. He describes his years of addiction in *Confessions*, as well as its effects on his life and writing and his efforts to overcome his addiction. From time to time, he was able to withdraw from use of the drug but, a point noted by some of his biographers, the quantity and quality of his literary work suffered significantly during these periods of abstinence.

In 1816, De Quincey married Margaret Simpson, who was eventually to bear him eight children. She has been described as the "anchor" in his life, and, after her death in 1837, De Quincey's use of opium increased significantly.

De Quincey survived for most of his life after about 1820 partially through the financial support of his family and partially through his own literary efforts. In the early 1820s, he moved to London where he worked as a novelist, essayist, translator, reporter, and critic. Publication of *Confessions* in 1821 essentially made his career as a writer, although he never again produced a work with such wide popularity. In addition to his opium addiction, De Quincey spent most of his life battling financial problems, and he was convicted and imprisoned on five occasions for nonpayment of his debts.

Biographers have noted De Quincey's substantial influence on later writers and artists, including Edgar Allan Poe, Charles Baudelaire, Nikolai Gogol, Aldous Huxley, William Burroughs, and Hector Berlioz, whose "Symphonie Fantastique" is reputedly loosely based on *Confessions*. The most recent collection of De Quincey's works was published in 21 volumes between 2000 and 2003. De Quincey died in Glasgow on December 8, 1859.

Drug Enforcement Administration

The Drug Enforcement Administration (DEA) has a long bureaucratic history. Its original predecessors were the Bureau of Narcotics, created within the Department of the Treasury in 1930, and the Bureau of Drug Abuse Control, established as a part of the Food and Drug Administration in 1966. The two agencies were then combined in 1968 with the creation of the Bureau of Narcotics and Dangerous Drugs (BNDD) by the Reorganization Plan No. 1 and placed within the Department of Justice. Five years later, another reorganization plan created the DEA in the merger of the BNDD with four other drug-related agencies, the Office of National Narcotics Intelligence in the Department of Justice; the drug investigation arm of the U.S. Customs Services, in the Department of the Treasury; the Narcotics Advance Research Management Team, in the Executive Office of the President; and the Office of Drug Abuse Law Enforcement, also in the Department of Justice. At the time it was created, DEA had 1,470 special agents and a budget of less than $75 million. Today it has more than 5,000 special agents and a budget of $2.02 billion. It maintains 21 district offices in the United States and 86 overseas offices in 67 countries.

The mission of the DEA is to enforce the controlled substances laws and regulations of the U.S. government and to bring to justice those individuals and organizations that violate those laws and regulations. In achieving this objective, the agency carries out a number of specific activities, such as

- investigating and preparing for prosecution violators of controlled substance laws operating at interstate and international levels;
- investigating and preparing for prosecution individuals and gangs who use violence to terrorize individuals and communities in their sale and trafficking of drugs;

- managing a national drug intelligence program, in cooperation with other federal agencies, as well as state, local, and international agencies, to collect, analyze, and distribute information on drug activities;

- seizing assets that can be shown to be associated with illicit drug activities;

- enforcing, in particular, the provisions of the Controlled Substances Act of 1970 and its later amendments pertaining to the manufacture and distribution of substances listed under that act;

- working with state and local agencies to deal with interstate and international illicit drug activities;

- working with the United Nations, Interpol, and other organizations on matters related to international drug control programs.

DEA activities are organized under 16 distinct programs: Asset Forfeiture, Aviation, Cannabis Eradication, Clandestine Drug Laboratory Cleanup, DEA Museum, Diversion Control/Prescription Drug Abuse, Drug Prevention/Demand Reduction, Foreign Cooperative Investigations, Forensic Sciences, High Intensity Drug Trafficking Areas, Money Laundering, Office of the Administrative Law Judges, Organized Crime and Drug Enforcement Task Force, State and Local Task Forces, Southwest Border Initiative, and Victim-Witness Assistance Program. In the Diversion Control/Prescription Drug Abuse program, DEA agents are involved in the monitoring of physicians and pharmacists who provide prescription drugs to those not qualified to receive such drugs or who falsify their records about such transactions; identifying employees who steal such drugs or falsify records to cover illegal sales, individuals who steal or forge prescriptions, and criminals who rob pharmacies or other facilities to obtain prescription drugs. In addition, agents in the program have a variety of other non-field work, such as coordinating major investigations, fulfilling U.S.

obligations under international drug treaties and agreements, advising state and local policy makers, controlling the import and export of controlled substances, and liaising with industry representatives.

In addition to its investigative, enforcement, advisory, and other functions, the DEA has an active program of prevention, housed within its Demand Reduction Section. As its title suggests, the goal of this department is to reduce the demand of drugs among existing and potential drug users and addicts by providing good education about the nature of drugs for populations thought to be most at risk for drug problems. The section has created and maintains two major Internet programs in this area, Just Think Twice (www.justthinktwice.com) and Get Smart about Drugs (www.getsmartaboutdrugs.com), the former designed primarily for teenagers, and the latter for parents, educators, and other adults.

The DEA website is also a useful source of information about all aspects of drug use and abuse. Its Drug Information page contains documents on Drug Scheduling, the Controlled Substances Act, and Federal Trafficking Penalties, as well as fact sheets with information about more than two dozen commonly abused drugs, such as various opioids, stimulants, and depressants, as well as certain over-the-counter products, such as inhalants and bath salts. The fact sheets are sections taken from the agency's 2011 publication "Drugs of Abuse," which provides basic information about all forms of illegal drugs presented in a clear and understandable format.

Carl Durham (1892–1974)

Durham was coauthor with Senator Hubert Humphrey (D-MN) of an amendment to the Federal Food, Drug, and Cosmetic Act of 1938 that required certain types of drugs to be sold only through prescription and to be labeled as noting that they were available only by prescription. The act was significant because prior to its adoption there was no legal or formal process for distinguishing between drugs that might pose a threat to one's health or life and those that were completely safe to take, the classes of drugs now known as *prescription* and *over-the-counter*, respectively. In a sense, then, Durham and Humphrey can be known as the "fathers of prescription drugs." Additional provisions of the Durham-Humphrey amendment allowed a pharmacist to refill a prescription without receiving additional instructions from the prescriber and permitted prescriptions to be ordered verbally as well as in writing.

Carl Thomas Durham was born at White Cross, in Orange County, North Carolina, on August 28, 1892. He was the oldest of the six children of Claude and Delia Ann (Lloyd) Durham. Carl Durham attended the local elementary school in White Cross before continuing his education at the privately run Manndale Academy at Saxapahaw, just west of White Cross. In the summer of 1913, at the age of 21, Durham began work as an apprentice pharmacist at Eubanks Drugstore in Chapel Hill. Three years later, he had achieved sufficient experience to qualify for the pharmacy program at the University of North Carolina, from which he graduated in 1917. He then enlisted in the U.S. Navy, following the United States' entering World War I. Durham served as a pharmacist's mate for one year, before leaving the navy at the end of the war and returning to the Eubanks Drugstore as a professional pharmacist.

Even as a young man, Durham was active in civic and religious groups, serving as a deacon in his church and as president of his Bible class at the church. His first foray into politics occurred in 1921, when he was elected to the Chapel Hill Board of Alderman, a post he held until 1930. He was also elected to the Chapel Hill School Board, where he served from 1924 to 1938, and the Orange County Board of Commissioners, where he was a member from 1932 to 1938. Throughout this period, Durham continued to work as a pharmacist at Eubanks.

In 1938, Representative William B. Umstead, from North Carolina's Sixth Congressional District, retired and the candidate selected by the Democratic Party to replace him died before the election was held. With less than two weeks before the election, the party then selected Durham to run for the post, and he was elected without Republican opposition. Durham later ran and was reelected 10 more times before finally retiring from the body in 1961. While serving in the House, his major position was as chair of the Joint Committee on Atomic Energy in the 82nd and 85th Congresses. He also served on the House Military Affairs and Armed Services Committees. During his tenure, he was acknowledged by the Library of Congress as "the only pharmacist in Congress," although that accolade was not precisely true since his cosponsor for the prescription drug bill, Senator Hubert Humphrey, also had earned his license in pharmacy.

During the latter portion of his career, he became especially interested and active in issues related to the use of atomic energy, which had arisen at the end of World War II with the debate over control of the powerful new source of energy. Durham was a persistent spokesperson for the position that control of the new energy source should remain in civilian hands, in contrast to the position of military leaders who hoped to maintain control over atomic power themselves. Durham was a delegate to the Atoms for Peace Conference held in Geneva in 1955 and attended the initial meeting of the Atomic Energy Agency in Vienna two years later.

After he retired from Congress in 1961, Durham was named honorary president of the American Pharmaceutical Association and hired as a special consultant to the organization. An article in the association's publication, *Drug Topics*, observed that, if an award existed for the pharmacist who had performed the greatest service for his country, it would have to go to Carl Durham. Durham died in Durham, North Carolina, on April 29, 1974, and was interred at the Antioch Baptist Church Cemetery, in Chapel Hill. He had been married twice, and had 8 children and 26 grandchildren.

European Monitoring Centre for Drugs and Drug Addiction

The European Monitoring Centre for Drugs and Drug Addiction (EMCDDA) was established in 1993 to provide member state of the European Union with a comprehensive and coordinated system for collecting, organizing, and distributing information about substance abuse issues within the EU. Prior to that time, various countries had different methods of collecting and analyzing these data, and a poorly developed system for exchanging information with each other. Today, EMCDDA employs about 100 specialists in the field of drug information and analysis with the responsibility of providing member states with the scientific information they need for the development of sound drug policies.

As a data-gathering organization, EMCDDA's activities are focused almost entirely on the collection of statistical information, review and analysis of that information, production of reports on the data, and distribution of those data to members of the European Union and other individuals and organizations interested in its many topics. Some of the topics on which the organization has reported recently are drug-related deaths and mortality indicators; drug-related research; harm reduction interventions; health and social responses to drug use; high risk drug use indicators; key epidemiological indicators; markets, crime and supply reduction; policy and law; prevention of drug use; social reintegration of drug abusers; treatment demand; treatment of drug use; and wastewater analysis.

EMCDDA has collected data and maintains reports on virtually every imaginable aspect of drug use and abuse in the European Union. Its index of publications lists the names of essentially all abused substances, ranging from amphetamine and benzodiazepine to synthetic cannabinoids and synthetic cathinones. It also contains references to other drug-related topics, such as mortality and morbidity data, control status of drugs, drug-related events on the continent, harm reduction, public expenditures on drug problems, and strategies and action plans.

As is to be expected, the EMCDDA library consists of a host of reports and other documents on drug issues, including regular publications such as its invaluable annual review of the drug situation in Europe, "European Drug Report," and the bimonthly newsletter "Drugnet Europe." In addition, the organization provides a variety of EMCDDA papers on specific topics, implementation reports, joint reports and publications, literature reviews, manuals and guidelines, monographs, national reports, technical reports, and thematic papers. Examples of the wide range of topics on which publications are available are drug demand reduction, responding to new psychoactive substances, khat use in Europe, responding to drug driving in Europe, treatment of cannabis-related disorders in Europe, impaired driving and traffic accidents, therapeutic communities for treating addictions in Europe, models of addiction, social reintegration and employment for drug users in treatment, cannabis production and markets in Europe, and new heroin-assisted treatment. Most of these publications are available at no charge and can be downloaded from the organization's website at http://www.emcdda.europa.eu/index.cfm.

Of particular interest on the EMCDDA website is the section called Perspectives on Drugs, which provide a multimedia overview of all the major drugs of abuse, providing a general detailed analysis of the drug, a video presentation on the drug, and interactive features for learning more about the nature of the drug, its abuse and misuse, and methods of prevention and treatment.

Information about prescription drug abuse in Europe is scattered through a wide variety of EMCDDA documents and can best be located by performing a search for the terms "prescription drugs" and "opioids" on the opening page of the website.

Francis B. Harrison (1873–1957)

Harrison is probably best known today as author of the Harrison Narcotics Tax Act of 1914, an act that was passed, somewhat ironically, only after Harrison himself had left office. The act did not specifically prohibit any illegal substance, but it provided for the registration and taxation of "all persons who produce, import, manufacture, compound, deal in, dispense, sell, distribute, or give away opium or coca leaves, their salts, derivatives, or preparations, and for other purposes." Law enforcement officers and the courts immediately began to interpret the law as restricting physicians from writing prescriptions for the nonmedical use of opiates, and they began arresting, prosecuting, and convicting individuals for such activities. To a significant extent, then the Harrison Act marked the beginning of a national campaign against the use of certain substances for other than medical uses.

Francis Burton Harrison was born in New York City on December 18, 1873, to Burton Harrison, an attorney and private secretary to Jefferson Davis, president of the Confederate States, and Constance Cary Harrison, a novelist and social activist. He attended the Cutler School, in New York City, and Yale University, from which he received his BA in 1895. He then earned his LLB at New York Law School in 1897. Harrison was elected to the U.S. Congress from the New York 13th district, but resigned after one term to run (unsuccessfully) for lieutenant governor of New York. After a brief hiatus in the private practice of law, he ran for Congress again in 1907, this time from the New York 20th district, and was elected. He served for three terms in the Congress before accepting an appointment as governor general of the Philippine Islands, where he remained until 1921. Following his service in the Philippines, Harrison essentially retired from public life, spending extended periods of time in Scotland and Spain. He returned to the Philippines on a number of occasions, however, as consultant and advisor, especially when the islands were granted their independence in 1934. Harrison was married six times, with five of those marriages ending in divorce. He died in Flemington, New Jersey, on November 21, 1957.

Felix Hoffmann (1868–1946)

Hoffmann was a German chemist who worked at the Bayer pharmaceutical company (then known as Farbenfabriken vorm. Friedr. Bayer & Company) from 1894 to 1928, where he was best known as the discoverer of two of the company's most successful products, aspirin and heroin, both within a two-week period in 1897. Hoffmann's research was based on his interest in a chemical process known as acetylation, a chemical reaction in which an acetyl group is added to some other substances to make a derivative of that substance.

That reaction had been used successfully by Bayer researchers in synthesizing the antipyretic phenacetin from the medically useless compound p-nitrophenol and the antidiarrheal medication Tannig from tannic acid, whose main use was in the tanning of leather.

In his own research, Hoffmann first attempted to acetylate salicylic acid, a compound extracted from willow bark that had long been used as an analgesic and antipyretic, but which tended to cause gastrointestinal distress. Hoffmann called the product of this acetylsalicylic acid, which became better known as aspirin. Although first rejected by Hoffmann's superiors as having no marketable value, the product went on to become by far the best known and best-selling of the company's pharmaceutical products in the form of Bayer aspirin.

Less than two weeks after his success with aspirin, Hoffmann studied the results of acetylating morphine, a reaction that resulted in the formation of the product diacetylmorphine, later better known as heroin. This reaction had been studied earlier by the English chemist C. R. Wright, who had, however, never pursued the practical medical applications of the product. As with aspirin, heroin eventually became one of the best-selling products of the Bayer company.

Felix Hoffmann was born in Ludwigsburg, Germany, on January 21, 1868. His father, Jakob, was a successful industrialist in the city who suffered from arthritis. Legend has it that Felix Hoffmann became interested in the development of a pain medication at least to some extent as a way of helping his father dealing with this painful condition. He entered the Ludwigs-Maximillian-University of Munich in 1889 to study chemistry, with an ultimate objective of becoming a pharmacist. He completed his studies a year later and passed the state examination in pharmacy. In 1891, he graduated from Munich and then stayed on to study for his doctorate, which he received in 1893. He then accepted a post as research chemist at Bayer, a company with which he remained for the rest of his working life. After completing his historic studies on aspirin and heroin, he left research to work in the company's marketing department. He retired from the company in 1928 and lived as a bachelor in Switzerland until his death on February 8, 1946. The details of his post-Bayer life are largely lost to a world which, until recently, knew little about his contributions to the development of two essential medical compounds.

Hubert Humphrey (1911–1978)

Humphrey was one of the leading members of the Democratic Party during the 1960s and 1970s. He served as vice president under President Lyndon B. Johnson from 1965 to 1969, was twice U.S. senator from the state of Minnesota (1949–1964 and 1971–1978), and was the nominee of the Democratic Party for president of the United States in 1968, when he lost to Richard M. Nixon. One of his many legislative accomplishments while serving in the Senate was cosponsorship of the Durham-Humphrey Amendment to the Federal Food, Drug, and Cosmetic Act of 1938 with Representative Carl Durham, of North Carolina. That act was of considerable importance because, for the first time in U.S. history, it created a category of drugs whose use involved sufficient risk to require that they not be freely available over the counter in a pharmacy. Such drugs, according to the act, could be dispensed only by prescription that could be filled at a registered pharmacy. The act, therefore, made a clear distinction between those *prescription drugs* and other types of medications that could be sold without a prescription, so-called *over-the-counter drugs.*

Hubert Horatio Humphrey, Jr., was born in the tiny town of Wallace, South Dakota, on May 27, 1911. His parents were Ragnild Kirstine (Sannes), a Norwegian immigrant, and Hubert Horatio Humphrey, Sr., ("H.H.") a pharmacist. When Hubert, Jr., was still young, his family moved to the only slightly larger town of Doland, South Carolina, where his father opened a drug store. The business struggled there, and H.H. tried his best to keep it going by selling anything he could think of, from paint to rakes to toys to chocolates. By the beginning of the Great Depression, however, Humphrey's Drug Store had been forced into foreclosure and H.H. was forced to sell the business and try his luck elsewhere, this time in the still slightly larger town of Huron, South Dakota. He had greater success there, and the business continues to operate today under the management of another family member, drawing its business more as a tourist site than as a purveyor of medicine. It was behind the soda fountain at the drug store that the young Humphrey had his introduction to the field of pharmacy during his after-school hours.

After completing high school in Doland, Humphrey enrolled at the University of Minnesota, with hopes of earning his doctorate in political science and becoming a college professor. With the difficult financial times developing, he had to leave Minnesota after the first year, and continued his studies instead at the Capitol College of Pharmacy, in Denver, from which he earned his two-year licensure program in six months. He then returned to Huron to help his father in the drug store, realizing that pharmacy might be the career in which he would remain.

By 1937, however, the nation's economic situation had begun to improve, and Humphrey was convinced that he could not spend the rest of his life in the Huron drug store. So he returned to Minnesota, where he earned his bachelor's degree in political science in 1939. He then moved on to Louisiana State University, from which he received his master's degree a year later. In 1940, he left Louisiana to return to Minnesota, where he enrolled as a doctoral student in political science. He never went very far in that program, however, has circumstances conspired to interrupt his long-held dream of earning a doctorate. The first of those circumstances was the outbreak of World War II, prompting Humphrey to attempt enlisting, first in the U.S. Navy, then in the U.S. Army. He was rejected multiple times by both arms of the service for a variety of physical problems, and he decided, instead, to involve himself in a variety of war-related activities, such as work on the War Manpower Commission.

In 1943, while serving as a professor of political science at Macalester College, in St. Paul, Humphrey decided to run for mayor of Minneapolis. He lost the election by a narrow margin, but achieved greater success two years later when he was elected with 61 percent of the vote. He served in that office until 1948, a year in which he made one of the most famous speeches at a Democratic National Convention in modern history. In that speech, he made an unabashed plea for greater progress in the field of civil rights, an issue that was, at the time, tearing the Democratic Party apart. The speech placed Humphrey on the national state in Democratic politics, a place where he remained for the rest of his life.

Humphrey followed up his success at the Democratic convention by gaining election to the U.S. Senate from the state of Minnesota in the fall of 1948, defeating incumbent Republican senator Joseph H. Ball with 60 percent of the vote. He was reelected twice more, in 1954 and 1960.

Throughout much of the last half of his tenure in the Senate, Humphrey was also angling for higher office, either that of the presidency or that of vice presidency. He never achieved these goals by way of an election, but he did become vice president on January 20, 1965, when he was chosen by President Lyndon B. Johnson to fill that office, which had been vacant since the assassination of President John F. Kennedy 14 months earlier. When Johnson decided not to run for another term in 1968, Humphrey at last had his chance for the highest office in the land when he was chosen as the Democratic nominee for the presidency at the 1968 national convention. In the general election, Humphrey garnered 42.7 percent of the popular vote compared to 43.4 percent for Republican nominee Richard M. Nixon. But that small difference translated into a landslide for Nixon, who earned 301 electoral votes compared to 191 for Humphrey. (Alabama governor George Wallace won 46 electoral votes in the Deep South.)

After the 1968 election, Humphrey returned to teaching at Macalester and the University of Minnesota. Then, in something of a twist of fate, he decided to run once more for the U.S. Senate from the state in the election of 1970, a contest he won handily. He was reelected in 1976, but was unable to serve out his term. In 1977, he announced that he had terminal bladder cancer, a disease from which he died on January 13, 1978, at his home in Waverly, Minnesota. Although the flashpoint of considerable political controversy throughout his career, Humphrey was generally well-liked and widely admired as a politician who always fought fervently for the causes in which he believed, the Happy Warrior of modern American politics, as his Senate colleagues were wont to call him.

The Medicine Abuse Project

The Medicine Abuse Project (MAP) is a working group of Partnership for Drug-Free Kids, an organization founded in 1987 by a group of advertising professionals who believed that, since one can "sell" almost any product with the right advertisement, it should also be possible to "unsell" kids on the notion of wanting to use illegal drugs. The organization, originally called Partnership for a Drug-Free America, produced its first ad in 1987, the now-famous image of an egg frying on the stove, with the caption, "This is your brain on drugs." MAP was founded as a project of the Partnership in 2012 largely in response to the growing concern over the misuse and abuse of prescription drugs by adolescents and young adults. The program has two major objectives: having responsible adults talk with young Americans about the health risks posed by using prescription drugs for purposes other than those for which they are intended, and having those adults ensure that they store and dispose of their own prescription drugs in ways that will prevent children and adolescents from gaining access to those drugs. The organization's long-term goal is to prevent a half million young people from becoming prescription drug abusers by the year 2017, and to develop prevention and treatment programs for those individuals who are already involved in the problem.

Resources developed by the MAP are designed for four groups of individuals: parent and grandparents, health care providers, educators, and community and law enforcement groups. For example, one of the most useful products available from MAP is a publication called the Parent Talk Kit, which provides information and talking points about a host of issues related to drug and alcohol abuse, such as what to say to kids and how to say it, how to choose "teachable moments," and how to involve other adults and organizations. Other materials available for parents and grandparents are publications on a guide on preventing abuse of over-the-counter medications by teens, a drug guide of commonly abused substances, a fact sheet on preventing prescription drug abuse, and a poster on what every parent needs to know about prescription drug abuse. Many of these resources are also available in Spanish.

Materials designed for health care providers fall into the general categories of becoming better educated about prescription drug abuse issues; educational materials for patients; tools for screening, intervention, and referral for treatment; best practices guidelines; and current news on the topic. Materials for educators are directed at four specific groups: teachers, administrators, school nurses, and college educators. The primary focus of materials designed for communities and law enforcement organizations is the PACT360 (for Police and Communities Together) program, which has developed a number of programs and activities designed for parents, youth, and individuals concerned about methamphetamine issues (METH360). Again, most of these materials are also available in Spanish (e.g., Padres360 and Latino360).

The "What You Can Do" section of the MAP website provides a concise list of activities in which one can become involved to help achieve the goals of the organization. The first item on the list is called "Take the Pledge," which refers to a pledge that appears on the first page of the organization's website: "I pledge to safeguard my medicines and to talk with my family about medicine abuse," a pledge that over 9,000 individuals had signed as of June 2015. The other "What You Can Do" activities involve safeguarding one's medicine and making sure that it is disposed of properly, educate oneself about the problem of prescription drug abuse and informing others about the issue, talking with kids about the problem, and seeking help for anyone who has become involved in prescription drug abuse.

One of the sections of the MAP website that is likely to be of greatest value to young people is the Stories section, where individuals have written about their own experiences with prescription drug abuse and, in most (but not all) cases, have successfully overcome that problem.

Mothers against Prescription Drug Abuse

Mothers against Prescription Drug Abuse (MAPDA) is an organization established by three mothers, all of whom had a child who became involved in the misuse or abuse of prescription drugs. Two of those children died as a result of their experiences, while one (Chesare Bono, the son of U.S. Representative Mary Bono Mack), survived and is now in recovery. The three mothers met to discuss their common experiences at

Palm Desert, California, on February 4, 2011, and decided to form a new organization to help fight the epidemic of prescription drug abuse then raging through the land. The organization, MAPDA, was officially incorporated only a month later, on March 15, 2011.

The primary focus of MAPDA activities is the development of materials that can be used by teachers, individuals, and community organizations to educate teenagers, their parents, and their friends about the dangers of prescription drugs that are used for nonmedical purposes. The Teacher's Page section of the organization's website lists resources that are especially suited for elementary school teachers, middle school teachers, and high school teachers. The community page provides document with basic information about the nature of prescription drugs, addiction, overdose, and abused medications. It also offers materials especially designed for teenagers, their parents, and their grandparents.

MAPDA is still a young and growing organization that offers limited personal appearance and opportunities for online exchanges of information and resources. Although relatively few in number, their resources are useful because they speak so directly to individual teenagers and their families who are often confronted with the specific realities of drug abuse and misuse.

The National Alliance of Advocates for Buprenorphine Treatment

The National Alliance of Advocates for Buprenorphine Treatment (NAABT) was founded on April 1, 2005, by three individuals, Timothy Lepak, Kathleen Gargano, and Nancy Jean Barmashi, who believed that the semisynthetic opioid buprenorphine held the potential for helping people addicted to other opioids recover from their addiction. The drug had been approved for use by the U.S. Food and Drug Administration three years earlier, but the three individuals felt that information about its potential value for opioid drug addiction was being ignored, that insufficient numbers of doctors were trained to use buprenorphine therapy, and that addicts themselves knew little or nothing about the procedure. They incorporated NAABT as a 501(c)(3) charitable foundation to work toward solving these problems and making the drug more widely used in the treatment of drug addictions.

NAABT says that its primary source of finances is donations from individuals in the organization's work. It also, however, asks for "unrestricted grants" from pharmaceutical companies to carry on its work. An "unrestricted grant" is one that a company provides an organization with "no strings attached," that is, that can be used by the organization for any purpose whatsoever. NAABT emphasizes the role of unrestricted grants in its work to avoid the impression that it is beholden to any of the companies that provide it with financial support.

NAABT makes use of a number of methods for advancing its core objective of promoting the use of buprenorphine for the treatment of opioid addictions. One of its primary approaches is a registry service that allows a person who wants assistance with his or her addiction to find a physician who is willing to treat him or her. The service also provides a place where physicians can also register so that their contact information can be provided to prospective patients. This matching system can be found on the NAABT website at http://www.treatmentmatch.org/. NAABT reports that it had registered 87,401 patients between 2006 and mid-2015, which produced a total of 72,859 contacts from providers, resulting in treatment programs for 50,780 individuals.

The NAABT website is also a valuable source of information on the basics of buprenorphine treatment. It includes a "frequently asked questions" section, a number of educational essays that provide information about various aspects of the drug and its use in the treatment of addiction, information on the "30–100 patient limit" that restricts the number of patients that can be treated by a single provider, patient stories about the use of buprenorphine therapy, laws dealing with buprenorphine, print and electronic resources, and links to other online sources of information and assistance. Of particular value to those who need further information about buprenorphine treatment is the organization's free resource kit, which contains a collection of NAABT materials about the issue.

Other publications available from NAABT include a patient discussion guide and physician discussion guide about buprenorphine and its use in treating addictions; online peer support forums on a number of specific issues, such as starting treatment, side effects, cost and insurance, tapering off and post-taper, and friends and family; a list of local resources; and a large number of publications on specific issues relating to buprenorphine treatment. Examples of these publications are a brochure on buprenorphine basics, a pamphlet about "precipitated withdrawal," a brochure on the ways in which peer support works, an emergency contact card, a counter-display card explaining how the NAABT matching system works, and the National Institute on Drug Abuse booklet on "The Science of Addiction." The website also has a section that provides detailed information about treatment programs specifically for physicians, counselors, pharmacists, and nurses.

National Association of State Controlled Substances Authorities

The National Association of State Controlled Substances Authorities (NASCSA) is a 501(C)(3) non-profit educational organization established in 1985. Its primary objective is to provide a mechanism through which state and federal agencies can work together to increase the effectiveness of efforts to monitor and prevent the diversion of prescription drugs to nonmedical purposes for which they are not intended. The organization consists of representatives from all 50 states, the District of Columbia, and Guam. Representatives come from a variety of agencies within each state, such as the board of pharmacy, office of the attorney general, bureau of drug control, consumer and industry services, division of professional licensing, and department of health. A number of associate members come from organizations interested in issues surrounding controlled substances, such as Abbvie pharmaceuticals, Associated Pharmacies Incorporated, Cardinal Health, CVS Pharmacy, Express Scripts, GW Pharmaceuticals, Healthcare Distribution Management Association, Janssen Pharmaceuticals, Inc., Mallincrodt, National Association of Chain Drug Stores, Optimum Technology, Omnicare, Purdue Pharma L.P., Quarles & Brady, LLP, Rite Aid, Walgreens, and Wal-Mart.

The organization's two main activities are an annual conference at which new information of drug diversion and related topics is shared, and a variety of educational programs on legislation, regulation, and enforcement of laws relating to controlled substances. The 2014 conference, for example, featured sessions on topics such as prescription drug monitoring programs, electronic prescribing of controlled substances, legislative and regulatory updates, telemedicine as a new diversion tool, abuse and diversion of amphetamines, the use of naloxone to save lives, and drug take-backs and drug disposal programs.

NASCSA makes use of resolutions to express its views on a variety of prescription drug-related issues. Some topics of resolutions adopted in 2014 are the model policy on the use of opioid analgesics in the treatment of pain developed by the Federation of State Medical Boards, the organization's position on an FDA program for the development of abuse deterrent medications, support for the development of special educational programs for individuals who must routinely deal with controlled substances, approval of a policy by which institutions are required to report the names of employees who divert controlled substances, and a statement encouraging state agencies to develop policies about the prescribing of opioid drugs for patients upon discharge from medical and dental procedures.

An important feature of the organization's website is an interactive map that provides information about prescription drug monitoring programs in all member states and territories. One can click on any one of the states or territories and receive a detailed description of that state's program, contact information for the responsible official, and relevant legislation. Access is also available through the website to surveys that NASCSA has conducted in the past on topics such as issues of importance and information and opinion surveys of state and territory representatives on PMPD issues.

NASCSA publishes an online newsletter that is available for general viewing. It contains information about the organization's activities and events occurring in member states and territories.

National Coalition Against Prescription Drug Abuse

The National Coalition Against Prescription Drug Abuse (NCAPDA) was founded in June 2010 following the death of Joseph John (Joey) Rovero, III, the son of April and Joseph Rovero. Rovero was a student at Arizona State University when he died from a lethal combination of alcohol and prescription medications, provided by prescription from Dr. Hsiu-Ying "Lisa" Teng, of Rowland Heights, California. Teng was later charged with second-degree murder in the deaths of Rovero and two other students, Vu Nguyen and Steven Ogle. Today, April Rovero serves as CEO of NCAPDA and Joseph Rovero is the organization's treasurer.

NCAPDA is a 501(c)3 nonprofit volunteer organization whose purpose it is to create nationwide awareness about the dangers of prescription drug misuse and abuse. It has developed partnership with a number of other institutions and organizations, including schools, colleges, community organizations, medical associations, law enforcement agencies, and other groups interested in the prescription drug abuse problem. Among NCAPDA's current partners are the Discovery Counseling Center of San Ramon Valley, SRV Community against Substance Abuse, Teen Esteem, the Troy and Alana Pack Foundation, and the Sacramento Youth Drug and Alcohol

Coalition. One of the organization's primary goals is to work for policy changes and new state and federal laws designed to combat the current prescription drug abuse epidemic.

The primary activities of NCAPDA are speaking engagements, panel discussions, and roundtable discussions conducted at a variety of venues to increase awareness of the prescription drug abuse problem and its prevention. Some examples of the programs offered include the showing of two documentary films, "Out of Reach" and "Behind the Orange Curtain" about prescription drug abuse; presentation of the original play, "Pharming," on the topic; lectures on "Overdosed America," "Adolescent Subcultures and Current Drug Trends;" prescription drug take back days at local police stations; candle light vigils held in memory of those lost to prescription drug problems; and Addiction by Prescription panel discussions. These presentations are made at a wide variety of venues, including local middle and high schools, service clubs, governmental offices, social clubs, restaurants and bars, and police stations.

The NCAPDA website has a number of useful resources for those interested in the prescription drug abuse problem, some designed specifically for parents, and others, specifically for young adults. In addition to background information on potentially dangerous drugs and the nature of drug addiction, the Resources section of the website provides a number of valuable links to other sources of information and a collection of downloadable files on the topic of prescription drug abuse. The Stories section of the website also offers essays relating the personal experiences of individuals who have lost relatives and friends to prescription drug causes and an option for adding one's own story to the collection.

National Council on Alcoholism and Drug Dependence, Inc.

The National Council on Alcoholism and Drug Dependence, Inc. (NCADD) was founded in 1944 by Marty Mann, the first woman who is said to have achieved sustained sobriety through the Alcoholic Anonymous program. Inspired by the work of reformer Dorothea Dix, who had developed a breakthrough program in mental health care, Mann wondered if she could create a similar program for alcoholics, like herself. She was able to obtain a modest grant from the Yale University Center of Alcohol Studies to establish such an organization, which she called the National Committee for Education on Alcoholism (NCEA). Over the years, the organization evolved into a variety of formats, eventually becoming the National Council on Alcoholism and, in 1990, adding "and Drug Dependence" to its name, to reflect an emphasis that had been added to the organization's mission three years earlier.

Mann created the NCEA on three simple principles, which continue to guide the organization's work today:

- Alcoholism is a disease and the alcoholic is a sick person.
- The alcoholic can be helped and is worth helping.
- This is a public health problem and therefore a public responsibility.

In its literature today, NCADD points out that it was formed at a time when the public perception of alcoholism and drug dependence was very different, one in which the attitude was one of "let[ting] the existing population of alcoholics and addicts die off and prevent the creation of future alcoholics and addicts by legally prohibiting the sale of alcohol and legally controlling the distribution of opium, morphine and cocaine." Mann's approach, of course, was entirely different from that view, and it is one that continues to inspire the organization today.

The mission of the NCADD focuses on a half dozen major themes, the most important of which is the message to alcoholics and drug addicts to "get help," an offer that is fleshed out by the organization with a number of specific suggestions for

dealing with one's addiction. Additional themes focus on becoming educated about the nature of alcohol and drugs, with
special recommendations for parents, youth, friends and family, and those in recovery. The organization's website contains
a very useful section on prescription drug abuse, which talks
about the types of drugs most commonly abused and their
characteristic features and effects, the nature of the problem for
various age groups, methods of prevention and treatment, and
useful resources on the topic.

National Council on Patient Information and Education

The National Council on Patient Information and Education (NCPIE) was founded in 1982 to provide a mechanism
for providing information about the appropriate use of drugs
to consumers and health care providers. The organization
currently consists of more than 100 members from a wide
variety of professions and business, including consumer organizations, patient advocacy groups, voluntary health agencies; organizations representing health care professionals and
health educators; schools of pharmacy, medicine, nursing
and allied health professions; local, state, and federal government agencies; health-related trade associations; national and
international for-profit companies including pharmaceutical
manufacturers, patient information and database companies,
managed care organizations, and communication and public
relations firms. Examples of current members of the council are the AARP Policy Institute, American Cancer Society,
American College of Clinical Pharmacy, American Heart Association, Auburn University Harrison School of Pharmacy,
First Data Bank, Generic Pharmaceutical Association, The
Gerontological Society of America, Merck, National Association of Chain Drug Store Foundation, North Dakota State
Board of Pharmacy, Ohio Pharmacists Association, Pfizer
Consumer Healthcare, and University of Michigan University
Health Service Pharmacy.

NCPIE focuses on a variety of topics related to the appropriate use of medications, including subjects such as improving patients' adherence to drug use, prevention of prescription drug abuse, treatment and recovery, reduction in the number of medication errors, improvements in the quality of health care provider behaviors, improving communications with patients about the use of medications, and safe storage and disposal of medicines.

One of NCPIE's major activities is the development of educational programs of various types that encourage a dialog between patients and drug providers at various levels. The programs currently available are the online programs talkaboutrx.org, bemedicinesmart.org, bemedwise.org, mustforseniors.org, and recoveryopensdoors.org. The first of these programs, talkaboutrx.org, provides ideas for both patients and providers as to ways of about a medication *before* an individual actually begins to take that medication. The program offers background information, as well as talking points and tools for both patient and provider. An additional section provides articles that have appeared in the media about the program in question (e.g., Talk before You Take).

The website bemedicinesmart.org offers an extensive array of information about a number of chronic diseases and medications available for treatment, along with suggestions for adhering to an appropriate schedule and tools and strategies for learning more about specific drugs. BeMedWise also suggests a number of ways in which a patient can become better informed about the properties of a medication and a provider can explain the uses and abuses of various drugs. The bemedwise.org website has sections on drug labeling, issues about self-medication, over-the-counter drug literacy, the safe use of acetaminophen, proper storage of medications at home, and other sources of information about drugs.

The website mustforseniors.org (**M**edication **U**se **S**afety **T**raining for Seniors) is aimed, as the name suggests, at the elderly and deals with special issues relating to drug use by seniors. The website explains how to use the materials provided there, special tips about medication use by seniors, some interesting facts about drug use risks among the elderly, safe use of acetaminophen, and additional sources of information about medication use by seniors. The recoveryopensdoors.org web page is designed specifically for individuals who have or are having problems with drug abuse or misuse. It provides suggestions, tools, and resources that can be helpful in overcoming a substance dependence or addiction. The theme of the web page is that there are concrete steps that one can take in recovering from drug-related problems and that recovery can open new doors for an individual emerging from drug dependence.

NCPIE sponsors, cosponsors, and participates in a variety of conferences and other meetings dealing with drug abuse and misuse issues. In 2014, those meetings included the International Pharmaceutical Federation World Congress of Pharmacy and Pharmaceutical Sciences; Generation Rx University Conference for Collegiate Prevention and Recovery; American Society for Automation in Pharmacy (ASAP) mid-year meeting; Stakeholders' Forum, Promoting OTC Literacy Beyond the Classroom; and NCPIE Campus Dialogue on Prescription Drug Abuse Prevention, Treatment and Recovery.

National Institute on Drug Abuse

The National Institute on Drug Abuse (NIDA) is an agency within the National Institutes of Health (NIH), a part of the U.S. Department of Health and Human Services. Its long history dates to 1935, when a research facility was established in Lexington, Kentucky, as part of a U.S. Public Health Service hospital located there. In 1948, the facility was renamed the Addiction Research Center, at which basic research on the nature of drug abuse and drug addiction was carried out. That initial effort was later expanded even further with the creation of the National Institute on Drug Abuse in 1974 as part of the Alcohol, Drug Abuse, and Mental Health Administration of the Public Health Service of the Department of Health, Education, and Welfare. In 1992, the agency was moved to its present home within NIH. In 2015, the agency had about 400 full-time employees with a budget of $1.05 billion.

The NIDA's mission is "to lead the Nation in bringing the power of science to bear on drug abuse and addiction." It takes a two-pronged approach to carrying out this mission, the first of which is the support and conduct of research on all aspects of drug use and abuse. The second prong is the dissemination of information obtained from this research as a guide for the development of programs of prevention and treatment for drug abuse and addiction. The agency allocates its activities to seven major departments: the Intramural Research Program, where research is conducted by NIDA staff; the Center for Clinical Trials Network, which manages the agency's clinical trials; the Division of Basic Neuroscience and Behavioral Research; Division of Clinical Neuroscience and Behavioral Research; Division of Epidemiology, Services and Prevention Research; Division of Extramural Research, which is responsible for research carried out by individuals outside of NIDA itself; Office of Extramural Policy and Review; and the Division of Pharmacotherapies and Medical Consequences of Drug Abuse.

In addition to these standing departments, NIDA supports a number of working groups, special interest groups, and other groups interested in more specific issues. The current list of such groups includes those working on HIV/AIDS, cannabis science, child and adolescent issues, community epidemiology, comorbidity problems, genetic factors in drug abuse, prescription opioid and pain issues, translationally oriented approaches, devices and strategies, women and sex/gender differences research, nicotine and tobacco, neuroscience research, and the NIDA Genetics Consortium. The prescription drug group was organized in 2006 to study the growing problem of prescription drug abuse, with a special interest in learning more about the interrelationship between appropriate pain treatment procedures and the potential misuse and abuse of traditional opioid narcotic medicines. The group currently meets monthly to share information and ideas about the prescription drug abuse problem.

The NIDA website is a rich source of information about nearly all aspects of drug abuse issues, such as the current prescription drug abuse epidemic. One section of the website, for example, provides detailed information about the nature of drugs most commonly abused, along with the effects produced by such drugs on the human body, along with related publications, news releases, and additional resources on each substance, as well as information about clinical trials that may be starting or are in operation on prevention and treatment for abuse of the drug. This section has information about bath salts, hallucinogens, heroin, inhalants, and prescription and over-the-counter drugs, as well as nonprescription illegal drugs.

A second section of the website focuses on topics related to drug abuse and addiction, such as addiction science, comorbidity, college-age and young adults, criminal justice and drug abuse, drug testing, drugged driving, drugs and the brain, global health, viral hepatitis, HIV/AIDS, medical consequences of drug abuse, mental health, pain, prevention, substance abuse in military life, treatment, and trends and statistics.

Many of NIDA's most popular publications appear as part of its four major publications series: DrugFacts, Research Reports, Mind over Matter, and Brain Power. The first of these series consists of comprehensive articles that provide all of the information one might wish to have about a particular controlled substance. The second series provide updates on the most recent research available on specific drugs. Mind over Matter consists of nine booklets that describe the effects of nine specific drugs—cocaine, hallucinogens, inhalants, marijuana, methamphetamine, nicotine, opiates, prescription drugs, and steroids—on the human brain. Brain Power consists of four curriculum programs designed for students in grades K-1, 2–3, 4–5, and 6–9.

NOPE Task Force

The NOPE Task Force is a 501(c)(3) nonprofit organization created to combat the illegal use of prescription drugs, narcotics, and other illegal drugs. The organization was formed in 2002 when the Florida Office of Drug Control asked community leaders in Palm Beach County to form a task force to deal with drug overdose deaths in the county, which at the time had the highest death rate from that cause of any county in the state. Community leaders and parents who had lost children to drug overdoses met to plan a multimedia presentation on the risks posed by illegal drug use, a presentation that was called Narcotics Overdose and Prevention Education (NOPE). The group offered this presentation at a number of middle and high schools in Palm Beach County during the school year 2002–2003.

Recognizing the success of this initial effort in arousing interest and providing information about drug abuse, three members of the group, Richard and Karen Perry and Maryann Carey, recommended creating a formal, nonprofit organization to facilitate continuation of the program as well as its possible expansion. As a result, the group was awarded tax-free status by the Internal Revenue Service on June 24, 2004. At that time, the group also decided to change its name somewhat to its present title of the N.O.P.E. (or NOPE) Task Force. The organization has since created a broad category of partners and sponsors. Among the former are a number of national organizations, such as the Office of National Drug Control Policy, Partnership for a Drug Free America, and Safe and Drug Free Schools; state agencies, such as the Office of the Attorney General of Florida, Florida Coalition Alliance, Florida Office of Drug Control, Florida Police Chiefs Association, and Florida Sheriff's Association; and a number of local police and sheriff's departments, including those from Altamonte Springs, Casselberry, Daytona Beach, Delray Beach, Lake Mary, Longwood, Oviedo, Sanford, Tarpon Springs, Winter Springs, Broward

County, Hillsborough County, Indian River County, Martin County, Okeechobee County, Palm Beach County, Pinellas County, Sarasota County, Seminole County, St. Lucie County, and Volusia County; as well as private facilities and organizations, including the Caron Renaissance Center, Hanley Center, DACCO, Inc. of Hillsborough County, Holcomb Behavioral Health Systems, and Tykes and Teens of Martin County. The organization also works with Lynn University in Boca Raton, Florida, which provides evaluation services for NOPE programs.

NOPE sponsors also cover the wide range of helping organizations and facilities with an interest in drug abuse issues, such as Kings Point Capital Management, Waterview Kitchens, Caswell F. and Marie B. Holloway Foundation, Clear Channel, Florida News Network, East Coast Plastics, Enterprise Rent-a-Car Foundation, Citizens Bank, Florida Power and Light, and Recovery Associates of the Palm Beaches.

The services offered by NOPE have expanded substantially since its earliest years of existence. The organization continues to offer its multimedia presentation to middle and high schools, and has extended its audiences to university campuses. It also offers parent and community forums, support groups, a drug take-back program, an annual candlelight vigil, and a variety of brochures, pamphlets, and other publications on the topic of drug abuse.

NOPE has emphasized the importance of extending its programs to communities outside the Palm Beach region of Florida. It currently has more than a dozen other chapters in Florida (10 chapters), California (1 chapter), and Pennsylvania (4 chapters).

Office of National Drug Control Policy

The Office of National Drug Control Policy (ONDCP) was created by the Anti-Drug Abuse Act of 1988, which required that the office carry out three functions: (1) set priorities for a national drug control policy, (2) implement a national strategy for that purpose, and (3) certify federal drug-control budgets. The activities of the office have greatly expanded since its creation through a series of laws and executive orders that

- extended its responsibility for monitoring of drug control budgets and reporting on drug abuse (Violent Crime Control and Law Enforcement Act of 1994),
- required to development of outcome-measurement systems for the office's work (Executive Orders 12880, 12992, and 13023),
- authorized the office to award federal grants to community coalitions developed to deal with drug abuse (the Drug Free Communities Act of 1997),
- ordered the office to develop and conduct national media campaigns to prompt reduction and prevention of drug abuse in the country (the Media Campaign Act of 1998),
- vastly increased the scope of the office's responsibility in dealing with the nation's drug abuse and misuse crisis (the Office of National Drug Control Policy Reauthorization Act of 1998), and
- further increased the office's responsibilities in a variety of areas related to federal drug policy (the Office of National Drug Control Policy Reauthorization Act of 2006).

(A complete summary of these actions is available on the ONDCP website, https://www.whitehouse.gov/ondcp/authorization-language.)

Arguably the most important single product of the ONDCP work is its annual report, "National Drug Control Strategy," in which the agency reviews the current state of drug abuse in the United States and proposes a number of actions for dealing with the problem. The 2014 version of the report, for example, focused on strengthening efforts to prevent drug use in local communities; seeking methods of early intervention opportunities in health care systems; integrating treatment for drug problems into the overall health care system; breaking the cycle of drug use, crime, delinquency, and incarceration; disrupting domestic drug production and trafficking; strengthening international partnerships to reduce the flow of illegal drugs into the United States; and improving the use of information systems and analysis in deal with drug issues. The 2014 version also chose two areas of special concern for discussion and planning: drugged driving and prescription drug abuse.

As of 2015, ONDCP has selected seven policy areas on which it plans to focus in the near future: prescription drug abuse, drugged driving, community-based drug prevention, health care, marijuana, methamphetamine, and public lands. In addition, it has identified four groups of individuals to whom special attention should be paid in the battle against drug abuse: military, veterans, and families; women, children, and families; colleges and universities; and Native Americans and Alaskan Natives. More detailed information about these campaigns is available on the ONDCP website at https://www .whitehouse.gov/ondcp/issues-info.

Among the most useful of the office's publications are a group of fact sheets on topics of special importance to U.S. policy on drug abuse and misuse. Some of the topics covered in fact sheets that are currently available are, under U.S. Drug Policy: Our Strategy, Our Record of Reform, Lifting the Stigma of Addiction, and Política de los Estados Unidos sobre drogas (En Español); under Our Priorities: Opioid Abuse, Prescription Drugs, Drugged Driving, Prevention; under Criminal Justice Reform: Alternatives to Incarceration, Drug Courts, Mandatory Minimum Policy in Certain Drug Cases, and Compassionate Release Reductions in Sentence; under the Public Health Approach: A Medical Approach to Substance Abuse Prevention, Medication Assisted Treatment, Economic Benefits of Early Intervention and Substance Abuse Treatment, Addressing Substance Abuse and HIV/AIDS, Preventing, Treating and Surviving Overdose; and under Other Issues: Synthetic Drugs and Consequences of Illicit Drug Use.

Pain Therapy Access Physicians Working Group

The Pain Therapy Access Physicians Working Group (PTAPWG) is a group within the Alliance of Patient Access, a national network of physicians who work to ensure that patients are able to receive access to approved therapies and appropriate clinical care. PTAPWG was formed in 2013, at least partly in response to governmental efforts to gain greater control over the misuse and abuse of opioid pain medications, in order to work for policies and practices that make it possible for patients who are legitimate need of pain medications are able to obtain adequate types of forms of those drugs. The organization focuses on developing educational resource that will help inform the general public as well as provide the basis for informed policy-making.

Among the white papers and policy briefings prepared by the group are the health policy briefings "Access to Integrated Care for Chronic Pain" and "Abuse-Deterrent Opioid Formulations: Promising Technology, Unique Challenges," and a white paper, "Prescription Pain Medication: Preserving Patient Access While Curbing Abuse." A variety of educational resources are also available from the group, including and infographic, "Integrated Care Addresses the Multiple Issues of Chronic Pain; a policy briefing, "The Pain Debate: Treatment, Abuse, and Deterrence;" a video presentation, "Prescription Pain Medication: Preserving Access While Curing Abuse;" a radio presentation, "Aches and Gains;" information on state prescription drug policies; and a call to action, "Curbing Prescription Drug Abuse While Safeguarding Patient Access."

The PTAPWG website (http://allianceforpatientaccess.org/pain-therapy-access-physicians-working-group/) also provides a wealth of articles on the subject of prescription drug abuse and medications for legitimate pain needs from newspaper, magazine, Internet, and other sources.

PhRMA, the Pharmaceutical Research and Manufacturers of America

PhRMA was founded in 1958 as the Pharmaceutical Manufacturers Association. The organization changed its name to the present title in 1994, reflecting the increasing importance of research in the activities of pharmaceutical companies in contrast to their previous marketing and sales emphasis. PhRMA's mission statement reflects this change in emphasis by pointing out that its goal is "to conduct effective advocacy for public policies that encourage discovery of important new medicines for patients by pharmaceutical and biotechnology research companies." The organization's three goals for carrying out this mission are:

• to provide patients with access to safe and effect medications that can be produced and sold on the free market without price controls;

• to encourage strong guarantee of intellectual property rights for inventions and discoveries; and

• to support transparent and effective regulation of drugs and free access to relevant information about medications for patients.

More than 50 pharmaceutical companies with primary or other offices in the United States are members of PhRMA. The organization's main office is in Washington, D.C., with additional offices in Albany, New York; Atlanta, Georgia; Baton Rouge, Louisiana; Denver, Colorado; Foxboro, Massachusetts; Indianapolis, Indiana; Olympia, Washington; Sacramento, California; St. Paul, Minnesota; and Tokyo, Japan.

The PhRMA website is divided into four major sections called Access, Innovation, Value, and Safety. Each section provides a number of extended discussions of specific topics within the general rubric. For example, the Access page has detailed information about the Affordable Care Act, public problems such as Medicare and Medicaid, the Partnership for Prescription Assistance, health care communications, international issues, and disaster relief. The Innovation section focuses on a variety of topics related to pharmaceutical research, such as intellectual property issues, clinical trials, updates on new research, medicines in development, and STEM (science, technology, engineering, and math) education, and "I am research, progress, hope," a series of biographical sketches of people involved in pharmaceutical research.

The Value section of the web page focuses on economic issues relating to the development and distribution of drugs, covering topics such as cost and the economic impact of the pharmaceutical industry. The Safety section has essays on prescription drug abuse, counterfeit drugs, safe use and disposal of drugs, drug shortages, and the work of the U.S. Food and Drug Administration.

A particularly useful section of the PhRMA web page is its PhRMApedia, an interactive tool that allows one to search for specific articles on the website with a number of filtering factors, such as keywords and/or topic, disease, and type of document (blog post, fact sheet, press release, testimony, chart pack, infographic, conversations, newsletters, reports, etc.) Another source of articles on current topics of interest is the organization's blog, The Catalyst, which carries stories on topics such as "Out-of-Pocket Cost Burden for Patients Treating HIV/AIDS," "Big Strides in Fight against Cancer," "Recognizing Emerging Value in Oncology Treatments," "How Manufacturing Advances Can Make Medicines More Effective," and "How Successful Negotiation Takes Place in Medicare."

Harold ("Hal") Rogers (1937–)

Rogers was responsible for the creation of a grant program that carries his name, the Harold Rogers Prescription Drug

Monitoring Program, that was created in the FY2002 appropriations bill for the U.S. Department of Justice (Public Law 107–77). That program provides grants to state governments and other agencies to improve their ability to collect and analyze data with regard to the nonmedical use of prescription drugs within a state, territory, or Indian tribal government. The program has been funded by the U.S. Congress on an annual basis ever since it was first established. Rogers is also cochair of the Congressional Prescription Drug Abuse Caucus, which consists of 13 members: 7 Republicans and 6 Democrats. The caucus was created in 2010 by Rogers and Representative Mary Bono Mack (R-CA) to raise awareness of the prescription drug abuse problem and to work toward solutions for that problem that involve research, treatment, prevention, education, and law enforcement programs.

Harold Dallas "Hal" Rogers was born in Barrier, Kentucky, on December 31, 1937. He graduated from Wayne County High School, in Monticello, Kentucky, in 1955, before matriculating at Western Kentucky University, in Bowling Green, Kentucky. He later transferred to the University of Kentucky, from which he received his bachelor of arts degree in 1962 and his law degree in 1964. From 1956 to 1963, he also served in the Kentucky and North Carolina National Guard as a staff sergeant. After completing his law degree at Kentucky, Rogers went into private practice until he was elected Commonwealth's Attorney for Pulaski and Rockcastle counties in Kentucky. He held that post from 1969 to 1980, when he made his first run for public office, in an attempt to become U.S. representative from Kentucky's Fifth Congressional District. Rogers won that election handily, receiving 67 percent of the total vote. He has since been elected 17 more times, never with less than 65 percent of the total vote. On six occasions, he had no opposition in the election. He is currently the longest-serving Republican ever elected to federal office from the state of Kentucky. (His tenure is surpassed, however, by a number of Democratic representatives.)

Rogers is currently one of the most powerful members of the House of Representatives, serving as chair of the influential House Appropriations Committee. He is also a member of the Republican House Steering Committee. In addition to the Prescription Drug Abuse Caucus, he is a member of the Coal Caucus, Sportsmen Caucus, Pro-Life Caucus, Rural Caucus, Rural Health Caucus, National Guard and Reserve Caucus, and Caucus to Fight and Control Meth. He has been honored with honorary degrees from a number of institutions of higher learning, including Morehead State University, Cumberland College, Lincoln Memorial University, Lindsey Wilson College, Pikeville College, Union College, and Coastal Carolina University.

Friedrich Sertürner (1783–1841)

While still a young pharmacist's apprentice, Sertürner isolated the psychoactive agent morphine from the opium plant. His accomplishment is especially important, not only because it was the first such agent extracted from opium but also the first alkaloid obtained from any plant. Sertürner named his new discovery after the Greek god of dreams, Morpheus, for its powerful analgesic and sedative properties.

Friedrich Wilhelm Adam Ferdinand Sertürner was born in Neuhaus, Prussia, on June 19, 1783. His parents, Joseph Simon Serdinner (the spelling of his name varies somewhat) and Marie Therese Brockmann, were in service to Prince Friedrich Wilhelm, who was also his godfather. When both his father and the prince died in 1794, Sertürner was left without means of support and, therefore, was apprenticed to a court apothecary by the name of Cramer. One of the topics in which he became interested in his new job was the chemical composition of opium, a plant that had long been known for its powerful analgesic and sedative properties. By 1803, he had extracted from opium seeds a white crystalline powder clearly responsible for the pharmacological properties of the plant. He named the new substance *morphine* and proceeded to test its properties, first on stray animals available at the castle, and later on his friends and himself. His friends soon withdrew from the experiments because, while pleasurable enough in its initial moderate doses, the compound ultimately caused unpleasant physical effects, including nausea and vomiting. Sertürner continued, however, to test the drug on himself, unaware of its ultimate addictive properties.

Sertürner was awarded his apothecary license in 1806 and established his own pharmacy in the Prussian town of Einbeck. In addition to operating his business, he continued to study the chemical and pharmacological properties of morphine for a number of years. His work drew little attention from professional scientists, however, and he eventually turned his attention to other topics, including the development of improved firearms and ammunition. During the last few years of his life, he became increasingly depressed about his failure to interest the scientific community in his research on opium. He withdrew into his own world and turned to morphine for comfort against his disillusionment with what he saw as the failure of his life. He did receive some comfort in 1831 when he was awarded a Montyon Prize by the Académie Française, sometimes described as the forerunner of the Nobel Prizes, with its cash award of 2,000 francs. By the time of his death in Hamelin, Prussia, on February 20, 1841, however, the scientific world in general had still not appreciated the enormous significance of his research on morphine.

Substance Abuse and Mental Health Services Administration

The Substance Abuse and Mental Health Services Administration (SAMHSA) was created in 1992 during the reorganization of the federal government's agencies responsible for mental health services. It assumed most of the responsibilities of the Alcohol, Drug Abuse, and Mental Health Administration

(ADAMHA), which was disbanded in the reorganization. The organization is charged with developing and supporting programs that improve the quality and availability of prevention, treatment, and rehabilitation for abusers of both legal and illegal drugs. As of 2015, it had about 660 employees and a budget of about $3.7 billion. Its headquarters are in Rockville, Maryland, and it maintains four primary research centers there, the Center for Behavioral Health Statistics and Quality, Center for Mental Health Services, Center for Substance Abuse Prevention, and Center for Substance Abuse Treatment.

From time to time, SAMHSA selects a small number of strategic initiatives on which it focuses its efforts over a specific and limited period of time. Currently those initiatives are:

- Prevention of Substance Abuse and Mental Health, the current form of an ongoing effort to make use of existing research knowledge to reduce the risk of substance abuse and mental health among Americans, especially high-risk populations of transition-age youth; college students; American Indian/Alaska Natives; ethnic minorities experiencing health and behavioral health disparities; service members, veterans, and their families; and lesbian, gay, bisexual, and transgender individuals.

- Health Care and Health Systems Integration, designed to make the best available therapies available to all individuals in the areas of both substance abuse and mental health.

- Trauma and Justice, an effort to increase the availability of mental health and substance abuse services to individuals in the criminal justice and juvenile justice systems.

- Recovery Support, which focuses on providing assistance to individuals who are in recovery from both mental health and substance abuse disorders.

- Health Information Technology, designed to promote the use of existing technology, such as electronic health records, to transform the fundamental nature of behavioral health care.

- Workforce Development, an effort to train more workers in methods for using modern technology to address the behavioral health needs of the nation.

More detailed information about these initiatives is available at http://store.samhsa.gov/shin/content//PEP14-LEADCHAN GE2/PEP14-LEADCHANGE2.pdf.

In addition to its specialized strategic initiatives, SAMHSA maintains a large number of ongoing programs and campaigns on specific issues within the areas of substance abuse and mental health. Some of these topics are Behavioral Health Equity, the Buprenorphine Information Center, the Center for Application of Prevention Technologies, National Prevention Week, the Partners for Recovery Initiative, the Recovery to Practice program, the Safe Schools/Healthy Students Initiative, the Disaster Technical Assistance Center, the Division of Workplace Programs, the Fetal Alcohol Spectrum Disorders Center, the Homelessness Resource Center, the SAMHSA Knowledge Applications Project, and the Tribal Training and Technical Assistance Center.

The SAMHSA website is one of the best resources for information on virtually all aspects of substance abuse. This information is organized under about two dozen rubrics, including alcohol, tobacco, and other drugs; behavioral health treatments and services; criminal and juvenile justice; data, outcomes, and quality; disaster preparedness, response, and recovery; health care and health systems integration; health disparities; health financing; health information technology; HIV, AIDS, and viral hepatitis; homelessness and housing; laws, regulations, and guidelines; mental and substance use disorders; prescription drug misuse and abuse; prevention of substance abuse and mental illness; recovery and recovery support; school and campus health; specific populations; state and local government partnerships; suicide prevention; trauma and violence; tribal affairs; underage drinking; veterans and military families; wellness; and workforce. The Prescription Drug Abuse page provides basic information obtained from a number of essential studies, such as the 2013 National Survey on Drug Use and Health, a 2011 analysis by the Centers for Disease Control and Prevention, a 2008 report by the Coalition Against Insurance Fraud, and the 2014 National Drug Control Strategy. Other sections of this part of the website deal with additional issues such as types of commonly misused or abused drugs, specific populations and prescription drug misuse and abuse, SAMHSA's efforts to fight prescription drug misuse and abuse, grants related to prescription drug misuse and abuse, and publications and resources on prescription drug misuse and abuse. SAMHSA also maintains and extensive library of brochures, pamphlets, reports, toolkits, digital downloads, comic books, guidelines, manuals, and other publications on the range of topics in which it is interested and involved.

Charles E. Terry (1878–1945)

Terry is perhaps best known for his monumental work on opium, *The Opium Problem*, which he wrote in 1928 with his then associate executive, Mildred Pellens, who was later to become his third wife. Terry was one of the most outspoken advocates of his time for the position that drug addiction was primarily a medical problem, rather than a crime, a philosophy that put him largely at odds with many physicians, law enforcement officers, government officials, and others of the period.

Charles Edward Terry was born in Hartford, Connecticut, on February 14, 1878. His family moved to Florida while he was still a young boy in hopes that warmer weather there would aid in his father's recovery from tuberculosis. When the move failed to achieve that result, his father died of the disease, an event that motivated Terry to consider become a physician so that he could contributed to the solution of medical problems such as the one that disrupted his family's own life. He enrolled at the University of Maryland Medical School in 1899, from which he earned his medical degree in 1903. He then returned to Florida, where he joined his brother-in-law in private practice in Jacksonville. In 1910 he was elected president of the Duval County Medical Society and, in the same year, was invited to become the city's first full-time medical officer, a post he held until 1917.

During his tenure as medical officer in Jacksonville, Terry instituted a number of progressive policies concerning the city's drug abuse and addiction problems. For example, he established a drug clinic at which drug addicts could receive free prescriptions for the narcotic drugs they needed, largely in hopes of weaning them off their addiction. The clinic was, in a way, a forerunner of modern methadone clinics that also aim to wean users away from heroin or other opioids by offering them treatment with a milder narcotic, methadone.

Terry also introduced the concept of multiple prescription copies, an early form of the duplicate and triplicate prescriptions forms that later became routine in most parts of the country. This practice allowed Terry to track physicians and pharmacists who wrote and filled prescriptions for larger quantities of drugs than would normally be required for medical purposes. Possession of such large quantities of a drug by an individual became a misdemeanor, but the city health office was allowed to contact anyone accused of such an act in order to offer them access to the health department drug clinic and its services.

Beyond his work with drug addiction, Terry introduced a number of other reforms in the city health program, including a more aggressive program of smallpox vaccinations, a rat-eradication project, improvements in the city's sewage disposal system, and creation of midwifery and visiting nurse programs.

Terry was also active in public health issues on a national level, which led to his election in 1914 as president of the American Public Health Association (APHA). He also served as chair of the APHA Committee on Habit-Forming Drugs, where he continued to push for a greater acceptance among professionals for the concept of drug addiction as a medical problem and a more compassionate philosophy for dealing with those addicted to drugs.

In 1917, Terry left the Jacksonville health department to become medical editor of the *Delineator* magazine, a woman's magazine that claimed to be "A Journal of Fashion, Culture, and Fine Arts." Four years later, he left Florida to accept a position as executive secretary of the newly formed Committee on Drug Addictions of the Bureau of Social Hygiene in New York, an organization funded by a wealthy group of philanthropists that included John D. Rockefeller Jr., and Paul Warburg. One of the first problems with which Terry had to deal on the committee was the lack of a common understanding as to exactly what the nature of drug addiction was. As a consequence, the committee decided to conduct a comprehensive study on the nature of opium addiction, a study to be led by Terry, assisted by Pellens. They study continued for a number of years, resulting in a report of more than a thousand pages covering topics such as the development and extent of the problem, its etiology and general nature, its pathology and symptomatology, the nature of users, and national and international laws and regulations about opium use and trafficking. Seldom in the history of drug studies has a research project dealt with such a comprehensive range of topics in so much detail.

As the Terry-Peller study was being completed, a debate was going on within the Committee on Drug Addictions between those who saw addiction as a medical problem, and those who viewed it as an issue of crime and punishment. Over time it was the latter view that became predominant, and Terry eventually decided that he could no longer continue his work on the committee. After completing a survey in Detroit that he was conducting in the early 1930s, Terry resigned from the committee and accepted a position at the Harlem Valley Hospital, in Dover, New York, where he remained until his death in 1945. After leaving the Committee on Drug Addictions, he was never again involved in the field of drug addiction.

United Nations Office on Drugs and Crime

The United Nations Office on Drugs and Crime (UNODC) was established in 1997 through the merger of the United Nations Drug Control Programme and the Centre for International Crime Prevention. The agency's mission is to assist member states in their battles against illegal substance abuse, crime, and terrorism. The agency employs about 1,500 staff located at its headquarters in Vienna, Austria, and 21 field offices that supervise its work in more than 150 countries.

The vast majority of the agency's work is based on a number of treaties, protocols, conventions, and other international agreements dealing with crime and drug issues. In the area of crime, those treaties include such agreements as the Convention against Transnational Organized Crime, the Protocol to Prevent, Suppress and Punish Trafficking in Persons, especially Women and Children, and the Protocol against the Smuggling of Migrants by Land, Sea and Air. Relevant drug agreements include the Single Convention on Narcotic Drugs of 1961, as amended by the 1972 Protocol; the Convention on Psychotropic Substances of 1971; and the United Nations Convention Against Illicit Traffic in Narcotic Drugs and Psychotropic Substances of 1988.

UNODC makes use of a number of activities to carry out its responsibilities, such as campaigns, commissions, data gathering and analysis, legal tools, laboratory and forensic science services, and e-learning opportunities. Examples of the types of campaigns conducted by the agency are World Drug Day, International Day against Drug Abuse and Illicit Trafficking, International Anti-Corruption Day, and World AIDS Day, special events at which a wide range of activities are carried out at locations around the world to raise awareness and knowledge of the topic at hand. The Blue Heart Campaign is focused on educating the public about human trafficking and steps that can be taken to reduce the problem. The two most important commissions sponsored by the organization are the Commission on

Narcotic Drugs and the Commission on Crime Prevention and Criminal Justice. These commissions meet annually to review the status of the field for which they are responsible, on which they base their resolutions, decisions, and other actions to be taken by subsidiary committees that serve the commissions.

One of the most important activities carried out by the office is extensive and detailed research on the status of drug use and abuse and all forms of criminal behavior in nations around the world. The data produced from these studies then form the basis for a number of reports on specific aspects of drug use and crime worldwide, such as the World Drug Report, almost certainly the most important single publication on drug issues worldwide currently available; the Global Report on Trafficking in Persons; and the Global Study on Homicide. Other publications available from UNODC include research studies on topics such as "One Hundred Years of Drug Control," "Amphetamines and Ecstasy," Sweden's Successful Drug Policy," and "The Opium Economy in Afghanistan," as well as two regular journals, the *Bulletin on Narcotics* and *Forum on Crime and Society*.

Another important function of UNODC is its Laboratory and Scientific Section, whose goal it is to improve the forensic capabilities of member states in their efforts to meet international standards. The section provides a host of tools for forensic agencies around the world to achieve this goal, tools such as drug testing kits developed by the agency that make use of the best technology currently available, publications on a wide variety of specific topics in forensic science, links to a number of useful resources and organizations, and online lessons and classes intended for updating and educating about current developments in the forensic sciences.

The UNODC website is a rich source of reports, commentaries, papers, and other publications dealing with many topics relating to drug use and crime. Those resources are categorized under a number of topics, such as alternative development, corruption, crime prevention and criminal justice, drug prevention, treatment and care, drug trafficking, firearms, fraudulent medicines, HIV and AIDS, human trafficking, and migrant smuggling, money-laundering, organized crime, maritime crime and piracy, terrorism prevention, and wildlife and forest crime. The drug sections have a number of very useful publications on prescription drug abuse, one of which is the agency's 2011 discussion paper, "The Non-Medical Use of Prescription Drugs: Policy Direction Issues," which provides a comprehensive overview of the status of prescription drug abuse in various regions of the world among groups of individuals especially at risk for the problem. Other papers and reports available on the topic include "Opioid Overdose: Preventing and Reducing Opioid Overdose Mortality," "International Standards On Drug Use Prevention," "TREATNET Quality Standards For Drug Dependence Treatment And Care Services," and "Ensuring Availability of Controlled Medications for the Relief of Pain and Preventing Diversion and Abuse."

Hamilton Wright (1867–1917)

Wright has been described as the "father of drug laws" in the United States because of his strong objections to the use of illegal drugs and his vigorous efforts to have laws passed against the manufacture, transport, sale, and consumption of illegal substances. Although he was not a member of Congress at the time, he is generally regarded as the author of the Harrison Narcotics Tax Act of 1914 which instituted taxes on opiates for the first time in U.S. history.

Hamilton Wright was born in Cleveland, Ohio, on August 2, 1867. After graduating from high school in Boston, he enlisted in the U.S. Army, where he served in the 7th Fusiliers in the Reale Rebellion, earning a medal for his valor during the war. He then attended McGill University, in Montreál, Canada, from which he received his M.D. in 1895. From 1895 to 1908, he was engaged in a variety of research projects at a number of sites around the world, studying tropical diseases such as beri-beri, plague, and malaria. His work took him to China, Japan, Malaya, Great Britain, Germany, and France. In 1908, President Teddy Roosevelt appointed Wright the nation's first commissioner on international opium, a capacity in which he represented the United States at the International Opium Conference held at The Hague, The Netherlands, in 1911. He spent the rest of his life campaigning against opium use in the United States, which, as he wrote in a 1911 article for The *New York Times*, had the highest proportion of opium users of any country in the world.

Wright is known today for his willingness to use inflammatory, often inaccurate statements about the dangers posed by opium. He was especially critical of blacks and Chinese Americans for their use of the drug, suggesting at one point that "one of the most unfortunate phases of the habit of smoking opium in this country is the large number of women who have become involved and are living as common-law wives or cohabiting with Chinese in the Chinatowns of our various cities." He also railed against cocaine use, suggesting at one time that "cocaine is often the direct incentive to the crime of rape by the Negroes of the South and other sections of the country."

Wright was very successful in pushing his antiopium agenda both domestically and internationally. At home, his greatest achievement was adoption of the Harrison Act in 1914 and overseas, adoption of the International Opium Convention in 1912. In both cases, Wright had pushed for even broader, more comprehensive control over drugs other than opium, especially marijuana, but without success. Wright died at his home in Washington, D.C. on January 9, 1917, as the result of complications resulting from an automobile accident in France two years earlier. He was assisting in U.S. relief efforts in that country following the conclusion of World War II.

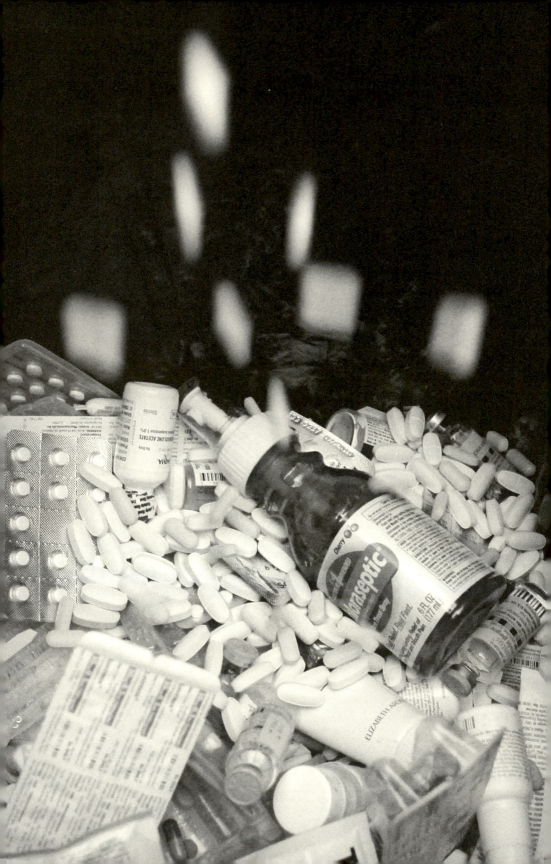

Introduction

Useful information about the status of prescription drug abuse in the United States and the rest of the world can often be gleaned from national, state, and local laws; court cases dealing with the topic; and statistics and data about the production and use of prescription drugs. This chapter provides some of this basic information on the topic of prescription drug abuse.

Data

Table 5.1 Prescription Drug Overdose Death Rates by Selected Characteristics (2008)

Characteristic	All Drugs*	Prescription Drugs*	Opioid Pain Relievers*	Illicit Drugs**
Sex				
Male	14.8	7.7	5.9	4.3
Female	9.0	5.3	3.7	1.4
Race/Ethnicity				
White	13.2	7.4	5.6	2.8
Hispanic	6.1	3.0	2.1	2.5

(continued)

Blue pills fall into the disposal receptacle for expired prescription drugs as they are poured out at the Allegheny County police station in Allison Park, Pennsylvania, on April 28, 2012. This collection point was a part of the fourth National Prescription Drug Take Back Day hosted by the federal Drug Enforcement Administration. The goal was to help prevent abuse of their purpose, to keep the drugs away from children they weren't intended for, and to dispose of them in a safe and controlled manner. (AP Photo/Keith Srakocic)

233

Table 5.1   *(continued)*

Characteristic	All Drugs*	Prescription Drugs*	Opioid Pain Relievers*	Illicit Drugs**
Non-Hispanic	14.7	8.4	6.3	2.9
Black	8.3	3.0	1.9	4.0
Asian/Native Hawaiian or Pacific Islander	1.8	1.0	0.5	0.6
American Indian/ Alaska Native	13.0	8.4	6.2	2.7
Age Group (in Years)				
0–14	0.2	0.2	0.1	†
15–24	8.2	4.5	3.7	2.2
25–34	16.5	8.8	7.1	4.4
35–44	20.9	11.0	8.3	5.3
45–54	25.3	13.8	10.4	6.0
55–64	13.0	7.3	5.0	2.5
≥65	4.1	3.0	1.0	0.3
Intent				
Unintentional	9.2	4.8	3.9	2.6
Undetermined	1.1	0.6	0.5	0.2
Suicide	1.6	1.1	0.5	0.1

* Rate per 100,000 population age-adjusted to the 2000 U.S. standard population using the vintage 2008 population. Because deaths might involve both prescription and illicit drugs, some deaths are included in both categories.

** Drug overdose deaths that have heroin cocaine, hallucinogens, or stimulants as contributing causes.

† Less than 20 deaths; unstable data.

Source: Table 1. Drug Overdose Death Rates by Selected Characteristics. Morbidity and Mortality Weekly Report (MMWR). Centers for Disease Control and Prevention. November 4, 2011. http://www.cdc.gov/mmwr/preview/mmwrhtml/mm6043a4.htm. Accessed on April 6, 2015.

Table 5.2   **Nonmedical Use of Any Psychotherapeutic Drug in the Past Month among Persons Aged 12 and Over, by Age, Sex, Race, and Race/Ethnicity: United States, Selected Years 2002–2012 (Percentage of Population)**

Characteristic	2002	2011	2012
≥12 years of age	2.7	2.4	2.6
12–13 years	1.7	1.3	1.7

Characteristic	2002	2011	2012
14–15 years	4.0	2.6	2.5
16–17 years	6.3	4.2	4.0
18–25 years	5.5	5.0	5.3
26–34 years	3.7	3.9	4.1
≥35 years of age	1.6	1.4	1.7
Males	2.8	2.6	2.8
Females	2.6	2.2	2.4
Not Hispanic or Latino			
White only	2.8	2.6	2.8
Black or African American only	2.0	1.6	2.3
Native Hawaiian or Pacific Islander only	3.8	3.7	1.3
Asian only	0.7	0.9	1.2
Two or more races	3.5	3.2	2.4
Hispanic or Latino	2.9	2.2	2.4

Source: "Use of Selected Substances in the past Month among Persons Aged 12 and Over, by Age, Sex, Race, and Hispanic Origin: United States, Selected Years." Health, United States, 2013. Centers for Disease Control. National Center for Health Statistics. Table 60, p. 203. http://www.cdc.gov/nchs/data/hus/hus13.pdf#060. Accessed on April 6, 2015.

Table 5.3   Rates of Drug Overdose Death, Nonmedical Use of Opioid Pain Relievers (OPR), and OPR Sales, by State (2008)

State*	OPR Nonmedical Use (%)	OPR Sales (kg per 100,000 population)
National	4.8	7.1
New Mexico	5.7	6.7
West Virginia	5.9	9.4
Nevada	5.9	11.8
Utah	5.3	7.4
Alaska	5.2	8.2
Kentucky	6.0	9.0
Rhode Island	6.1	5.9
Florida	4.1	12.6
Oklahoma	8.1	9.2

(continued)

Table 5.3   (*continued*)

State*	OPR Nonmedical Use (%)	OPR Sales (kg per 100,000 population)
Ohio	5.5	7.9
Louisiana	5.3	6.8
Pennsylvania	4.1	8.0
Tennessee	4.9	11.8
Washington	6.1	9.2
Colorado	5.7	6.3
Delaware	5.6	10.2
Wyoming	3.9	6.0
Montana	5.3	8.4
Indiana	5.7	8.1
Alabama	5.1	9.7
Arizona	6.0	8.4
Arkansas	5.1	8.7
Missouri	4.4	7.2
North Carolina	5.0	6.9
South Carolina	4.7	7.2
Maine	4.7	9.8
Michigan	5.7	8.1
Maryland	3.8	7.3
Massachusetts	5.3	5.8
Oregon	6.8	11.6
Vermont	4.6	8.1
Connecticut	3.8	6.7
Mississippi	4.7	6.1
Illinois	4.1	3.7
Wisconsin	4.8	6.5
California	4.8	6.2
Idaho	5.8	7.5
Georgia	4.6	6.5
District of Columbia	3.7	3.9
Hawaii	5.1	5.9
New Hampshire	5.9	8.1
Virginia	4.6	5.6

State*	OPR Nonmedical Use (%)	OPR Sales (kg per 100,000 population)
Texas	4.6	4.2
New York	4.4	5.3
Kansas	5.0	6.8
New Jersey	3.8	6.0
North Dakota	3.9	5.0
South Dakota	3.8	5.5
Minnesota	4.4	4.2
Iowa	3.6	4.6
Nebraska	3.6	4.2

* States are arranged in sequence according to number of drug overdose deaths from all causes.

Source: Table 2. Rates of Drug Overdose Death, Nonmedical Use of Opioid Pain Relievers (OPR), and OPR Sales, by State. Morbidity and Mortality Weekly Report (MMWR). Centers for Disease Control and Prevention. November 4, 2011. http://www.cdc.gov/mmwr/preview/mmwrhtml/mm6043a4.htm. Accessed on April 6, 2015.

Table 5.4 Death Rates for Drug Poisoning and Drug Poisoning Involving Opioid Analgesics, by Sex, Age, Race and Race/Ethnicity Origin: United States, Selected Years 1999–2010. (Drug poisoning deaths involving opioid analgesics per 100,000 resident population)

Characteristic	1999	2000	2001	2002	2003	2004	2005	2009	2010
All ages, age-adjusted*	1.4	1.5	1.9	2.6	2.9	3.4	3.7	5.0	5.4
<15 years of age	0.0**	0.0	0.1	0.1	0.1	0.1	0.1	0.1	0.1
15–24 years	0.7	0.8	1.3	1.7	2.2	2.7	2.7	3.6	3.9
25–34 years	1.9	1.9	2.3	3.3	3.7	4.4	5.3	7.6	8.5
35–44 years	3.5	3.7	4.4	5.7	6.2	6.8	6.9	8.6	9.1
45–54 years	2.9	3.2	4.0	5.5	6.2	7.1	7.9	10.6	10.9
55–64 years	1.0	1.1	1.4	1.8	2.2	2.6	3.1	5.8	6.2
65–74 years	0.4	0.4	0.4	0.7	0.7	0.8	1.0	1.7	1.5
75–84 years	0.3	0.2	0.3	0.4	0.4	0.5	0.6	0.8	0.7
≥85 years	**	**	**	0.6	0.7	0.5	0.9	0.7	1.1
Males, age-adjusted*	2.0	2.0	2.5	3.3	3.7	4.2	4.6	6.2	6.5
Females, age-adjusted*	0.9	1.1	1.4	1.9	2.2	2.5	2.8	3.9	4.2

(continued)

Table 5.4   (*continued*)

Characteristic	1999	2000	2001	2002	2003	2004	2005	2009	2010
Males, age-adjusted*									
White	2.2	2.3	2.8	3.7	4.3	4.8	5.3	7.2	7.7
Black or African American	1.2	1.2	1.4	1.6	1.5	1.8	2.1	2.4	2.2
American Indian or Alaska Native	**	1.9	1.6	2.7	3.1	4.5	4.4	7.5	5.3
Asian or Pacific Islander	**	**	**	0.6	**	0.4	0.5	0.7	0.8
Hispanic or Latino	2.9	1.7	1.8	2.1	2.3	2.1	2.2	2.6	2.4
White, not Hispanic or Latino	2.1	2.3	3.0	4.0	4.7	5.3	5.9	8.2	9.0
Females, age-adjusted*									
White	1.0	1.2	1.5	2.1	2.5	2.9	3.2	4.5	4.8
Black or African American	0.6	0.6	0.8	1.0	1.0	1.2	1.4	1.8	2.0
American Indian or Alaska Native	**	**	1.8	2.1	2.9	2.7	3.8	4.7	4.9
Asian or Pacific Islander	**	**	**	**	**	**	0.4	0.4	0.5
Hispanic or Latina	0.5	0.5	0.5	1.0	0.9	1.0	1.0	1.3	1.3
White, not Hispanic or Latina	1.1	1.3	1.7	2.3	2.7	3.2	3.5	5.2	5.6

* Age-adjusted. For definition, see original text.

** Based on fewer than 20 deaths; data statistically unreliable.

Source: "Death Rates for Drug Poisoning and Drug Poisoning Involving Opioid Analgesics, by Sex, Age, Race, and Hispanic Origin: United States, Selected Years 1999–2010. Health, United States, 2013. Centers for Disease Control. National Center for Health Statistics. Table 32, pp .124–25. http://www.cdc.gov/nchs/data/hus/hus13.pdf#032. Accessed on April 6, 2015.

Table 5.5   Emergency Department (ED) Visits Involving Nonmedical Use of Pharmaceuticals, by Selected Drugs, 2011

Drug category and specific drug*	Number of ED visits	Percent of all ED visits	RSE**
Total Pharmaceuticals	1,244,872	100.0	7.2
Anorexiants	1,042	0.1	32.8

Drug category and specific drug*	Number of ED visits	Percent of all ED visits	RSE**
Anticonvulsants	44,235	3.6	10.7
Anti-Parkinson agents	6,200	0.5	29.4
Anxiolytics, sedatives, and hypnotics	421,940	33.9	11.9
Barbiturates	18,282	1.5	14.1
Benzodiazepines	357,836	28.7	14.3
Alprazolam	123,744	9.9	15.1
Clonazepam	61,219	4.9	6.7
Diazepam	24,118	1.9	8.8
Lorazepam	42,874	3.4	8.8
Diphenhydramine	19,012	1.5	19.7
Hydroxyzine	4,978	0.4	20.2
Zolpidem	30,149	2.4	8.0
Cardiovascular agents	47,699	3.8	9.0
ACE inhibitors	6,980	0.6	14.0
Alpha agonists, central	9,080	0.7	22.8
Beta blockers	14,585	1.2	10.7
Calcium channel blocking agents	7,043	0.6	18.3
Diuretics	7,829	0.6	17.4
Central nervous system stimulants	40,648	3.3	12.3
Amphetamine-dextroamphetamine	17,272	1.4	14.8
Caffeine	1,848	0.1	40.9
Methylphenidate	4,918	0.4	25.4
Gastrointestinal agents	13,060	1.0	15.1
Hormones	12,539	1.0	16.6
Metabolic agents	27,794	2.2	11.3
Muscle relaxants	46,269	3.7	11.5
Carisoprodol	25,528	2.1	16.9
Cyclobenzaprine	11,551	0.9	15.2
Nutritional products	11,090	0.9	14.1
Pain relievers	573,497	46.1	9.5
Acetaminophen products	39,783	3.2	6.2
Aspirin products	11,074	0.9	17.1
Nonsteroidal anti-inflammatories	33,034	2.7	6.5

(continued)

Table 5.5   (*continued*)

Drug category and specific drug*	Number of ED visits	Percent of all ED visits	RSE**
Ibuprofen	22,663	1.8	9.0
Naproxen	7,223	0.6	24.4
Opiates/opioids	488,004	39.2	10.7
Narcotic pain relievers	366,181	29.4	9.2
Buprenorphine products	21,483	1.7	21.1
Codeine products	9,927	0.8	19.5
Fentanyl products	20,034	1.6	19.7
Hydrocodone products	82,480	6.6	9.3
Hydromorphone products	18,224	1.5	17.2
Methadone	66,870	5.4	11.0
Morphine products	34,593	2.8	10.5
Oxycodone products	151,218	12.1	16.5
Propoxyphene products	1,655	0.1	36.9
Opiates/opioids, unspecified	138,130	11.1	20.3
Tramadol products	20,000	1.6	18.6
Psychotherapeutic agents	135,455	10.9	7.2
Antidepressants	88,965	7.1	7.0
SSRI antidepressants	41,257	3.3	6.9
Tricyclic antidepressants	15,307	1.2	22.2
Antipsychotics	61,951	5.0	11.4
Respiratory agents	41,377	3.3	9.9
Antihistamines	8,441	0.7	17.8
Bronchodilators	3,762	0.3	23.3
Expectorants	5,336	0.4	24.4
Upper respiratory products	17,726	1.4	13.3

* For a detailed description of each drug listed in the table, see Drugs.com at http://www.drugs.com/drug-classes.html.

** Relative standard error (RSE) is a measure of the precision of a measurement. The higher the RSE, the lower the precision of the measurement.

Source: "ED Visits Involving Nonmedical Use of Pharmaceuticals, by Selected Drugs, 2011." 2011. National Estimates of Drug-Related Emergency Department Visits. Drug Abuse Warning Network, Table 18, pp. 49–50. http://www.samhsa .gov/data/sites/default/files/DAWN2k11ED/DAWN2k11ED/DAWN2k11ED.pdf. Accessed on April 7, 2015.

Table 5.6   **Trends in Annual Prevalence of Use of Various Drug for Grades 8, 10, and 12 Combined (as Percentages)**

Year	OxyContin	Vicodin	Ritalin	Adderall	Bath Salts	OTC Cough/Cold Medicines
2001	—		4.2	—	—	—
2002	2.7	6.0	3.8	—	—	—
2003	3.2	6.6	3.5	—	—	—
2004	3.3	5.8	3.6	—	—	—
2005	3.4	5.7	3.3	—	—	—
2006	3.5	6.3	3.5	—	—	5.4
2007	3.5	6.2	2.8	—	—	5.0
2008	3.4	6.1	2.6	—	—	4.7
2009	3.9	6.5	2.5	4.3	—	5.2
2010	3.8	5.9	2.2	4.5	—	4.8
2011	3.4	5.1	2.1	4.1	—	4.4
2012	2.9	4.3	1.7	4.4	0.9	4.4
2013	2.9	3.7	1.7	4.4	0.9	4.0
2014	2.4	3.0	1.5	4.1	0.8	3.2

— = No data.

Source: Table 2. Trends in Annual Prevalence of Use of Various Drug for Grades 8, 10, and 12 Combined. 2015. 2014 Data from In-School Surveys of 8th-, 10th-, and 12th-Grade Students. Monitoring the Future. http://www.monitoringthefuture .org/data/14data.html#2014data-drugs. Accessed on May 11, 2015.

Table 5.7   **Trends in Harmfulness of Drugs as Perceived by 12th Graders (as Percentages)**

Category	2010	2011	2012	2013	2014
Try any narcotic other than heroin (codeine, Vicodin, OxyContin, Percocet, etc.) once or twice	40.4	39.9	38.4	43.1	42.7
Take any narcotic other than heroin occasionally	54.3	54.8	53.8	57.3	59.0
Take any narcotic other than heroin regularly	74.9	75.5	73.9	75.8	72.7
Try Adderall once or twice	33.3	31.2	27.2	31.8	33.6
Try Adderall regularly	41.6	40.8	35.3	38.8	41.5

(continued)

Table 5.7   (continued)

Category	2010	2011	2012	2013	2014
Try bath salts (synthetic stimulants) once or twice	—	—	33.2	59.5	59.2
Take bath salts (synthetic stimulants) occasionally	—	—	45.0	69.9	68.8
Try sedatives (barbiturates) once or twice*	28.0	27.8	27.8	29.4	29.6
Try sedatives (barbiturates) regularly*	52.1	52.4	53.9	53.3	50.5

— = No data.

* Data from 1975 are available in original table.

Source: Table 8. Trends in Harmfulness of Drugs as Perceived by 12th Graders. 2014 Data from In-School Surveys of 8th-, 10th-, and 12th-Grade Students. Monitoring the Future. http://www.monitoringthefuture.org/data/14data.html#2014data-drugs. Accessed on May 11, 2015.

Documents

Opium Exclusion Act of 1909

As the United States prepared to send its representatives to the Shanghai Conference on opium of 1909, it was in the somewhat awkward position of having no legislation limiting the importation, sale, or use of opium in this country. To remedy that problem, the U.S. Congress adopted the Opium Exclusion Act of 1909 that was somewhat limited in its coverage of the issue, but sufficient to convince other nations at the Shanghai Conference of its commitment to limit the sale and use of opium in other countries. The body of the new law was as follows.

AN ACT to prohibit the importation and use of opium for other than medicinal purposes.

Be it enacted by the Senate and House of Representatives of the United States in Congress assembled, That after the first day of April, nineteen hundred and nine, it shall be unlawful to import in the United States opium in any form or any preparation or derivative thereof: *Provided,* That opium and preparations and derivatives thereof, other than smoking opium or opium prepared for smoking, may be imported for medicinal purposes only, under regulations which the Secretary of the Treasury is hereby authorized to prescribe, and when so imported shall be subject to the duties which are now and may hereafter be imposed by law.

SEC. 2. That if any person shall fraudulently or knowingly import or bring into the United States, or assist in doing so, any opium or any preparation or derivative thereof contrary to law, or shall receive, conceal, buy, sell, or in any manner facilitate the transportation, concealment, or sale of such opium or preparation or derivative thereof after importation, knowing the same to have been imported contrary to law, such opium or preparation or derivative thereof shall be forfeited and shall be destroyed, and the offender shall be fined in any sum not exceeding five thousand dollars nor less than fifty dollars, or by imprisonment for any time not exceeding two years, or both. Whenever, on trial for a violation of this section, the defendant is shown to have, or have had, possession of such opium or preparation or derivative thereof, such possession shall be deemed sufficient evidence to authorize conviction unless the defendant shall explain to the satisfaction of the jury. Approved February 9, 1909.

Source: *Comparison of the Tariffs of 1897 and 1909.* 1910. Washington, DC: Government Printing Office. https://archive.org/details/cu31924018727697. Accessed on April 19, 2015.

Harrison Narcotic Act (1914)

Probably the first effort by the U.S. government to exert some control over the production, distribution, and consumption of recreational drugs was the Harrison Narcotic Act of 1914. Although this act did not make the drugs with which it dealt—opiates—illegal, it did place a tax on their production, distribution, and sale. In retrospect, the Harrison Act was a weak effort to control substance abuse, but it is historically significant because of its being the first attempt to interrupt substance abuse in any way whatsoever by the federal government. The core of the act is expressed in its first section, reproduced here.

Be it enacted by the Senate and House of Representatives of the United States of America in Congress assembled, that on and after the first day of March, nineteen hundred and fifteen, every person who produces, imports, manufactures, compounds, deals in, dispenses, distributes, or gives away opium or coca leaves or any compound, manufacture, salt, derivative, or preparation thereof, shall register with the collector of internal revenue of the district, his name or style, place of business, and place or places where such business is to be carried on: Provided, that the office, or if none, then the residence of any person shall be considered for purposes of this Act to be his place of business. At the time of such registry and on or before the first of July annually thereafter, every person who produces, imports, manufactures, compounds, deals in, dispenses, distributes, or gives away any of the aforesaid drugs shall pay to the said collector a special tax at the rate of $1 per annum: Provided, that no employee of any person who produces, imports, manufactures, compounds, deals in, dispenses, distributes, or gives away any of the aforesaid drugs, acting within the scope of his employment, shall be required to register or to pay the special tax provided by this section: Provided further, That officers of the United States Government who are lawfully engaged in making purchases of the above-named drugs for the various departments of the Army and Navy, the Public Health Service, and for Government hospitals and prisons, and officers of State governments or any municipality therein, who are lawfully engaged in making purchases of the above-named drugs for State, county, or municipal hospitals or prisons, and officials of any Territory or insular possession, or the District of Columbia or of the United States who are lawfully engaged in making purchases of the above-named drugs for hospitals or prisons therein shall not be required to register and pay the special tax as herein required.

Source: "63rd Congress. Public Law 223. 38 Stat. 785. Public Acts of the Sixty-Third Congress of the United States." http://legisworks.org/sal/38/stats/STATUTE-38-Pg785.pdf. Accessed on April 8, 2015.

United States v. Jin Fuey Moy (1916)

United States v. Doremus (1919)

Webb v. United States (1919)

The Harrison Narcotic Tax Act of 1914 was of considerable significance because it was the first piece of federal legislation designed to deal with almost any aspect of opium and other narcotics. But as the first piece of such legislation, it was subject to later interpretation by the court system and was followed by a number of clarifying decisions by the U.S. Supreme Court in succeeding years. One such case involved the interpretation of a provision of the act that " [n]othing contained in this section shall apply [t]o the dispensing or distribution of any of the aforesaid drugs to a patient by a physician, dentist, or veterinary surgeon registered under this Act in the course of his professional practice only" (Section 2(a)). In a series of three decisions, the Court declared exactly how this phrase was to be interpreted.

In United States v. Jin Fuey Moy *(1916), the Court ruled that a physician could distribute heroin tablets to a known addict under terms of the Harrison Act. Three years later, in* United States v. Doremus *(1919), the Court changed its mind and said that one of the reasons that Congress wrote the Harrison Act as it did was to prevent physicians and others involved in the distribution of prescription drugs from supplying addicts with narcotics. In the same year, the Court confirmed its previous decision in* Webb v. United States *(1919), saying that it was a perversion to think that the Congress would approve of anyone distributing narcotics to a drug addict. The relevant parts of each decision are given here.*

United States v. Jin Fuey Moy (1916)

This is an indictment under § 8 of the Act of December 17, 1914, c. 1, 38 Stat. 785, 789. It was quashed by the district court on the ground that the statute did not apply to the case. 225 F. 1003. The indictment charges a conspiracy with Willie Martin to have in Martin's possession opium and salts thereof, to wit, one dram of morphine sulphate. It alleges that Martin was not registered with the collector of internal revenue of the district, and had not paid the special tax required; that the defendant *[Jin Fuey Moy]*, for the purpose of executing the conspiracy, issued to Martin a written prescription for the morphine sulphate, and that he did not issue it in good faith, but knew that the drug was not given for medicinal purposes, but for the purpose of supplying one addicted to the use of opium. The question is whether the possession conspired for is within the prohibitions of the act.

. . .

Approaching the issue from this point of view, we conclude that "any person not registered" in § 8 cannot be taken to mean any person in the United States, but must be taken to refer to the class with which the statute undertakes to deal—the persons who are required to register by § 1. It is true that the exemption of possession of drugs prescribed in good faith by a physician is a powerful argument, taken by itself, for a broader meaning. But every question of construction is unique, and an argument that would prevail in one case may be inadequate in another. This exemption stands alongside of one that saves employees of registered persons, as do §§ 1 and 4, and nurses under the supervision of a physician, etc., as does § 4, and is so far vague that it may have had in mind other persons carrying out a doctor's orders, rather than the patients. The general purpose seems to be to apply to possession exemptions similar to those applied to registration. Even if for a moment the scope and intent of the act were lost sight of, the proviso is not enough to overcome the dominant considerations that prevail in our mind.

Judgment affirmed.

United States v. Doremus (1919)

There are ten counts in the indictment. . . .

The second count charges in substance that Doremus did unlawfully and knowingly sell, dispense, and distribute to one Ameris five hundred one-sixth grain tablets of heroin not in the course of the regular professional practice of Doremus and not for the treatment of any disease from which Ameris was suffering, but, as was well known by Doremus, Ameris was addicted to the use of the drug as a habit, being a person popularly known as a "dope fiend," and that Doremus did sell, dispense, and distribute the drug heroin to Ameris for the purpose of gratifying his appetite for the drug as an habitual user thereof.

. . .

Considering the full power of Congress over excise taxation, the decisive question here is: have the provisions in question any relation to the raising of revenue? That Congress might levy an excise tax upon such dealers, and others who are named in § 1 of the act, cannot be successfully disputed. The provisions of § 2 to which we have referred aim to confine sales to registered dealers and to those dispensing the drugs as physicians, and to those who come to dealers with legitimate prescriptions of physicians. Congress, with full power over the subject, short of arbitrary and unreasonable action which is not to be assumed, inserted these provisions in an act specifically providing for the raising of revenue. Considered of themselves, we think they tend to keep the traffic above-board and subject to inspection by those authorized to collect the revenue. They tend to diminish the opportunity of unauthorized persons to obtain the drugs and sell them clandestinely without paying the tax imposed by the federal law. This case well illustrates the possibility which may have induced Congress to insert the provisions limiting sales to registered dealers and requiring patients to obtain these drugs as a medicine from physicians or upon regular prescriptions. Ameris, being, as the indictment charges, an addict, may not have used this great number of doses for himself. He might sell some to others without paying the tax—at least Congress may have deemed it wise to prevent such possible dealings because of their effect upon the collection of the revenue.

We cannot agree with the contention that the provisions of § 2, controlling the disposition of these drugs in the ways described, can have nothing to do with facilitating the collection of the revenue, as we should be obliged to do if we were to declare this act beyond the power of Congress acting under its constitutional authority to impose excise taxes. It follows that the judgment of the district court must be reversed.

Reversed.

Webb v. United States (1919)

. . . the circuit court of appeals propounds to this Court three questions:

"1. Does the first sentence of § 2 of the Harrison Act prohibit retail sales of morphine by druggists to persons who have no physician's prescription, who have no order blank therefor, and who cannot obtain an order blank because not of the class to which such blanks are allowed to be issued?"

"2. If the answer to question one is in the affirmative, does this construction make unconstitutional the prohibition of such sale?"

"3. If a practicing and registered physician issues an order for morphine to an habitual user thereof, the order not being issued by him in the course of professional treatment in the attempted cure of the habit, but being issued for the purpose of providing the user with morphine sufficient to keep him comfortable by maintaining his customary use, is such order a physician's prescription under exception (b) of § 2?"

. . .

What we have said of the construction and purpose of the act in No. 367 *[United States v. Doremus]* plainly requires that question one should be answered in the affirmative. Question two should be answered in the negative for the reasons stated in the opinion in No. 367. As to question three, to call such an order for the use of morphine a physician's prescription would be so plain a perversion of meaning that no discussion of the subject is required. That question should be answered in the negative.

Sources: *United States v. Jin Fuey Moy* 241 U.S. 394 (1916). https://supreme.justia.com/cases/federal/us/241/394/case.html; *United States v. Doremus* 249 U.S. 86 (1919). https://supreme.justia.com/cases/federal/us/249/86/case.html; *Webb v. United States* 249 U.S. 96 (1919). https://supreme.justia.com/cases/federal/us/249/96/case.html. All accessed on May 10, 2015.

Durham-Humphrey Amendment (1951)

One of the most important pieces of legislation concerning prescription drugs was the Durham-Humphrey Amendment to the Food, Drug, and Cosmetics Act of 1938 adopted in 1951. The amendment was important because it defined precisely what was meant by a "prescription drug" and what the conditions were under which such a drug could be sold. The basic part of the amendment was as follows:

[A "prescription drug" is:]

"(b)   (1)   A drug intended for use by man which—

"(A) is a habit-forming drug to which section 502 (d) applies;

or

"(B) because of its toxicity or other potentiality for harmful effect, or the method of its use, or the collateral measures necessary to its use, is not safe for use except under the supervision of a practitioner licensed by law to administer such drug; or

"(C) is limited by an effective application under section 505 to use under the professional supervision of a practitioner licensed by law to administer such drug,

shall be dispensed only (i) upon a written prescription of a practitioner licensed by law to administer such drug, or (ii) upon an oral prescription of such practitioner which is reduced promptly to writing and filed by the pharmacist, or (iii) by refilling any such written or oral prescription if such refilling is authorized by the prescriber either in the original prescription or by oral order which is reduced promptly to writing and filed by the pharmacist. The act of dispensing a drug contrary to the provisions of this paragraph shall be deemed to be an act which results in the drug being misbranded while held for sale.

["Section 502" referred to here is now Section 352 of Title 21 of the U.S. Code, available online at http://www.gpo.gov/fdsys/ pkg/USCODE-2010-title21/pdf/USCODE-2010-title21-chap9-subchapV-partA-sec352.pdf.]

Source: Public Law 215, Chapter 578. U.S. Statutes. Available online at http://www.gpo.gov/fdsys/pkg/STATUTE-65/pdf/ STATUTE-65-Pg648.pdf. Accessed on May 8, 2015.

Controlled Substances Act (1970)

The cornerstone of the U.S. government's efforts to control substance abuse is the Controlled Substances Act of 1970, now a part of the U.S. Code, Title 21, Chapter 13. That act established the system of "schedules" for various categories of drugs that is still used by agencies of the U.S. government today. It also provides extensive background information about the domestic and international status of drug abuse efforts. Some of the most relevant sections for the domestic portion of the act are reprinted here.

Section 801 of the act presents Congress's findings and declarations about controlled substances, with special mention in Section 801a of psychotropic drugs.

§ 801. Congressional findings and declarations: controlled substances

The Congress makes the following findings and declarations:

(1) Many of the drugs included within this subchapter have a useful and legitimate medical purpose and are necessary to maintain the health and general welfare of the American people.
(2) The illegal importation, manufacture, distribution, and possession and improper use of controlled substances have a substantial and detrimental effect on the health and general welfare of the American people.

. . .

Section 802 deals with definitions used in the act, and section 803 deals with a minor housekeeping issue of financing for the act. Section 811 deals with the Attorney General's authority for classifying and declassifying drugs and the manner in which these steps are to be taken. In general:

§ 811. Authority and criteria for classification of substances
(a) Rules and regulations of Attorney General; hearing

The Attorney General shall apply the provisions of this subchapter to the controlled substances listed in the schedules established by section 812 of this title and to any other drug or other substance added to such schedules under this subchapter. Except as provided in subsections (d) and (e) of this section, the Attorney General may by rule—

(1) add to such a schedule or transfer between such schedules any drug or other substance if he—

(A) finds that such drug or other substance has a potential for abuse, and

(B) makes with respect to such drug or other substance the findings prescribed by subsection (b) of section 812 of this title for the schedule in which such drug is to be placed; or

(2) remove any drug or other substance from the schedules if he finds that the drug or other substance does not meet the requirements for inclusion in any schedule.

. . .

Section (b) provides guidelines for the evaluation of drugs and other substances. The next section, (c), is a key element of the act:

(c) Factors determinative of control or removal from schedules

In making any finding under subsection (a) of this section or under subsection (b) of section 812 of this title, the Attorney General shall consider the following factors with respect to each drug or other substance proposed to be controlled or removed from the schedules:

(1) Its actual or relative potential for abuse.
(2) Scientific evidence of its pharmacological effect, if known.
(3) The state of current scientific knowledge regarding the drug or other substance.
(4) Its history and current pattern of abuse.
(5) The scope, duration, and significance of abuse.
(6) What, if any, risk there is to the public health.
(7) Its psychic or physiological dependence liability.

(8)   Whether the substance is an immediate precursor of a substance already controlled under this subchapter.

Section (d) is a lengthy discussion of international aspects of the nation's efforts to control substance abuse. Section (e) through (h) deal with related, but less important, issues of the control of substance abuse. Section 812 is perhaps of greatest interest to the general reader in that it establishes the system of classifying drugs still used in the United States, along with the criteria for classification and the original list of drugs to be included in each schedule (since greatly expanded):

§ 812. Schedules of controlled substances

(a) Establishment

> There are established five schedules of controlled substances, to be known as schedules I, II, III, IV, and V. Such schedules shall initially consist of the substances listed in this section. The schedules established by this section shall be updated and republished on a semiannual basis during the two-year period beginning one year after October 27, 1970, and shall be updated and republished on an annual basis thereafter.

(b) Placement on schedules; findings required

> Except where control is required by United States obligations under an international treaty, convention, or protocol, in effect on October 27, 1970, and except in the case of an immediate precursor, a drug or other substance may not be placed in any schedule unless the findings required for such schedule are made with respect to such drug or other substance. The findings required for each of the schedules are as follows:

> > (1)   Schedule I.—

> > (A)   The drug or other substance has a high potential for abuse.

> > (B)   The drug or other substance has no currently accepted medical use in treatment in the United States.

(C) There is a lack of accepted safety for use of the drug or other substance under medical supervision.

(2) Schedule II.—

(A) The drug or other substance has a high potential for abuse.

(B) The drug or other substance has a currently accepted medical use in treatment in the United States or a currently accepted medical use with severe restrictions.

(C) Abuse of the drug or other substances may lead to severe psychological or physical dependence.

(3) Schedule III.—

(A) The drug or other substance has a potential for abuse less than the drugs or other substances in schedules I and II.

(B) The drug or other substance has a currently accepted medical use in treatment in the United States.

(C) Abuse of the drug or other substance may lead to moderate or low physical dependence or high psychological dependence.

(4) Schedule IV.—

(A) The drug or other substance has a low potential for abuse relative to the drugs or other substances in schedule III.

(B) The drug or other substance has a currently accepted medical use in treatment in the United States.

(C) Abuse of the drug or other substance may lead to limited physical dependence or psychological dependence relative to the drugs or other substances in schedule III.

(5) Schedule V.—

(A) The drug or other substance has a low potential for abuse relative to the drugs or other substances in schedule IV.

(B) The drug or other substance has a currently accepted medical use in treatment in the United States.

(C) Abuse of the drug or other substance may lead to limited physical dependence or psychological dependence relative to the drugs or other substances in schedule IV.

(c) Initial schedules of controlled substances

Schedules I, II, III, IV, and V shall, unless and until amended [1] pursuant to section 811 of this title, consist of the following drugs or other substances, by whatever official name, common or usual name, chemical name, or brand name designated: *The initial list of drugs under each schedule follows.*

Source: "Controlled Substances Act." U.S. Food and Drug Administration.   http://www.fda.gov/regulatoryinformation/ legislation/ucm148726.htm. Accessed on April 8, 2015.

Ryan Haight Online Pharmacy Consumer Protection Act of 2008

As a way of dealing with the problem of online sales of prescription drugs without a valid prescription, the U.S. Congress adopted the Ryan Haight Online Pharmacy Consumer Protection Act of 2008. One provision of that act requires that a consumer have a "valid prescription" in order to purchase a controlled substance online. That provision reads:

(e) Controlled substances dispensed by means of the Internet

(1) No controlled substance that is a prescription drug as determined under the Federal Food, Drug, and Cosmetic

Act [21 U.S.C. 301 et seq.] may be delivered, distributed, or dispensed by means of the Internet without a valid prescription.

(2) As used in this subsection:

    (A) The term "valid prescription" means a prescription that is issued for a legitimate medical purpose in the usual course of professional practice by—

        (i)   a practitioner who has conducted at least 1 in-person medical evaluation of the patient; or

        (ii) a covering practitioner.

    (B) (i)   The term "in-person medical evaluation" means a medical evaluation that is conducted with the patient in the physical presence of the practitioner, without regard to whether portions of the evaluation are conducted by other health professionals.

        (ii) Nothing in clause (i) shall be construed to imply that 1 in-person medical evaluation demonstrates that a prescription has been issued for a legitimate medical purpose within the usual course of professional practice.

    (C) The term "covering practitioner" means, with respect to a patient, a practitioner who conducts a medical evaluation (other than an in-person medical evaluation) at the request of a practitioner who—

        (i)   has conducted at least 1 in-person medical evaluation of the patient or an evaluation of the patient through the practice of telemedicine, within the previous 24 months; and

        (ii) is temporarily unavailable to conduct the evaluation of the patient.

(3) Nothing in this subsection shall apply to—

(A) the delivery, distribution, or dispensing of a controlled substance by a practitioner engaged in the practice of telemedicine; or

(B) the dispensing or selling of a controlled substance pursuant to practices as determined by the Attorney General by regulation, which shall be consistent with effective controls against diversion.

A second provision of the act calls for the registration of pharmacies that wish to sell prescription drugs on the Internet, as follows:

(f) Research by practitioners; pharmacies; research applications; construction of Article 7 of the Convention on Psychotropic Substances

The Attorney General shall register practitioners (including pharmacies, as distinguished from pharmacists) to dispense, or conduct research with, controlled substances in schedule II, III, IV, or V and shall modify the registrations of pharmacies so registered to authorize them to dispense controlled substances by means of the Internet, if the applicant is authorized to dispense, or conduct research with respect to, controlled substances under the laws of the State in which he practices. The Attorney General may deny an application for such registration or such modification of registration if the Attorney General determines that the issuance of such registration or modification would be inconsistent with the public interest. In determining the public interest, the following factors shall be considered:

(1) The recommendation of the appropriate State licensing board or professional disciplinary authority.
(2) The applicant's experience in dispensing, or conducting research with respect to controlled substances.
(3) The applicant's conviction record under Federal or State laws relating to the manufacture, distribution, or dispensing of controlled substances.

(4) Compliance with applicable State, Federal, or local laws relating to controlled substances.

(5) Such other conduct which may threaten the public health and safety.

Sources: U.S. Code. Title 21—Food and Drugs. Sections 823 and 829, pages 530, 541. http://www.gpo.gov/fdsys/pkg/ USCODE-2011-title21/pdf/USCODE-2011-title21-chap13-subchapI-partC-sec823.pdf; http://www.gpo.gov/fdsys/pkg/ USCODE-2011-title21/pdf/ USCODE-2011-title21-chap13-subchapI-partC-sec829.pdf. Accessed on May 10, 2015.

Prescription Monitoring Program. State of Oregon (2009)

As of mid-2015, 49 states and the District of Columbia had adopted legislation establishing prescription drug monitoring programs, Missouri being the only exception. These state laws are generally quite complex, with sections dealing with a variety of aspects of such programs. The following excerpt from Oregon's law shows the subjects typically covered in such laws. For the most complete information on all state PDMP laws, see "Prescription Drug Monitoring Programs," National Alliance for Model State Drug Laws, at http://www.namsdl.org/prescription-monitoring-programs.cfm.

431.962 Establishment of program; rules; report to commission. (1)(a) The Department of Human Services, in consultation with the Prescription Monitoring Program Advisory Commission, shall establish and maintain a prescription monitoring program for monitoring and reporting prescription drugs dispensed by pharmacies in Oregon that are classified in schedules II through IV under the federal Controlled Substances Act, 21 U.S.C. 811 and 812, as modified under ORS 475.035.

(b)(A) To fulfill the requirements of this subsection, the department shall establish, maintain and operate an electronic system to monitor and report drugs described in paragraph (a) of this subsection that are dispensed by prescription.

(B) The system must operate and be accessible by practitioners and pharmacies 24 hours a day, seven days a week.

(C) The department may contract with a state agency or private entity to ensure the effective operation of the electronic system.

(2) In consultation with the commission, the department shall adopt rules for the operation of the electronic prescription monitoring program established under subsection (1) of this section, including but not limited to standards for:

(a) Reporting data;

(b) Providing maintenance, security and disclosure of data;

(c) Ensuring accuracy and completeness of data;

(d) Complying with the federal Health Insurance Portability and Accountability Act of 1996 (P.L. 104-191) and regulations adopted under it, including 45 C.F.R. parts 160 and 164, federal alcohol and drug treatment confidentiality laws and regulations adopted under those laws, including 42 C.F.R. part 2, and state health and mental health confidentiality laws, including ORS 179.505, 192.517 and 192.518 to 192.529;

(e) Ensuring accurate identification of persons or entities requesting information from the database;

(f) Accepting printed or nonelectronic reports from pharmacies that do not have the capability to provide electronic reports; and

(g) Notifying a patient, before or when a drug classified in schedules II through IV is dispensed to the patient, about the prescription monitoring program and the entry of the prescription in the system.

(3) The department shall submit an annual report to the commission regarding the prescription monitoring program established under this section.

[The sections that follow describe each of the functions of the PDMP.]

431.964 Duty of pharmacy to report to program; exceptions.

431.966 Disclosure of information; corrections; records; immunity from liability.

431.968 Duty of pharmacist to fill prescription.

431.970 Reports to health professional regulatory boards.

431.972 Fees.

431.974 Electronic Prescription Monitoring Fund.

431.976 Prescription Monitoring Program Advisory Commission; purposes; members.

431.978 Term; meetings; rules; quorum; expenses.

431.992 Civil penalty for violation of ORS 431.964 to 431.968.

Source: Title 36. Public Health and Safety. Chapter 431—State and Local Administration and Enforcement of Health Laws. http://www.orpdmp.com/orpdmpfiles/PDF_Files/ORS%20 431.960%20PDMP.pdf. Accessed on May 9, 2015.

Secure and Responsible Drug Disposal Act of 2010 (Public Law 111–273, 124 Stat. 2858)

One of the fundamental problems with the prescription drug abuse problem is that individuals who no longer need prescription drugs that they may have legitimately received have no easy legal way to dispose of those prescriptions, other than flushing them down the drain. In an effort to solve this problem, the U.S. Congress in 2010 adopted a bill simplifying the process by which legal drug users could dispose of their unneeded prescription drugs.

The Congress adopted the following amendment to the Controlled Substances Act of 1970 to deal with this issue. The amendment reads as follows.

(1) An ultimate user who has lawfully obtained a controlled substance in accordance with this title may, without being registered, deliver the controlled substance to another person for the purpose of disposal of the controlled substance if—

   (A) the person receiving the controlled substance is authorized under this title to engage in such activity; and

   (B) the disposal takes place in accordance with regulations issued by the Attorney General to prevent diversion of controlled substances.

(2) In developing regulations under this subsection, the Attorney General shall take into consideration the public health and safety, as well as the ease and cost of program implementation and participation by various communities. Such regulations may not require any entity to establish or operate a delivery or disposal program.

(3) The Attorney General may, by regulation, authorize long-term care facilities, as defined by the Attorney General by regulation, to dispose of controlled substances on behalf of ultimate users who reside, or have resided, at such long-term care facilities in a manner that the Attorney General determines will provide effective controls against diversion and be consistent with the public health and safety.

(4) If a person dies while lawfully in possession of a controlled substance for personal use, any person lawfully entitled to dispose of the decedent's property may deliver the controlled substance to another person for the purpose of disposal under the same conditions as provided in paragraph (1) for an ultimate user.

[The regulations developed by the Drug Enforcement Administration required by this act can be found in the Federal Register,

volume 79, number 174, pages 53520–70. Available online at http://www.deadiversion.usdoj.gov/fed_regs/rules/2014/2014-20926.pdf.]

Source: Text of the Secure and Responsible Drug Disposal Act of 2010. https://www.govtrack.us/congress/bills/111/s3397/text. Accessed on May 8, 2015.

Between Peril and Promise: Facing the Dangers of VA's Skyrocketing Use of Prescription Painkillers to Treat Veterans (2013)

One of the issues in the current prescription drug abuse epidemic has to do with the overuse of opioid painkillers by current and former members of the U.S. military who are being treated for combat-related medical problems. Some critics have argued that the Veterans Administration (VA) relies too heavily on the use of prescription drugs for treating these men and women, rather than addressing the root problems of a veteran's pain issues. In October 2013, the Subcommittee on Health of the Committee on Veterans' Affairs of the U.S. House of Representatives held hearings on this issue. Some comments from those hearings are reprinted here.

Rep. Jeff Miller (R-FL): . . . when these veterans reach out and entrust the VA to relieve their pain, the treatment they often receive is the systemwide default of prescribing prescription painkillers. CBS News has recently reported that based on VA data, over the past 11 years, the number of patients treated by the VA is up 29 percent, while the narcotic prescriptions written by VA doctors and nurse practitioners are up 259 percent.

Look, veterans depend upon VA to uphold its mission of restoring the health of those who have borne battle. But instead of helping them manage their battles with pain, VA has opted instead to use a treatment that has the power to destroy rather than to restore their lives.

VA can and must change course and act now to reduce their reliance on the use of prescription drugs. The veterans and their loved ones must be listened to, must be followed up with closely, and supported with a treatment that can best help them regain happy and healthy lives. Anything less is unacceptable.

Heather McDonald, wife of Specialist Scott McDonald (deceased): On April 30, 2011, [Scott] began seeking the treatment from the VA for back pain and mental illness. The Chalmers P. Wylie Ambulatory Care Center in Columbus, Ohio immediately starting prescribing medications. Beginning with Ibuprofen, Neurontin, and Meloxicam, and graduating to Vicodin, Klonopin, Celexa, Zoloft, Valium, and Percocet. This is where the roller coaster began.

My husband was taking up to 15 pills a day within the first six months of treatment. Every time Scott came home from an appointment, he had different medications, different dosages, different directions on how to take them. And progressively over the course of a year and a half of starting his treatment, the medications had changed so many times by adding and changing that Scott began changing. We researched many of the drugs that he was prescribed online and saw the dangerous interactions that they cause. Yet my husband was conditioned to follow orders. And he did so.

On September 12, 2012, Scott attended another of his scheduled appointments. This is when they added Percocet. This was a much different medication than he was used to taking, and which they prescribed him not to exceed 500 milligrams of Acetaminophen. Again, my husband followed orders.

Approximately 01:00 hours on the 13th of September, I arrived home from my job. I found Scott disoriented and very lethargic. I woke him and asked him if he was okay. He told me he was fine and that he just took what the doctors told him to take. At approximately 07:30 I found my husband cold and unresponsive. At 35 years old this father of two was gone.

. . .

When our men and women signed that contract they gave their bodies to their country. And I ask now, as the people that have the power and the ability to make these changes happen, to force regulations to change on behalf of all of the veterans out there that have died. And for their families, I beg you to reopen this issue and reevaluate the distribution of narcotics to our men and women when they come home.

Source: "Between Peril and Promise: Facing the Dangers of VA's Skyrocketing Use of Prescription Painkillers to Treat Veterans." Hearing before the Subcommittee on Health of the Committee on Veterans' Affairs. U.S. House of Representatives, 113th Congress, first Session. Thursday, October 10, 2013. http://www.gpo.gov/fdsys/pkg/CHRG-113hhrg85864/html/CHRG-113hhrg85864.htm. Accessed on May 9, 2015.

Prescription Drug Monitoring Programs (2014)

In 2014, the nonpartisan Congressional Research Service conducted a study of the nation's prescription drug monitoring programs (PDMPs). It reviewed the nature of these programs, the role of the federal government in their execution, and research on their effectiveness. The two sections of the report included here review (1) available evidence on the effectiveness of PMDPs and (2) potential unintended consequences resulting in their withholding of valid prescription drugs needed by some patients (citations omitted).

Effectiveness Research

Research on PDMP effectiveness suggests that existence of a PDMP has an impact on both law enforcement and health care. A 2002 GAO study found that "the time and effort required by law enforcement and regulatory investigators to explore leads and the merits of possible drug diversion cases" declined after PDMP implementation. The study found that

Kentucky investigations of alleged doctor shoppers took an average of 156 days prior to PDMP implementation and 16 days after PDMP implementation (a 90% decrease). Nevada and Utah reported decreases in investigation time of 83% and 80%, respectively. These decreases in investigation time do not necessarily translate into less prescription drug abuse.

A 2012 review article summarized all peer-reviewed research articles about PDMPs published between 2001 and 2011, which amounted to 11 articles (not all of which addressed effectiveness). The author concluded that PDMPs reduce "doctor shopping," change prescribing behavior, and reduce prescription drug abuse. For example, a 2006 federally funded study (included in the 2012 review article) found that PDMPs—especially ones that issue reports proactively—change prescriber behavior in a way that reduces the per capita supply of prescription pain relievers and stimulants, which in turn reduces the likelihood of abuse. A study published in 2012 (and therefore not included in the review) found that while opioid abuse was increasing over time, the rate of increase was slower in states with PDMPs than in states without PDMPs.

. . .

Potential Unintended Consequences

PDMPs may have unintended consequences beyond reducing prescription drug diversion and abuse. Prescribers may hesitate to prescribe medications monitored by the PDMP—even for appropriate medical use—if they are concerned about potentially coming under scrutiny from law enforcement or licensing authorities. Studies of paper-based prescription monitoring programs that preceded the electronic PDMPs found that many prescribers did not order the required prescription forms, rendering them unable to prescribe specified controlled substances at all. Their concerns may lead prescribers to replace medications that are monitored by the PDMP with medications that are not monitored by the PDMP, even if the unmonitored medications are inferior in terms of effectiveness or side effects. Studies showed that after benzodiazepines were added to New York's paper-based program in 1989, a decrease in benzodiazepine prescriptions was accompanied by an increase in prescriptions for other sedatives. Individuals whose intent is to use controlled substances for nonmedical purposes may also substitute unmonitored prescription drugs or street drugs for those that are monitored by the PDMP.

Like prescribers, patients may fear coming under scrutiny from law enforcement if they use medications monitored by the PDMP, even if they have a legitimate medical need for the medications. Patients may worry about changes in prescribing behavior, which may limit their access to needed medications. Patients may worry about the additional cost of more frequent office visits if prescribers become more cautious about writing prescriptions with refills. Patients may also have concerns about the privacy and security of their prescription information if it is submitted to a PDMP.

Another potential unintended consequence of a state PDMP is that it may push drug diversion activities over the border into a neighboring state with no PDMP. A GAO study, completed in 2002, identified evidence of this spillover across state lines. This concern is one of the reasons interstate data sharing and interoperability have become priorities. Similarly, a PDMP may push drug diversion activities into a neighboring state with a PDMP that does not monitor as many medications. In any of these cases, the effectiveness of the PDMP may be offset by unintended consequences.

An additional possible unintended consequence of state PDMP activity may be an uptick in the abuse of non-prescription opioids such as heroin. As mentioned, some academic and government experts link the comparatively higher cost of prescription drugs and the crackdown on prescription drug abuse to the recent rise in heroin abuse. If PDMPs indeed change patient and doctor behavior and/or access to and the cost of prescription drugs, patients may turn to a cheaper illicit alternative such as heroin.

A PDMP may also have positive unintended consequences. For example, when accessing information from a PDMP, a prescriber or dispenser may identify a patient who is receiving legitimate prescriptions for multiple controlled substances and who is therefore at risk of harmful drug interactions. PDMPs may also enable prescribers to monitor their own DEA number to determine whether someone else is using it to forge prescriptions.

Source: Finklea, Kristin, Lisa N. Sacco, and Erin Bagalman. *Prescription Drug Monitoring Programs.* Congressional Research Service. http://www.fas.org/sgp/crs/misc/R42593.pdf. Accessed on May 10, 2015.

State Doctor Shopping Laws

The so-called doctor shopping laws differ to only a limited extent from state to state in the United States. The one area in which laws do differ from each other is the extent, if at all, to which they specifically exclude information produced by such laws from patient-provider privileged communication provisions. The first law given here is typical of the type of doctor shopping laws enacted by states, while the second law illustrates the specific exclusion of privileged communication from doctor shopping data.

South Dakota

22-42-17. Controlled substances obtained concurrently from different medical practitioners—Misdemeanor. Any person who knowingly obtains a controlled substance from a medical practitioner and who knowingly withholds information from that medical practitioner that he has obtained a controlled substance of similar therapeutic use in a concurrent time period from another medical practitioner is guilty of a Class 1 misdemeanor.

Source: SL 1990, Chapter 168. http://legis.sd.gov/Statutes/ Codified_Laws/DisplayStatute.aspx?Type=Statute&Stat ute=22-42-17. Accessed on May 10, 2015.

Connecticut

Sec. 21a-266. (Formerly Sec. 19-472). Prohibited acts. (a) No person shall obtain or attempt to obtain a controlled substance or procure or attempt to procure the administration of a controlled substance (1) by fraud, deceit, misrepresentation or subterfuge, or (2) by the forgery or alteration of a prescription or of any written order, or (3) by the concealment of a material fact, or (4) by the use of a false name or the giving of a false address.

(b) Information communicated to a practitioner in an effort unlawfully to procure a controlled substance, or unlawfully to procure the administration of any such substance, shall not be deemed a privileged communication.

(c) No person shall wilfully make a false statement in any prescription, order, report or record required by this part.

(d) No person shall, for the purpose of obtaining a controlled substance, falsely assume the title of, or claim to be, a manufacturer, wholesaler, pharmacist, physician, dentist, veterinarian, podiatrist or other authorized person.

(e) No person shall make or utter any false or forged prescription or false or forged written order.

(f) No person shall affix any false or forged label to a package or receptacle containing controlled substances.

(g) No person shall alter an otherwise valid written order or prescription except upon express authorization of the issuing practitioner.

(h) No person who, in the course of treatment, is supplied with controlled substances or a prescription therefore by one practitioner shall, knowingly, without disclosing such fact, accept during such treatment controlled substances or a prescription therefor from another practitioner with intent to obtain a quantity of controlled substances for abuse of such substances.

(i) The provisions of subsections (a), (d) and (e) shall not apply to manufacturers of controlled substances, or their agents or employees, when such manufacturers or their authorized agents or employees are actually engaged in investigative activities directed toward safeguarding of the manufacturer's trademark, provided prior written approval for such investigative activities is obtained from the Commissioner of Consumer Protection.

Source: Chapter 420b. Dependency-Producing Drugs. http://www.cga.ct.gov/2011/pub/chap420b.htm#Sec21a-266.htm. Accessed on May 10, 2015.

Bitter Pill
.IN.gov

Prescription drug abu
is a bitter pill for
Indiana to swallow.

 EVERY 25 MINUTES
SOMEONE <u>DIES</u> FROM
PRESCRIPTION DRUG OVER

MORE PEOPLE ABUSE PRESCRIPTION
THAN COCAINE, HEROIN, HALLUCIN
AND INHALANTS <u>COMBINED.</u>

 IN THE U.S. **1 IN 20** PEOPL
USED PRESCRIPTION PAINK
FOR <u>NON-MEDICAL</u> REAS

Introduction

Problems with the illicit use of prescription drugs are a relatively new phenomenon in modern society. Still, people have been writing about drug abuse in general and some potential risks associated with the illicit use of some prescription drugs for many years. This chapter presents a selection of some of the most useful books, articles, reports, and Internet references on the topic of prescription drug abuse. Most of the items listed here deal specifically with prescription drug abuse, although many are concerned with the more general problem of drug abuse of all kinds, with at least some mention of prescription (and sometimes over-the-counter) drugs.

Some resources are available in more than one format, usually as articles and as Internet reproductions of those articles. In such cases, information about both formats is provided. The reader is reminded that this list of resources is not meant to be exhaustive, but is provided as a source of references with which one might continue his or her research on the topic. The reader is also encouraged to review the reference lists for Chapters 1 and 2, which contain a number of other valuable resources, most of which are not duplicated in this bibliography.

Indiana state legislators and a prescription drug task force unveil a new website that includes information on the symptoms exhibited by people abusing prescription drugs as a part of the state's effort to combat its prescription drug rate on August 16, 2013. (AP Photo/Rick Callahan)

Books

Adams, Taite. 2013. *Opiate Addiction: The Painkiller Epidemic, Heroin Addiction, and the Way Out.* St. Petersburg, FL: Rapid Response Press.

> The major sections of this book deal with a general introduction to opiates, an explanation of how opiates work in the human body, how addiction occurs with pain killers, prescription drug abuse and chronic pain, the nature of heroin addiction, herbal opiates, opiate maintenance drugs and opiate substitution therapy, opiate addiction, and treatment for prescription drug addiction.

Bodden, Valerie. 2015. *Club and Prescription Drug Abuse.* Minneapolis: ABDO Publishing.

> This book is intended for young adults. It provides a general introduction to the topic of club and prescription drug abuse with chapters on the history of drug abuse, drug abuse among young adults and children, why young people use drugs, club drugs and inhalants, prescription and OTC drugs, the cost of drug use, drugs and the law, and other prevention efforts.

Bramness, Jørgen G. 2015. "Prescription Drug Abuse: Risks and Prevention." In Nady el-Guebaly, Gisueppe Carrà, and Marc Galanter, eds. *Textbook of Addiction Treatment: International Perspectives*, vol. 1, 637–661. Milan: Springer Reference.

> This chapter reviews the major classes of prescription drugs currently being abused, the terminology and diagnosis involved with such drugs, epidemiology of prescription drug abuse, strategies for prevention, and treatment alternatives.

Colvin, Rod. 2008. *Overcoming Prescription Drug Addiction: A Guide to Coping and Understanding*, 3rd ed. Omaha, NE: Addicus Books.

This book provides a good basic introduction to the topic of prescription drug abuse. Its three main sections deal with coping with addiction, obtaining fraudulent prescriptions, and efforts to curb drug abuse.

Dabu-Bondoc, Susan, Amit A. Shah, and Philip R. Effraim. 2015. "Prescription Drug Abuse." In Alan David Kaye, Nalini Vadivelu, and Richard D. Urman, eds. *Substance Abuse: Inpatient and Outpatient Management for Every Clinician.* New York: Springer.
This chapter is written especially for specialists in the field, but is accessible for the general reader. It deals with the definition, classification, and pathophysiology of prescription drug abuse; diagnosis and management; and strategies of prevention and management.

Estren, Mark James. 2013. *Prescription Drug Abuse.* Berkeley, CA: Ronin Publishing.
This book explains the process by which prescription drug abuse has become such a widespread problem in the 2010s. It then goes on to discuss some of the harmful effects that government efforts to deal with this problem may have had on people who are in chronic pain.

Fields, Rene, and Stuart R. Banks, eds. 2012. *Prescription Drug Abuse, Doctor Shopping & the Role of Medicaid.* Hauppauge, NY: Nova Science.
This book is a collection of articles and documents dealing with the growing problem of doctor shopping and other procedures designed by individuals to obtain prescription medications for nonmedical purposes.

Foreman, Judy. 2014. *A Nation in Pain: Healing Our Nation's Biggest Health Problem.* Oxford, UK: Oxford University Press.
This book is about pain primarily, but it includes an extended discussion of the way that efforts to curb

prescription drug abuse is having unexpected and undesirable effects on efforts to treat individuals with chronic pain problems.

Galanter, Marc, Herbert D. Kleber, and Kathleen Brady. 2015. *The American Psychiatric Publishing Textbook of Substance Abuse Treatment.* Washington, DC: American Psychiatric Publishing.

This book is the ultimate resource for professionals in the field of psychiatry on the diagnosis and treatment of all forms of substance abuse. Section III contains chapters that focus specifically on a variety of prescription drugs.

Greer, Darla B., ed. 2015. *Prescription Drug Abuse: Reduction Efforts and Federal Role.* New York: Nova Science Publishers.

This book is divided into three major sections dealing with prescription drug abuse in general: prescription drug monitoring programs, addressing prescription drug abuse in the United States: current activities and future opportunities.

Inciardi, James A., and Karen McElrath, eds. *The American Drug Scene: Readings in a Global Context.* New York: Oxford University Press.

This book contains a collection of 39 articles previously published in other places dealing with a variety of drug-related issues. The essays discuss topics such as the history of drug taking in the United States, the history of marijuana use in Australia, why people take drugs, the use of crack cocaine on college campuses, and drug abuse among "nice" people.

O'Neil, Michael. 2015. *The ADA Practical Guide to Substance Use Disorders and Safe Prescribing.* Hoboken, NJ: John Wiley and Sons.

This book provides a comprehensive introduction to substance abuse problems with which dental practitioners might come into contact, along with a discussion of methods of prevention and treatment of such problems. A number of excellent sections deal with specific issues related to the types of prescription drugs used primarily for pain with which dentists and related workers might come into contact.

Quinones, Sam. 2015. *Dreamland the True Tale of America's Opiate Epidemic*. New York: Bloomsbury Press.
  The author provides a popular description of the process by which heroin and other opiate addictions have come to be the nation's "most serious drug problem" in the 21st century.

Waters, Rosa. 2015. *Prescription Painkillers: Oxycontin, Percocet, Vicodin, & Other Addictive Analgesics*. Broomall, PA: Mason Crest.
  This short book is designed for young adults. It provides a broad, general overview of the problem of prescription drug abuse, with particular emphasis on the substances mentioned in its title.

Articles

Arria, Amelia M., et al. 2010. "Increased Alcohol Consumption, Nonmedical Prescription Drug Use, and Illicit Drug Use Are Associated with Energy Drink Consumption among College Students." *Journal of Addiction Medicine* 4 (2): 74–80.
  This research study produced the rather intriguing finding that college students who had high rates of energy drink consumption are significantly more likely to also become involved in the use of prescription medications for nonmedical purposes.

Barlas, Stephen. 2013. "Prescription Drug Abuse Hits Hospitals Hard: Tighter Federal Steps Aim to Deflate Crisis." *P&T (Pharmacy and Therapeutics)* 38 (9): 531–34.
  The author explains the special problems of prescription drug abuse for hospitals and the new challenges created

by these problems for the federal government and the federal efforts to reduce the illegal use of prescription drugs.

Beletsky, Leo, Josiah D. Rich, and Alexander Y. Walley. 2012. "Prevention of Fatal Opioid Overdose." *JAMA* 308 (18): 1863–64.

The authors point out that federal efforts for dealing with the prescription drug abuse issue have focused almost entirely on monitoring and securing the drug supply. They suggest that attention should also be paid to the use of naloxone, an antagonist to opioids, which can prevent death if supplied early enough in the respiratory failure experienced by a patient.

Butler, Stephen F. 2013. "Abuse Rates and Routes of Administration of Reformulated Extended-Release Oxycodone: Initial Findings from a Sentinel Surveillance Sample of Individuals Assessed for Substance Abuse Treatment." *The Journal of Pain* 14 (4): 351–58.

The authors report on one of the earliest studies on the efficacy of drug reformulations as a way of reducing the use of prescription medications for nonmedical purposes. They found that the reformulated drugs were significantly more effective in reducing illicit use on eight separate measures.

Butler, Stephen F., Emily C. McNaughton, and Ryan A. Black. 2015. "Tapentadol Abuse Potential: A Postmarketing Evaluation Using a Sample of Individuals Evaluated for Substance Abuse Treatment." *Pain Medicine* 16 (1): 119–30.

Tapentadol is a relatively new opioid analgesic of considerable interest to the medical profession because it is a powerful painkiller, but is much less subject to nonmedical use than are most other opioids. This study was designed to measure the extent the compound was used illicitly compared to oxymorphone, hydromorphone, hydrocodone, morphine, fentanyl, oxycodone, tramadol, and buprenorphine. Researchers found that the expected claims for the high effectiveness and low abuse potential for the compound were confirmed. Also see the companion study on the same compound at Emily C McNaughton, Ryan A. Black, Sarah E. Weber, and Stephen F Butler, "Assessing Abuse Potential of New Analgesic Medications Following Market Release: An Evaluation of Internet Discussion of Tapentadol Abuse," *Pain Medicine* 16(1): 131–40.

Casati, Alicia, Roumen Sedefov, and Tim Pfeiffer-Gerschel. 2012. "Misuse of Medicines in the European Union: A Systematic Review of the Literature." *European Addiction Research* 18 (5): 228–45. http://ift.de/fileadmin/user_upload/Literatur/Zeitschriften/Casati_Sedefov_Pfeiffer-Gerschel_2012.pdf. Accessed on May 23, 2015.

This article summarizes research on the prevalence and characteristic features of prescription drug misuse and abuse in the European Union.

Chakravarthy, Bharath, Shyam Shah, and Shahram Lotfipour. 2012. "Vital Signs: Prescription Drug Monitoring Programs and Other Interventions to Combat Prescription Opioid Abuse." *Western Journal of Emergency Medicine* 13 (5): 422–25. https://escholarship.org/uc/item/4zz8q955. Accessed on May 22, 2015.

The authors use data from the CDC Morbidity and Mortality Weekly Report to assess the efficacy of state programs for prescription drug monitoring in preventing injury and death from the nonmedical use of prescription drugs and find that states with strong programs of this kind tend to be more effective in reducing injury and death from prescription drug overdose.

Conn, Bridgid M., and Amy K. Marks. 2014. "Ethnic/Racial Differences in Peer and Parent Influence on Adolescent Prescription Drug Misuse." *Advances in Nursing Science* 37 (2): 257–65.

The authors report on their research attempting to determine whether prescription drug abuse exists among subgroups of adolescents. They find that white young adults are most likely to abuse prescription drugs and African Americans are least likely to do so. Hispanic youth fall between whites and African Americans.

Cronin, Michael, Susan Berger, and Paul J. Seligman. 2014. "Risk Evaluation and Mitigation Strategies with Elements to Assure Safe Use: Alignment of the Goals with the Tools to Manage Risk." *Therapeutic Innovation and Regulatory Science* 48 (6): 724–33.

The authors provide an analysis of the effectiveness of the U.S. Food and Drug Administration's (FDA) risk evaluation and mitigation strategies programs that have been developed since the agency announced the initiation of this program in 2010.

Culberson, John W., and Martin Ziska. 2008. "Prescription Drug Misuse/Abuse in the Elderly." *Geriatrics* 63 (9): 22–31. http://vulnerable-families.wikispaces.com/file/view/elderly.pdf. Accessed on May 21, 2015.

The authors provide an overview of the problem of prescription drug misuse/abuse in the elderly with a special focus on the types of medications that seniors may abuse or misuse and the effects produced by each category of drugs.

David, Jonathan M., et al. 2014. "Using Poison Center Exposure Calls to Predict Prescription Opioid Abuse and Misuse-Related Emergency Department Visits." *Pharmacoepidemiology and Drug Safety* 23 (1): 18–25.

The authors use data from the Researched Abuse, Diversion and Addiction-Related Surveillance System poison center program and from the Drug Abuse Warning Network to determine the effectiveness of poison centers as early-warning systems for possible prescription drug abuse. They find that poison centers can play an essential role in this method of diagnosis.

Francoeur, Richard B. 2011. "Ensuring Safe Access to Medication for Palliative Care While Preventing Prescription Drug Abuse: Innovations for American Inner Cities, Rural Areas, and Communities Overwhelmed by Addiction." *Risk Management Healthcare Policy* 4: 97–105.

The author describes a system he has developed for more safely dispensing prescription drugs that are likely to be used illicitly, especially in areas that tend to be high risk for elevated levels of prescription drug abuse.

Garcia, Andrea M. 2013. "State Laws Regulating Prescribing of Controlled Substances: Balancing the Public Health Problems of Chronic Pain and Prescription Painkiller Abuse and Overdose." *The Journal of Law, Medicine & Ethics* 41: 42–45.

The author considers the issue as to how the illegal use of prescription medications can be prevented while still guaranteeing that patients are able to receive the pain medications that they need. She reviews the variety of approaches that are being taken by states that have passed legislation attempting to resolve this question.

Gugelmann, Hallam, Jeanmarie Perrone, and Lewis Nelson. 2012. "Windmills and Pill Mills: Can PDMPs Tilt the Prescription Drug Epidemic?" *Journal of Medical Toxicology* 8 (4): 378–86.

The authors provide a history of prescription drug monitoring programs, the mechanisms by which such programs operate, and current evidence about their success in reducing the illegal use of prescription medications. They say that such programs are "an essential component in ongoing efforts to establish safe and compassionate prescription opioid stewardship."

Herry, C., et al. 2013. "Reducing Abuse of Orally Administered Prescription Opioids Using Formulation Technologies." *Journal of Drug Delivery Science and Technology* 23 (2): 103–10.

The authors review some of the methods that are now available for producing drugs in formats that make them less likely to be used for nonmedical purposes, while retaining their legitimate access for patients for whom they are intended.

Hildebran, Christi, et al. 2014. "How Clinicians Use Prescription Drug Monitoring Programs: A Qualitative Inquiry." *Pain Medicine* 15 (7): 1179–86.

Prescription drug monitoring programs (PDMPs) have become nearly universal in the United States today. However, it is not yet clear as to how physicians and other medical workers take advantage of the resources provided by these programs. This study attempts to provide information on that question. Researchers learned that there is a very wide variation in the way clinicians actually make use of state PDMPs (also see Irvine reference later in this section.)

Hwang, Catherine S., et al. 2015. "Prescription Drug Abuse." *JAMA Internal Medicine* 175 (2): 302–4.

The authors report on a survey of 420 primary physicians in the United States concerning their attitudes about prescription drug abuse. The primary findings were that 90 percent of respondents thought that prescription drug abuse was a "big" or "moderate" problem in their communities; 85 percent said that opioids were misused in clinical practice; and 45 percent said they were less likely to prescribe opioids than they were in the previous year.

Irvine, Jessica M., et al. 2014. "Who Uses a Prescription Drug Monitoring Program and How? Insights from a Statewide Survey of Oregon Clinicians." *The Journal of Pain* 15 (7): 747–55.

As its title suggests, this article attempts to find out how clinicians in Oregon make use of the state's PDMP. They find that clients often express anger or denial when presented with their prescription drug abuse problem and only seldom ask for help with such issues.

Jena, Anupam, and Dana P. Goldman. 2011. "Growing Internet Use May Help Explain the Rise in Prescription Drug Abuse in the United States." *Health Affairs* 30 (6): 1192–99.

> The author's research supports the notion that the growth of the Internet may have some effect on the growth of prescription drug abuse, primarily because of the increased availability of prescription drugs on the web.

Katz, Cara, R. El-Gabalawy, K. M. Keyes, S. S. Martins, and J. Sareen. 2013. "Risk Factors for Incident Nonmedical Prescription Opioid Use and Abuse and Dependence: Results from a Longitudinal Nationally Representative Sample." *Drug and Alcohol Dependence* 132 (1–2): 107–13.

> This study attempted to identify mental and physical health factors that might be related to the use of prescription drugs for nonmedical purposes. It found a number of such factors and discussed the implications of these findings for prevention programs.

Katz, Nathaniel P., et al. 2013. "Prescription Opioid Abuse: Challenges and Opportunities for Payers." *American Journal of Managed Care* 19 (4): 295–302.

> The prescription drug abuse crisis has the potential for greatly increasing the cost of both legitimate health care and problems related to the illegal use of prescription drugs. This article reviews the economic consequences associated with prescription drug abuse and suggests some methods for keeping the costs of dealing with that problem under control.

Kirsh, Kenneth L., John F. Peppin, and John J. Coleman. 2010. "FDA's Proposed Risk Evaluation and Mitigation Strategy (REMS) for Opioids." *Practical Pain Management* 10 (6): 49–52. Available online at http://www.practicalpainmanagement.com/treatments/pharmacological/opioids/fda-proposed-risk-evaluation-mitigation-strategy-rems-opioids. Accessed on May 20, 2015.

The authors discuss the rationale behind the FDA's risk evaluation and mitigation strategy efforts as well as some of the problems involved with the specific program then being developed by the agency.

Kuramoto, Janet, Howard D. Chilcoat, Jean Ko, and Silvia S. Martins. 2012. "Suicidal Ideation and Suicide Attempt across Stages of Nonmedical Prescription Opioid Use and Presence of Prescription Opioid Disorders among U.S. Adults." *Journal of Studies on Alcohol and Drugs* 73 (2): 178–84.

Researchers found that people who had once abused prescription drugs and then quit were at greater risk for suicidal thoughts and actions than were those who had never used such drugs and those who were addicted to the drugs.

Lankenau, Stephen E., et al. 2012. "Initiation into Prescription Opioid Misuse amongst Young Injection Drug Users." *The International Journal on Drug Policy* 23 (1): 37–44.

This article reports on a study attempting to determine the factors that lead to intravenous drug users' initiation into prescription drug abuse. Researchers found that the main factor was easy access to drugs used by parents, family, and friends, and that prescription drug abuse was often the first step in transitioning to other forms of drug abuse, especially involving the use of heroin.

LeClair, Amy, et al. 2015. "Motivations for Prescription Drug Misuse among Young Adults: Considering Social and Developmental Contexts." *Drugs: Education, Prevention, and Policy* 14: 1–9.

The authors report on a study designed to identify the motivations behind young adults' interest in misusing and abusing prescription drugs for recreational purposes. Their sample was chosen from individuals involved in an active nightlife scene in New York City. They found that the "work hard, play hard" ethic was a major driver in the subjects' use of prescription drugs, but point out that this result may be very different for other groups of young adults in other social settings.

LeMire, Steven D., Sara G. Martner, and Cheryl Rising. 2012. "Advanced Practice Nurses' Use of Prescription Drug Monitoring Program Information." *The Journal for Nurse Practitioners* 8 (5): 383–88+.

> The authors describe the result of their study on attitudes about and practices with regard to PDMPs by advanced practice nurses.

Manchikanti, Laxmaiah, et al. 2010. "Therapeutic Use, Abuse, and Nonmedical Use of Opioids: A Ten-Year Perspective." *Pain Physician* 13 (5): 401–35.

> This article provides an excellent comprehensive review of the history of the use of opioids for pain relief since the 1990s with an analysis of the trends and factors that have led to a rapidly increasing use of such medications for nonmedical purposes.

Mastropietro, David J., and Hossein Omidian. 2014. "Abuse-Deterrent Formulations: Part 1—Development of a Formulation-Based Classification System." *Expert Opinion on Drug Metabolism & Toxicology* 11 (2): 193–204.

Mastropietro, David J., and Hossein Omidian. 2015. "Abuse-Deterrent Formulations: Part 2—Commercial Products and Proprietary Technologies." *Expert Opinion on Drug Metabolism & Toxicology* and 16 (3): 305–23.

> These two articles provide a comprehensive and up-to-date review of the variety of formulations that have been and are being developed as a way of making it more difficult to use prescription drugs for nonmedical purposes.

Maxwell, Jane Carlisle. 2011. "Prescription Drug Epidemic in the United States: A Perfect Storm." *Drug and Alcohol Review* 30 (3): 264–70.

> The author reports on a literature review of a range of information about prescription drug abuse and concludes that unless efforts to prevent or reduce drug diversion are successful, "clinicians may lose the ability to use some of the opioids for effective pain management or so many barriers will be raised that pain will go undertreated or untreated."

McCabe, Esteban, James A. Cranford, and Brady T. West. 2008. "Trends in Prescription Drug Abuse and Dependence, Co-occurrence with Other Substance Use Disorders, and Treatment Utilization: Results from Two National Surveys. *Addictive Behaviors* 33 (10): 1297–1305.

> The authors report on an analysis of trends in two national surveys of the illicit use of certain types of prescription drugs. They find significant increases in the percentage of users of all types of such drugs.

Nelson, Lewis S., Meredith Loh, and Jeanmarie Perrone. 2014. "Assuring Safety of Inherently Unsafe Medications: The FDA Risk Evaluation and Mitigation Strategies." *Journal of Medical Toxicology* 10 (2): 165–72.

> The authors provide a general introduction to the nature of risk evaluation and mitigation strategies programs, their historical background, the ways in which they work, and the benefits to be expected of them.

Nielsen, Suzanne, and Monica Jane Barratt. 2009. "Prescription Drug Misuse: Is Technology Friend or Foe?" *Drug and Alcohol Review* 28 (1): 81–86.

> The authors explain how the easy availability of prescription drugs on the Internet significantly increases the problem of misuse of such drugs, but describe some ways in

which electronic resources may become a valuable tool in preventing the further spread of this problem.

Pasquale, Margaret K., et al. 2014. "Cost Drivers of Prescription Opioid Abuse in Commercial and Medicare Populations." *Pain Practice* 14 (3): E116–E125.

> The prescription drug abuse epidemic has had serious consequences not only in the field of health care, social issues, personal well-being, and politics, but also in the field of economics. Thus study explores some of the factors in the prescription drug abuse epidemic that have affected health care costs for both the general population and those enrolled in the Medicare program.

Phillips, Janice. 2013. "Prescription Drug Abuse: Problem, Policies, and Implications." *Nursing Outlook* 61 (2): 78–84.

> This article provides a general overview of the prescription drug abuse problem in the United States as of 2013. The article pays special attention to legislation that was proposed in the U.S. Congress during the 112th Congress.

"Prescription Drug Abuse." 2015. *Journal of Substance Abuse Treatment* 48 (1): 1–138.

> This issue of the journal is devoted entirely to papers dealing with prescription drug abuse, covering topics such as the use of prescription drugs and future delinquency among adolescent offenders, prescription drug misuse among HIV positive individuals undergoing retroviral therapy, treatment outcomes for prescription drug abusers, and Oregon's program to deal with prescription opioid misuse. Articles in this journal are available to nonsubscribers and can be accessed at http://www.journalofsubstanceabuse-treatment.com/issue/S0740-5472%2814%29X0009-7.

Reifler, Liza M., et al. 2012. "Do Prescription Monitoring Programs Impact State Trends in Opioid Abuse/Misuse?" *Pain Medicine* 13 (3): 434–42.

Based on the results of the research, the authors of this article say the answer to the question in the title is "yes," although they suggest that further research is also necessary to obtain a more definitive answer.

Rigg, Khary K., and Gladys E. Ibañez. 2010. "Motivations for Non-Medical Prescription Drug Use: A Mixed Methods Analysis." *Journal of Substance Abuse Treatment* 39 (3): 236–47. http://www.ncbi.nlm.nih.gov/pmc/articles/PMC2937068/. Accessed on April 4, 2015.

The authors point out that researches still do not know very much about the factors that lead to a person's becoming a prescription drug abuser. They conduct this study to see if they can identify some of those factors. The three factors that they uncover in the study are "to get high," "to sleep," and "for the relief of anxiety and stress."

Rigg, Khary K., Samantha J. March, and James A. Inciardi. 2010. "Prescription Drug Abuse & Diversion: Role of the Pain Clinic." *Journal of Drug Issues* 40 (3): 681–702.

The authors examine the ways in which pain clinics may be contributing to the growing epidemic of prescription drug abuse. They find six factors that tend to be involved in the relationship: the existence of (1) "pill mills," (2) on-site pharmacies, (3) liberal prescribing habits, (4) "sponsoring" drug diversion (a method for paying for drugs), (5) pain doctor/pharmacy shopping, and (6) faking symptoms/documentation.

Ringwalt, Chris, Mariana Garrettson, and Apostolos Alexandridis. 2015. "The Effects of North Carolina's Prescription Drug Monitoring Program on the Prescribing Behaviors of the State's Providers." *The Journal of Primary Prevention* 36 (2): 131–37.

One of the concerns about the development of PDMPs is that they have a "chilling effect" on the willingness of medical providers to write prescriptions for legitimate uses, such as the control of severe pain. This study was designed to test whether that concern was valid for the PDMP program in the state of North Carolina, and found that it was not, as there was no change in the number of prescriptions for opioid medications written before and after the introduction of the state program.

Rosenblum, Andrew, et al. 2008. "Opioids and the Treatment of Chronic Pain: Controversies, Current Status, and Future Directions." *Experimental and Clinical Psychopharmacology* 16 (5): 405–16.

    This article provides an excellent general and technical introduction to the use of opioids for the treatment of pain and the problems that have resulted as a consequence of the diversion of these drugs for nonmedical uses.

Rutkow, Lainie, et al. 2015. "Most Primary Care Physicians Are Aware of Prescription Drug Monitoring Programs, but Many Find the Data Difficult to Access." *Health Affairs* 34 (3): 484–92.

    The authors report on a survey of 420 physicians in the United States to learn about their understanding and use of state-mandated programs for the reduction of prescription drug misuse. They find that about three quarters of respondents were familiar with state regulations and about half reported using the state program on occasion. The authors recommend some methods for increasing the effectiveness of state programs for dealing with this issue.

Sansone, Randy A., Justin S. Leung, and Michael W. Widerman. 2012. "The Abuse of Prescription Medications and Employment History." *International Journal of Psychiatry in Medicine* 43 (3): 273–78.

    The authors ask whether a person's employment history is associated in any way with his or her his tendency to become a prescription drug abuser. They find that all four of the employment variables they tested were correlated with prescription drug abuse.

Shimane, Takuya, Toshihiko Matsumoto, and Kiyoshi Wada. 2015. "Clinical Behavior of Japanese Community Pharmacists for Preventing Prescription Drug Overdose." *Psychiatry and Clinical Neurosciences* 69 (4): 220–27.

> The authors report on a study of pharmacists in Saitama Prefecture to learn the extent of prescription drug misuse among customers and the confidence that pharmacists have in dealing with this problem. They find that pharmacists have a key role in helping to deal with this issue, but they tend to lack confidence in participating in efforts to reduce the problem.

Simon, Kyle, et al. 2015. "Abuse-Deterrent Formulations: Transitioning the Pharmaceutical Market to Improve Public Health and Safety." *Therapeutic Advances in Drug Safety* 6 (2): 67–79. http://www.ncbi.nlm.nih.gov/pmc/articles/PMC4406920/. Accessed on May 16, 2015.

> The authors explore the results of and potential for the development of drug formulations that will reduce the risk of prescription drugs' being used for nonmedical purposes, while ensuring that they are also readily available to patients for the medical reasons for which they were developed.

Soledad Cepeda, M., et al. 2015. "Doctor Shopping for Medications Used in the Treatment of Attention Deficit Hyperactivity Disorder: Shoppers Often Pay in Cash and Cross State Lines." *The American Journal of Drug and Alcohol Abuse* 41 (3): 226–29.

> Investigators attempted to discover defining characteristics of individuals who doctor shopped for prescription drugs normally used in the treatment of attention deficit hyperactivity disorder. They found that such individuals traveled considerably greater distances to get prescriptions from more than one provider, visited more than one state, and more commonly paid cash than did nondoctor shoppers. A total of 0.4 percent of more than 4 million individuals included in the study were doctor shoppers.

Soledad Cepeda, M., et al. 2013. "Opioid Shopping Behavior: How Often, How Soon, Which Drugs, and What Payment Method." *The Journal of Clinical Pharmacology* 53 (1): 112–17.
The purpose of this research study was to determine the characteristic features displayed by so-called doctor shoppers who attempt to purchase prescription drugs from a variety of sources.

Stogner, John M., Amber Sanders, and Bryan Lee Miller. 2014. "Deception for Drugs: Self-reported "Doctor Shopping" among Young Adults." *Journal of the American Board of Family Medicine* 27 (5): 583–93.
The authors note that few data are available about "doctor shopping" by young adults in the United States. This study is an attempt to obtain such data. Information on the strategies and motivations relating to doctor shopping by young adults is provided in this report, along with a warning that the number of adolescents involved in such activities appears to be very small.

Surratt, Hilary L., et al. 2014. "Reductions in Prescription Opioid Diversion Following Recent Legislative Interventions in Florida." *Pharmacoepidemiology and Drug Safety* 23 (3): 314–20.
The authors attempt to identify changes in the illegal use of prescription drugs in Florida as the result of aggressive actions by the state legislature to improve prescribing practices and control the operation of pain clinics. They found that significant decreases in diversion rates for oxycodone, methadone, and morphine, and modest decreases for hydrocodone.

Taylor, Ozietta D. 2015. "The Cultural Influence of Adolescent Prescription Drug Abuse." *Journal of Human Behavior in the Social Environment* 25 (4): 304–11.
The author reviews available research to discover factors that tend to influence teenagers' likelihood (or not) of becoming a prescription drug abuser.

Twombly, Eric C., Kristen D. Holtz, and Christine B. Agnew. 2011. "Resonant Messages to Prevent Prescription Drug Misuse by Teens." *Journal of Alcohol and Drug Education* 55 (1): 38–52. Also available online in a slightly different form at http://www .kdhrc.com/publications/pdf/workingpapers/Working%20 Paper%2009-003.pdf.

The authors ask what types of messages about prescription drug abuse resonant best with adolescents and discover that "scare" messages are more powerful motivating devices than are "positive alternative" and "refusal skills" messages.

Weiner, Scott G. 2015. "Characteristics of Emergency Department 'Doctor Shoppers.'" *Journal of Emergency Medicine* 48 (4): 424–31.e1.

This study was focused on determining some defining characteristics of doctor shoppers. It found that there was no statistical difference in the behavior of males versus females, but there were statistical differences in age, race, chief complaint, and weekday versus weekend arrival. Another important different was that doctor-shopping patients utilized an average of 12.0 medical providers compared with a median of 1.0 for non-doctor-shoppers.

Weisberg, D., and C. Stannard. 2013. "Lost in Translation? Learning from the Opioid Epidemic in the USA." *Anaesthesia* 68 (12): 1215–19. http://onlinelibrary.wiley.com/doi/10.1111/ anae.12503/epdf. Accessed on May 23, 2015.

The authors compare the prescription drug abuse epidemic in the United States with similar problems in the United Kingdom and suggest that there are lessons to be learned in the United Kingdom based on the experience in the United States.

Wright, Eric R., Harold E. Kooreman, Marion S. Greene, R. Andrew Chambers, Aniruddha Banerjee, and Jeffrey Wilson.

2014. "The Iatrogenic Epidemic of Prescription Drug Abuse: County-level Determinants of Opioid Availability and Abuse." *Drug and Alcohol Dependence* 138: 209–15.

> This study explores the question as to the relationship between the availability of opioids in a geographical region compared to the amount of prescription drug abuse, and finds that such a relationship exists. Counties with a larger concentration of pharmacists and dentists tend to have a greater number of illicit prescription drug users, thus supporting an iatrogenic (i.e., caused by medical treatment itself) basis for prescription drug abuse.

Wu, Li-Tzy, D. G. Blazer, T. K. Li, and G. E. Woody. 2011. "Treatment Use and Barriers among Adolescents with Prescription Opioid Use Disorders." *Addictive Behaviors* 36 (12): 1233–39.

> Researchers report that only a small fraction of adolescents who abuse prescription drugs receive treatment for their problem. They find that nonfinancial factors are responsible for this statistic, primarily the perceived stigma involved with treatment and the lack of awareness of the need for treatment.

Wu, Li-Tzy, and Dan Blazer. 2011. "Illicit and Nonmedical Drug Use among Older Adults: A Review." *Journal of Aging and Health* 23 (3): 481–504.

> Much of the literature of prescription drug abuse focuses on the problem among adolescents. However, as these researchers point out, the problem is also a serious one for older adults and is likely to become more serious over time. They point out some of the characteristic features of prescription drug abuse among seniors and how they tend to differ from the characteristic features among younger individuals.

Young, April M., Natalie Glover, and Jennifer R. Havens. 2012. "Nonmedical Use of Prescription Medications among Adolescents in the United States: A Systematic Review." *Journal of Adolescent Health* 51 (1): 6–17.

> The author report on a review of 15 national studies on adolescent drug behavior to derive a list of factors that are associated with the use by young adults of prescription drugs for nonmedical purposes. They offer some suggestions for additional research in this area.

Zuzek, Crystal. 2013. "Pill Mills." *Texas Medicine* 109 (4): 18–24.

> The author provides an excellent review of the problem posed by pill mills in the state of Texas and how legal and medical authorities are trying to bring the illegal diversion of prescription drugs through such outlets.

Reports

"Addressing Prescription Drug Abuse in the United States: Current Activities and Future Opportunities." 2013. Behavioral Health Coordinating Committee. Prescription Drug Abuse Subcommittee. U.S. Department of Health and Human Services. http://www.cdc.gov/HomeandRecreationalSafety/pdf/HHS_Prescription_Drug_Abuse_Report_09.2013.pdf. Accessed on May 19, 2015.

> This report was developed and issued as required by a provision of Section 1122 of the Food and Drug Administration Safety and Innovation Act of 2012, for the purpose of developing an improved understanding of the current prescription drug abuse crisis in the United States and a summary of ways of ensuring the safe use of prescription drugs with the potential for abuse and the treatment of prescription drug dependence.

Bagalman, Erin, et al. 2014. "Prescription Drug Abuse." Congressional Research Service. http://claad.org/wp-content/uploads/2014/05/CRS-Drug-Abuse-Report-5-2014.pdf. Accessed on April 5, 2015.

This report focuses primarily on the role of federal agencies in dealing with the prescription drug abuse problem in the United States. It reviews the variety of methods that are now being used to deal with this problem, ranging from safe storage and disposal to focused law enforcement efforts, to new product development to increased awareness and improved education.

"Briefing on PDMP Effectiveness." 2013. PDMP Center of Excellence. Brandeis University. http://www.pdmpexcellence.org/sites/all/pdfs/briefing_PDMP_effectiveness_april_2013.pdf. Accessed on April 5, 2015.

One of the key questions about PDMPs is how effective they actually are. A number of research studies have been conducted to answer this question, but this publication is probably the best single source for an overview of the effectiveness of such programs.

"CDC Grand Rounds: Prescription Drug Overdoses—A U.S. Epidemic." 2012. Morbidity and Mortality Weekly Report (MMWR) 61(1): 10–13. http://www.cdc.gov/mmwr/preview/mmwrhtml/mm6101a3.htm. Accessed on April 4, 2015.

This issue of MMWR summarizes the current status of prescription drug abuse in the United States. The report notes that the problem has become "the fastest growing drug problem in the United States." It provides details on the nature of this epidemic.

Clark, Thomas, et al. 2012. "Prescription Drug Monitoring Programs: An Assessment of the Evidence for Best Practices." The Prescription Drug Monitoring Program Center of Excellence. Brandeis University. http://www.pdmpexcellence.org/sites/all/pdfs/Brandeis_PDMP_Report_final.pdf. Accessed on May 20, 2015.

This report was prepared by the Prescription Drug Monitoring Program at the Center of Excellence of the Heller

School for Social Policy and Management at Brandeis University to identify the elements that make up some of the most effective prescription drug monitoring programs now in action throughout the United States. The report provides an excellent summary of the goals and practices of a wide variety of types of PDMPs.

"DrugScope Street Drug Trends Survey 2014: UK Drug Scene Ever More Complex and Dangerous." DrugScope. http://www .drugscope.org.uk/Media/Press+office/pressreleases/Street-Drug-Trends-2014. Accessed on May 23, 2015.

The DrugScope organization in London conducts an annual survey of drug use in the United Kingdom. The 2014 report outlines in particular the growth of prescription drug abuse, especially gammapentin and pregabalin, which presages an epidemic in the United Kingdom that may parallel that which has already developed in the United States.

"Highlights of the 2009 Drug Abuse Warning Network (DAWN) Findings on Drug-Related Emergency Department Visits." 2010. Drug Abuse Warning Network. http://www.oas .samhsa.gov/2k10/DAWN034/EDHighlights.htm. Accessed on April 7, 2015.

This report provides the most recent data available from the federal government on the number of emergency department visits because of various factors, prescription drug misuse being one of them.

"Mandating PDMP Participation by Medical Providers: Current Status and Experience in Selected States." 2014. PDMP Center of Excellence. Brandeis University. http://www.pdmpexcellence .org/sites/all/pdfs/COE%20briefing%20on%20mandates%20 revised_a.pdf. Accessed on April 5, 2015.

Most PDMP programs are based on the voluntary participation of end users, such as prescribing physicians and pharmacists. But the participation rate of end users in some states is quite low, often less than 50 percent. To improve the effectiveness of such programs, some experts have recommended the adoption of laws that require end users to participate in such programs. This publication reviews the current status of this situation in selected states and offers recommendations about future direction for the concept.

"Medicaid. Fraud and Abuse Related to Controlled Substances Identified in Selected States." 2009. United States Government Accountability Office. Washington, DC: U.S. Government Accountability Office. http://www.gao.gov/assets/300/294710.pdf. Accessed on May 22, 2015.

In response to a Congressional inquiry, the GAO conducted a study to discover the extent and nature of so-called doctor shopping in the Medicaid program and the effectiveness of federal rules and regulations to control this activity. This report summarizes the results of that research and makes recommendations for more effective control of that activity.

"Medicare Part D: Instances of Questionable Access to Prescription Drugs: Report to Congressional Requesters." 2011. United States Government Accountability Office. Washington, DC: U.S. Government Accountability Office. http://gao.gov/new .items/d11699.pdf. Accessed on May 22, 2015.

This report was issued in response to a request from the U.S. Congress to (1) determine the extent to which Medicare beneficiaries obtained frequently abused drugs from multiple prescribers, (2) identify examples of doctor shopping activity, and (3) determine the actions taken by the Centers for Medicare & Medicaid Services to limit access to drugs for known abusers.

"Options for Unsolicited Reporting." 2014. PDMP Center of Excellence. Brandeis University. http://www.pdmpexcellence

.org/sites/all/pdfs/Brandeis_COE_Guidance_on_Unsolicited_
Reporting_final.pdf. Accessed on April 5, 2015.

Increasingly PDMPs are making use of unsolicited reporting, a process by which an agency sends information
about possible prescription drug abuse to end users even
though those end users have not requested such information. This publication describes some of the procedures currently being used by agencies to accomplish this
objective.

"State Substance Abuse Agencies and Prescription Drug Misuse and Abuse: Results from a NASADAD Membership Inquiry." 2012. National Association of State Alcohol and Drug
Abuse Directors. http://nationalrxdrugabusesummit.org/
wp-content/uploads/2012/10/NASADAD-Report-SSAs-and-
Prescription-Drug-Misuse-and-Abuse-09.20121.pdf. Accessed
on April 5, 2015.

This report is probably the most complete in-depth study
of the way in which states are dealing with prescription
drug abuse. It provides detailed information on state legislation, task forces and other study groups, education
and prevention programs, prescription drug monitoring
programs, and relevant data and statistics.

"2012 Partnership Attitude Tracking Study." 2013. MetLife
Foundation and the Partnership at DrugFree.org. http://www
.drugfree.org/wp-content/uploads/2013/04/PATS-2012-
FULL-REPORT2.pdf. Accessed on May 19, 2015.

The MetLife Foundation and The Partnership at Drug-
Free.org has been working together since 1987 to collected data on attitudes and behaviors of teenagers and
their parents about drug use. This report is the 24th in
that series and studied the attitudes and behaviors of families in which there was at least one child between the ages
of 10 and 19. The report is a gold mine of information on
these topics.

United Nations Office on Drugs and Crime. 2014. "World Drug Report." New York: United Nations. http://www.unodc.org/documents/wdr2014/World_Drug_Report_2014_web.pdf. Accessed on May 19, 2015.
  This report is probably the most complete and extensive of any study of the status of drug use of all kinds in every country of the world. The report is issued annually and runs more than a hundred pages with data, statistics, and interpretive commentaries about the status of drug use worldwide.

Yearwood, Douglas L. 2012. "Prescription Drug Abuse and Diversion: The Hidden Crisis." Raleigh: North Carolina Governor's Crime Commission.
  This report is a particularly good example of the type of study and report being conducted on the state level about the problem of prescription drug abuse.

Internet

"A Beginner's Guide to the Rx Drug Abuse Epidemic in America." 2015. Foundations Recovery Network. http://www.foundationsrecoverynetwork.com/beginners-guide-rx-drug-abuse-epidemic-america-part-5/. Accessed on May 16, 2015.
  This website is among the very best single resources for a comprehensive and in-depth coverage of the major points about prescription drug abuse. It consists of five sections that deal with a general overview of the "pill problem"; a review of the history of the problem; characteristic features of prescription drug addiction; related mental health issues; and steps that can be taken to deal with the problem.

Basca, Belinda. 2008. "The Elderly and Prescription Drug Misuse and Abuse." Community Prevention Initiative. http://www.cars-rp.org/publications/Prevention%20Tactics/PT09.02.08.pdf. Accessed on May 21, 2015.

This online pamphlet reviews the special issues involved in dealing with prescription drug abuse and misuse by the elderly, with suggestions for reducing and preventing the problem among seniors who may be at risk.

"The Brain: Understanding Neurobiology through the Study of Addiction." 2015. National Institutes of Health Curriculum Supplement Series. http://science.education.nih.gov/customers/ HSAddiction.html. Accessed on May 23, 2015.

This web page provides curriculum material for a unit on neurobiology and drug addiction produced by the National Institutes of Health. In addition to a number of excellent lessons on the topic, the website provides a host of clear, understandable drawings and images explaining the way in which drugs affect brain function.

"Call to Action and Issue Brief: Justice System Use of Prescription Drug Monitoring Programs—Addressing the Nation's Prescription Drug and Opioid Abuse Epidemic." 2015. Global Justice Information Sharing Initiative. https://it.ojp.gov/gist/174/ Call-to-Action-and-Issue-Brief—Justice-System-Use-of-Prescription-Drug-Monitoring-Programs—Addressing-the-Nations-Prescription-Drug-and-Opioid-Abuse-Epidemic. Accessed on May 21, 2015.

This brochure describes PDMPs in place in the various states and outlines some of the reasons that law enforcement agencies need to be intimately involved in these programs. It also provides some specific suggestions as to how the integration of law enforcement activities with PDMPs can be accomplished most successfully.

"Compound May Relieve Chronic Pain without CNS Side Effects." 2012. National Institute of Drug Abuse. http://www .drugabuse.gov/news-events/nida-notes/2012/09/potential-pain-medication-targets-peripheralnerves. Accessed on April 4, 2015.

One proposed method for dealing with the current epi-demic of prescription drug abuse is to find substances that will relieve pain without having harmful side effects as-sociated with currently popular drugs such as oxycodone, hydrocodone, morphine, and other opioids. This article describes progress in that line of research.

Converse, Deborah, and Kathryn Brohl. "Chapter 4: Prescrip-tion Drug Abuse: Etiology, Prevention and Treatment." 2013. Social Work and Mental Health Continuing Education. https:// s3.amazonaws.com/EliteCME_WebSite_2013/f/pdf/SWUS-06PDI15.pdf. Accessed on May 16, 2015.

This website provides instructional material for a course in prescription drug abuse for the Social Work and Men-tal Health Continuing Education web page. It provides an excellent introduction to all aspects of the prescription drug abuse issue.

"Cough and Cold Medicine Abuse." 2015. Kids Health. http:// kidshealth.org/parent/h1n1_center/h1n1_center_treatment/ cough_cold_medicine_abuse.html. Accessed on May 20, 2015.

This web page provides a good general introduction to the issues involved in the use of cough medicine for non-medical purposes, with special attention to the problem among teenagers.

"Diversion of Pharmaceutical Drugs." 2014. Get the Facts. Drug-WarFacts.org. http://www.drugwarfacts.org/cms/Diversion#sth ash.cV31vVPV.dpbs. Accessed on May 21, 2015.

This resource provides an extensive review of information on basic data associated with specific aspects of prescrip-tion drug abuse, such as sources of diverted prescription drugs, societal impact of diversion, use by high school seniors, first use of prescription drugs for nonmedical purposes, and availability of OxyContin. Additional ref-erences on PDMPs are provided.

"Drug Facts: Bath Salts." 2015. NIDA for Teens. http://teens.drugabuse.gov/drug-facts/bath-salts. Accessed on May 21, 2015.

This web page is among the most complete of all Internet resources on the subject of so-called bath salts, including information on what they are, how they are used, what their effects on the human body can be, and where one can get assistance in dealing with bath salts misuse and abuse issues.

"Drug Facts: Prescription Drugs." 2015. NIDA for Teens. http://teens.drugabuse.gov/drug-facts/prescription-drugs. Accessed on April 22, 2015.

This web page provides basic information on the current prescription drug crisis with suggestions for prevention and treatment, especially for young adults.

"DrugFacts: Synthetic Cathinones ("Bath Salts")." 2012. National Institute on Drug Abuse. http://www.drugabuse.gov/publications/drugfacts/synthetic-cathinones-bath-salts. Accessed on May 20, 2015.

This web page provides basic information about so-called bath salts, a misnomer for a variety of products in which compounds known as cathinones are the primary ingredient.

"Drug Interactions." 2015. Drug Watch. http://www.drugwatch.com/drug-interactions/. Accessed on May 21, 2015.

One of the problems associated with the misuse and abuse of prescription drugs is the risk of their interacting with other substances, such as other prescription drugs, over-the-counter medications, food supplements, or other substances. This article outlines some of those risks along with some specific examples of the interactions that may occur.

Ekern, Jacqueline, and Crystal Karges. 2015. "Tools for Recovering from Prescription Drugs." Addiction Hope. http://www

.addictionhope.com/prescription-drugs/tools-for-recovering-from-prescription-drugs. Accessed on May 21, 2015.

> The authors suggest steps in the road to recovery from dependence on or addiction to prescription drugs.

"Epidemic: Responding to America's Prescription Drug Abuse Crisis." 2011. Office of National Drug Control Policy. https://www.ncjrs.gov/pdffiles1/ondcp/rx_abuse_plan.pdf. Accessed on April 4, 2015.

> This publication outlines some of the ways of dealing with the prescription drug epidemic in the United States, including educational programs, tracking and monitoring of drugs, proper medication disposal, enforcement of existing laws, and prescription drug abuse planning.

Forest, Emily. 2008. "Atypical Drugs of Abuse." The Student Doctor Network. http://www.studentdoctor.net/2008/07/atypical-drugs-of-abuse/. Accessed on May 22, 2015.

> This article provides general information on the nature and long-term effects of exposure to diphenylhydramine for non-medical purposes. An extended list of responses contributes to an understanding of the characteristic features of this drug.

Griggs, Christopher A., Scott G. Weiner, and James A. Feldman. 2015. "Prescription Drug Monitoring Programs: Examining Limitations and Future Approaches." Western Journal of Emergency Medicine 16 (1). http://escholarship.org/uc/item/2147k2t1. Accessed on April 2, 2015.

> As of October 2014, 22 states at PDMPs that used one mechanism or another for attempting to reduce illicit use of prescription drugs in the state. The authors point out that such programs, while generally quite popular, do have limitations and that additional programs should be studied for reducing the rate of prescription drug misuse.

Kraman, Pilar. 2004. "Drug Abuse in America—Prescription Drug Diversion." The Council of State Governments. http://

www.csg.org/knowledgecenter/docs/TA0404DrugDiversion
.pdf. Accessed on May 21, 2015.

> This publication describes the prescription drug abuse and
> misuse problem as of 2004 with special focus on methods
> of diversion and steps that state governments can take to
> deal with this aspect of the overall problem.

Kraman, Pilar. 2004. "Rx for Prescription Drug Abuse." The Council of State Governments. http://www.csg.org/knowledgecenter/
docs/sn0405RxPrescriptionAbuse.pdf. Accessed on May 21, 2015.

> This web page provides a good general overview of the
> problem of prescription drug abuse with special attention
> to methods by which users obtain their drugs, commonly
> abused medications, and ways of dealing with the prob-
> lem of prescription drug abuse.

"Law Enforcement and Government." 2015. RxSafetyMatters.
http://www.rxsafetymatters.org/wp-content/uploads/2013/10/
RXSM_LawEnforceGov-V2.pdf. Accessed on May 7, 2015.

> This informational resource guide outlines the way in
> which law enforcement is and can be involved in dealing
> with the prevention of prescription drug abuse, includ-
> ing educational efforts, law enforcement grants, technical
> assistance, combating pharmacy theft, prescription moni-
> toring programs, and drug abuse surveillance.

Lee, Christine Sh-Teng. 2015. "Prescription Drug Monitoring
Programs: A Policy Review and Recommendations for States."
Thesis, Georgia State University. http://scholarworks.gsu.edu/
cgi/viewcontent.cgi?article=1391&context=iph_theses. Accessed
on April 2, 2015.

> The author reviews PDMPs and, on the basis of that re-
> view, develops a set of recommendations for the type of
> provisions that should be included in these and future
> PDMP legislation.

McDonald, Douglas C., and Kenneth E. Carlson. 2013. "Estimating the Prevalence of Opioid Diversion by "Doctor Shoppers" in the

United States." PLOS One. doi: 10.1371/journal.pone.0069241. http://journals.plos.org/plosone/article?id=10.1371/journal .pone.0069241. Accessed on April 4, 2015.

> The authors report on a study about the characteristics of "doctor shoppers," individuals who request (and usually get) prescriptions for drugs from more than one medical worker. Although they represent less than 1 percent of all purchasers of prescription medicines, doctor shoppers account for a much larger fraction of the total prescriptions dispensed.

"Medicaid Program Integrity. What Is a Prescriber's Role in Preventing the Diversion of Prescription Drugs?" 2014. Centers for Medicare & Medicaid Services. Department of Health and Human Services. http://www.cms.gov/Outreach-and-Education/ Medicare-Learning-Network-MLN/MLNProducts/Downloads/ Drug-Diversion-ICN901010.pdf. Accessed on May 21, 2015.

> This booklet explains the problem of prescription drug abuse for medical providers and explains their role and responsibilities with regard to this issue.

Merlo, Lisa J., Simone M. Cummings, and Linda B. Cottler. 2014. "Prescription Drug Diversion among Substance-Impaired Pharmacists." *The American Journal on Addictions* 23 (2): 123–28.

> This article reports on research conducted to determine the way in which dispensing pharmacists are able to divert prescription drugs for their own illicit use, or the use of others. The authors identify six primary methods used by such individuals, including the theft of drugs that are past their "sell-by" date and are awaiting disposal, volunteering to take responsibility for managing a pharmacy's stock, and forging prescriptions for desired drugs.

Morrison, Kyle W. 2012. "Injured and Addicted?" Safety+Health. http://www.safetyandhealthmagazine.com/articles/injured-and-addicted-2. Accessed on April 4, 2015.

> The author discusses the problems that arise when a worker is injured on the job, given painkillers, and then becomes addicted to those painkillers.

"NIDA Notes Articles: Prescription Drugs." 2015. National Institute on Drug Abuse. http://www.drugabuse.gov/news-events/nida-notes/articles/term/148/prescription-drugs. Accessed on May 20, 2015.

This web page contains about a dozen articles on various aspects of the epidemiology, prevention, treatment, and basic science of prescription drug abuse.

"The Non-Medical Use of Prescription Drugs: Policy Direction Issues." 2011. United Nations Office on Drugs and Crime. http://www.unodc.org/documents/drug-prevention-and-treatment/nonmedical-use-prescription-drugs.pdf. Accessed on May 21, 2015.

This publication provides an excellent overview of the prescription drug abuse problem worldwide, with sections on epidemiology in various regions of the world, particularly vulnerable groups, damage and consequences, international conventions that are relevant to the problem, the role of the medical and pharmaceutical professions, and prevention and treatment programs. The publication concludes with a number of recommendations for action by nations.

"Opioids." 2015. Opioids.net. http://www.opioids.net/. Accessed on April 8, 2015.

This website provides useful general information about opioids, their chemical composition, effects on the body, and use for both medical and recreational purposes. Some useful links are also to be found on the page.

"Opioids: How They Trick the Brain to Make You Feel Good." 2015. Vancouver Sun. http://www.vancouversun.com/Opioids+they+trick+brain+make+feel+good+with+video/9894363/story.html. Accessed on May 22, 2015.

This article and accompanying video illustrate the changes that occur in the brain when the body ingests an opioid.

"Oxycodone Vaccine Passes Early Tests." 2013. National Institute on Drug Abuse. http://www.drugabuse.gov/news-events/nida-notes/2013/05/oxycodone-vaccine-passes-early-tests. Accessed on April 4, 2015.

This web article describes the results of early testing on a possible vaccine for use against oxycodone abuse and addiction.

"The Physiological Mechanisms of Opioid Receptors." 2015. http://physiologicalmechanismsofopioids.weebly.com/. Accessed on May 22, 2015.

This web page with its accompanying videos provides a more detailed and advanced description of changes that take place in the brain when it is exposed to opioids.

"Popping Pills: Prescription Drug Abuse in America." 2015. National Institute on Drug Abuse. http://www.drugabuse.gov/related-topics/trends-statistics/infographics/popping-pills-prescription-drug-abuse-in-america. Accessed on May 16, 2015.

This website is an excellent source on a whole range of "fast facts" about prescription drug abuse in the United States.

"Prescription Drug Abuse." 2015. Huffington Post. http://www.huffingtonpost.com/news/prescription-drug-abuse/. Accessed on April 5, 2015.

This website contains a number of articles on specific aspects of the prescription drug abuse problem.

"Prescription Drug Abuse." 2015. Mayo Clinic. http://www.mayoclinic.org/diseases-conditions/prescription-drug-abuse/basics/definition/con-20032471. Accessed on April 5, 2015.

This highly respected medical resource provides a comprehensive review of the prescription drug abuse problem, with sections on symptoms, causes, risk factors, complications, tests, treatments, and prevention.

"Prescription Drug Abuse." 2014. National Institute on Drug Abuse. http://d14rmgtrwzf5a.cloudfront.net/sites/default/files/prescriptiondrugrrs_11_14.pdf. Accessed on April 8, 2015.

This excellent brochure provides a good general introduction to the problem of prescription drug abuse with sections on statistics, types of prescription drugs most commonly used illicitly, effects of these drugs on the human body, and treatment and prevention of prescription drug misuse. It is possibly the best single introductory reference on the topic.

"Prescription Drug Abuse." 2015. New York Times. http://top ics.nytimes.com/top/reference/timestopics/subjects/p/prescription_drug_abuse/index.html. Accessed on April 5, 2015.

This website contains a number of articles on specific aspects of the prescription drug abuse problem that have appeared in the newspaper over the years.

"Prescription Drug Abuse Statistics." 2015. Center for Lawful Access and Abuse Deterrence. http://claad.org/rx-drug-abuse-stats/#. Accessed on April 7, 2015.

In spite of the title of this website, it provides a very nice comprehensive overview of the current status of prescription drug abuse in the United States in the mid-2010s.

"Prescription Drug Addiction-Top 18 Facts for You and Your Family." Drugs.com. http://www.drugs.com/slideshow/prescription-drug-addiction-1075#slide-1. Accessed on April 8, 2015.

This website provides a number of interesting and useful facts and statistics about the current epidemic of prescription drug abuse in the United States.

"Prescription Drugs/Painkillers." 2015. https://www.hazelden.org/web/public/prescriptiondrugs.page. Accessed on April 5, 2015.

This website provides a good general introduction to the three categories of prescription drugs used for nonmedical purposes: opioids, central nervous system depressants, and stimulants.

"Prescription for Disaster: How Teens Abuse Medicine." 2012. Drug Enforcement Administration. http://www.dea.gov/pr/ multimedia-library/publications/prescription_for_disaster_ english.pdf. Accessed on April 5, 2015.

> The 10 chapters in this book deal with topics such as prescription drug basics; street drugs versus pharmaceuticals; common drugs of abuse; the Internet, drugs, and teens; and the role of the DEA in dealing with prescription drug abuse issues.

"Prescription for Peril: How Insurance Fraud Finances Theft and Abuse of Addictive Prescription Drugs." 2007. Coalition against Insurance Fraud. http://www.insurancefraud.org/downloads/ drugDiversion.pdf. Accessed on May 21, 2015.

> This report explains how insurance fraud finances the crime of prescription drug abuse, the economic costs of such activities, and steps that can be taken to reduce the economic losses resulting from drug diversion.

"Prescription Pain Medication: Preserving Patient Access While Curbing Abuse." 2015. Institute for Patient Access. http:// allianceforpatientaccess.org/wp-content/uploads/2013/01/ PT_White-Paper_Finala.pdf. Accessed on May 21, 2015.

> This white paper was prepared by the Pain Therapy Access Physicians Working Group of the Institute for Patient Access. It reviews the issues created by efforts to combat prescription drug abuse by imposing restrictions on the legitimate use of pain medications, and how this issue can be resolved without loss of access to pain medication for those who legitimately need it.

"Prescription Painkiller Overdoses." 2012. Centers for Disease Control and Prevention. http://www.cdc.gov/VitalSigns/ pdf/2012-07-vitalsigns.pdf. Accessed on April 4, 2015.

This CDC pamphlet provides a general overview of the issue of illicit methadone use, its causes, data, and consequences.

"Problem Behaviors Can Signal Risk in Prescribing Opioids to Teens." 2013. National Institute on Drug Abuse. http://www .drugabuse.gov/news-events/nida-notes/2013/07/problem-behaviors-can-signal-risk-in-prescribing-opioids-to-teens. Accessed on April 4, 2015.

This article summarizes two research studies on the characteristics of adolescents who become prescription drug abusers and the indications that these individuals may become more general substance abusers in the future.

"Schedules of Controlled Substances: Temporary Placement of 10 Synthetic Cathinones Into Schedule I." 2014. Office of Diversion Control. Drug Enforcement Administration. U.S. Department of Justice. http://www.deadiversion.usdoj.gov/fed_regs/rules/2014/fr0307_2.htm. Accessed on May 23, 2015.

This website announces the listing of 10 synthetic cathinones on Schedule I of the Controlled Substances Act. It provides detailed information about the chemical and pharmaceutical characteristics of these drugs, the reasons they are being placed in Schedule I, the scope and nature of the current problem of cathinone abuse, and regulatory issues relating to the new listing.

"STAMP Out Prescription Drug Misuse & Abuse!" 2012. American Society of Consulting Pharmacists. https://www.ascp .com/sites/default/files/SO-Background-v3.pdf. Accessed on May 21, 2015.

This backgrounder pamphlet is one of the most complete discussions of the problem of prescription drug abuse/misuse by the elderly. It lists the drugs most likely abused/misused, as well as their effects on the body, along with signs of abuse or misuse in an individual. The pamphlet also provides links to a large number of very useful references for further information on the topic.

"Strategies to Prevent the Non-Medical Use of Prescription Drugs. Using Prevention Research to Guide Prevention Practice." 2013. Center for the Application of Preventive Technologies. Substance Abuse and Mental Health Services Administration. https://cap tus.samhsa.gov/sites/default/files/capt_resource/strategies_to_prevent_nmupd_04-22-14_0.pdf. Accessed on May 23, 2015.

This publication presents the result of a meta-study of 15 outstanding approaches to the prevention of prescription drug abuse, gleaned from a review of published research appearing on the topic between 2006 and 2013. The recommended approaches are classified as suitable for a whole community or environment, an individual school, a family, or an individual. A useful list of references from which the recommendations were obtained is also part of the publication.

"Synthetic Cathinones (Bath Salts): An Emerging Domestic Threat." 2011. National Drug Intelligence Center. U.S. Department of Justice. http://www.justice.gov/archive/ndic/pubs44/44571/44571p.pdf. Accessed on May 23, 2015.

This publication by the U.S. Department of Justice provides an excellent general overview of the problems posed by the abuse of synthetic cathinones ("bath salts"), along with a review of efforts being made to attack this problem. The web page also has an excellent list of references on the topic.

"The Truth about Prescription Drug Abuse." 2008. Foundation for a Drug-Free World. http://f.edgesuite.net/data/www.drugfreeworld.org/files/truth-about-prescription-drug-abuse-booklet-en.pdf. Accessed on April 5, 2015.

This booklet is available in hard copy and online. It is designed primarily for young adults and consists mainly of information about specific prescription drugs that are most commonly used illicitly.

Turley, Ray. 2015. "Cough Medicine Abuse by Teens." University of Rochester Health Encyclopedia. http://www.urmc .rochester.edu/encyclopedia/content.aspx?ContentTypeID=1& ContentID=2617. Accessed on May 20, 2015.

This resource provides general information about the health effects of cough medicines and their main ingredient, dextromethorphan.

"Under the Counter: The Diversion and Abuse of Controlled Prescription Drugs in the U.S." 2005. The National Center on Addiction and Substance Abuse at Columbia University. http:// www.casacolumbia.org/addiction-research/reports/under-the-counter-diversion-abuse-controlled-perscription-drugs. Accessed on May 21, 2015.

This excellent, if somewhat dated, report deals with most of the major issues relating to prescription drug abuse, such as increased availability and increased abuse of drugs, abuse by young adults, controlled prescription drug only versus vs. poly-substance abusers, new abusers, consequences of drug abuse, prescription drug abuse and mental illness, prescription drug abuse and crime, prescription drug abuse and health care workers, regional differences, sources of diversion, regulation and control, prevention programs, and treating prescription drug abuse.

"Use, Abuse, Misuse, & Disposal of Prescription Pain Medication Time Tool Clinical Reference: A Resource from the American College of Preventive Medicine." 2011. American College of Preventive Medicine. http://www.acpm.org/?UseAbuseRxClin Ref. Accessed on May 21, 2015.

This web page is an extraordinary reference on virtually every major aspect of the prescription drug abuse issue, including sections on the right to pain control, terminology used in discussion of the issue, use and abuse trends, the economic burden of prescription drug abuse and misuse, regulation, role of the prescriber, and drug storage and disposal. An excellent list of resources and references is also provided.

"Veterans Voice Problems with VA's New Pain Killer Policy. Treating Veterans with Chronic Pain." 2014. WAVY News. http://wavy.com/2014/07/21/va-makes-changes-to-prescription-pain-killer-policy/. Accessed on May 23, 2015.

This article explains how new Veterans Administration policies and practices designed to reduce prescription drug abuse and misuse have resulted in veterans' having greater difficulty in obtaining the medications they legitimately need for their own pain problems.

Walter, Maureen. 2015. "Seven Processes in Neurotransmitter Action." http://bioserv.fiu.edu/~walterm/b/addicitions/dopamine.htm. Accessed on May 22, 2015.

This web page is taken from a biology class at Florida International University with excellent graphics that help understand how prescription drugs cause changes in the brain.

Zimam, A., Schmidt T., Nielsen A., and Wakeland W. 2013. "Data Sources Regarding the Nonmedical Use of Pharmaceutical Opioids in the United States." Portland State University Systems Science Graduate Program. https://www.pdx.edu/sysc/opioid-data-sources. Accessed on May 16, 2015.

This publication is a very useful resource for data, statistics, and other basic resources on the topic of prescription drug abuse.

7 Chronology

Introduction

The use of natural and synthetic products for nonmedical purposes dates to the very earliest periods of human civilization. Over the centuries, humans have apparently never ceased to look for plants, minerals, and other natural products that can be used for recreational purposes and to create synthetic products whose effects on the human body mimic those of such products. This chapter provides a brief history of some of the important events that have taken place in that long search for substances that produce psychoactive effects on the human body.

ca. 4000 BCE   The approximate period for which there is evidence that opium was used for its narcotic properties.

ca. 3400 BCE   Possible first mention of the *hul gil* plant in Sumerian texts, a plant (*gil*) that brings joy (*hul*) to anyone who ingests it.

ca. 2100 BCE   A clay tablet found in the area that was once Mesopotamia contains what might be the world's oldest prescription, instructions for using the bark of an apple tree for treating a wound. The elements of the treatment—washing,

Pharmacists may become suspicious about a customer having a prescription filled for painkillers, especially if it's someone they don't know. With so much concern about prescription drug abuse and so-called doctor shopping, they try to stay alert for potential trouble. State prescription drug monitoring programs make it easier for pharmacists, doctors, and law enforcement officers to monitor prescription drug sales and spot abuse. (AP Photo/Kiichiro Sato) applying a dressing, and bandaging—are essentially the same steps used today in treating a wound.

ca. 2000 BCE The Chinese emperor Shen Nung is said to have written the first (or one of the first) books on the use of drugs in medical treatment, *Pen Ts'ao.*

ca. 1550 BCE The Ebers papyrus from ancient Egypt is one of the earliest known books to describe the use of herbals for the treatment of disease and injury. It contains nearly 900 prescriptions that make use of more than 700 different drugs.

ca. 1300 BCE Approximate date of the "poppy goddess," or the "Minoan goddess of narcotics," whose characteristic features have suggested to some scholars a woman in a state of ecstasy supposedly induced by the ingestion of an opium-like substance.

ca. 1300 BCE The first evidence for the cultivation of the opium poppy in Egypt, near the city of Thebes. Opium produced in these fields is later exported to Mesopotamia, North Africa, Greece, and other parts of Europe.

ca. 600 BCE The text called *Sushruta Samhita* is generally regarded as the first medical/herbal text produced in ancient India.

ca. 500 BCE What were probably the first trademarked drugs were produced on the Greek island of Lemnos when, once each year, supposedly medicinal clay was dug from the earth, formed into pills, stamped with an official seal (the "Terra Sigillata") and sold as a certified and official type of medication.

ca. 460 BCE Hippocrates, the father of medicine, mentions a number of uses for opium as a medicine, including the treatment of "diseases of women."

ca. 330 BCE Alexander the Great is thought to have introduced opium to India and Persia.

50–75 CE The Roman physician Pedanius Dioscorides compiles one of the first materia medicas ever written, and certainly one of the most influential books of this type. In five volumes, the book describes more than 600 plants and minerals that can be used to produce more than a thousand medicinal substances.

ca. 150 CE The Roman physician Galen develops techniques for combining and blending a variety of herbs to produce substances for medical use. The procedure is said to be the origin of the process of *compounding* and is memorialized in the modern use of the term *galenical*, which refers to mixtures of natural substances prepared and used for medical purposes.

287 CE The twin brothers Damian and Cosmas are martyred and later named saints. They are known to have devoted their lives to the healing arts and are regarded by some as the patron saints of pharmacists and physicians, respectively.

ca. 400 CE Arab traders are thought to have introduced opium to China.

754 CE The world's first drugstore is thought to have opened at the central hospital of Baghdad.

1240 Frederick II of Hohenstaufen, emperor of Germany and king of Sicily, issues a decree separating the professions of pharmacy and medicine, two fields that had previously been practiced by the same individuals.

1498 The first official pharmacopoeia is published in Florence. It is compiled through the joint efforts of the Guild of Apothecaries and the Medical Society to serve as the official guide for the preparation and use of medications.

ca. 1500 Portuguese traders discover the benefits of smoking opium for recreational purposes because it produces nearly instantaneous psychoactive effects.

1527 The date on which Swiss-German alchemist and physician Paracelsus is said to have invented laudanum. The history of the product is far more complex, however, and other dates and inventors are also possible.

1680 One of the most famous versions of laudanum is invented and sold by English apothecary Thomas Sydenham under the name of Sydenham's Laudanum.

1729   Chinese emperor Yung Ching issues an edict prohibiting the smoking or other use of opium except for medical purposes. The edict reflects the growing objections to the use of opium as a recreational drug, in contrast to its medical applications.

1799   Chinese emperor Jiaqing bans growing, production, and use of all forms of opium.

1803   German chemist Friedrich Sertürner isolates morphine from opium.

1803   French chemist Jean-François Derosne discovers noscapine, known at the time as narcotine.

1821   English essayist Thomas De Quincey publishes his "Confessions of an English Opium-eater," an autobiographical account of his experiences in the use of opium as a recreational drug.

1827   The Merck company chooses morphine and aspirin as the two drugs it first begins producing in bulk quantities. Its success with these two drugs largely establishes Merck as one of the world's largest and most successful drug companies for well over a century.

1832   French chemist Pierre-Joseph Pelletier discovers narceine.

1832   French chemist Pierre Robiquet discovers codeine.

1835   French chemist Thibouméry (first name not available) discovers thebaine.

1839–1842   The First Opium War is fought between Great Britain and China over the importation of the drug into China by British traders, although other issues were also involved in the conflict.

1848   German chemist Georg Merck discovers papaverine.

1856–1860   The Second Opium War was fought between Great Britain and China over ongoing issues about the trade in opium and related political questions.

1861–1865   Morphine is used as a "miracle drug" during the American Civil War in bringing under control pain for which there was otherwise no treatment. The widespread use of morphine in the war, however, also leads to the development of thousands of cases of morphine addiction among veterans of the war who become dependent on the drug.

1874   English chemist Charles Romley (C. R.) Alder Wright prepares the first semisynthetic opioid, heroin. Wright does not pursue any commercial application for his discovery (but see **1897**).

1875   The city and county of San Francisco bans the smoking of opium outside of facilities designed specifically for that purpose, the so-called opium dens.

1879   An act is introduced into the U.S. Congress to create a system of controls over the production and sale of foods and drugs in the United States. The act fails in the Congress, and is reintroduced nearly 200 times over the next 27 years, before it is finally adopted in 1906.

1887   The U.S. Congress passes the first federal law dealing with opium, restricting the importation of opium containing less than 9 percent morphine, the form of opium normally used for smoking. Chinese individuals were prohibited from importing any form of opium whatsoever.

1897   German chemical researcher Felix Hoffmann rediscovers a method for making heroin (see **1874**), but also understands the potential of the drug for medical use. Heroin eventually becomes one of the best-selling drugs for Hoffman's employer, Aktiengesellschaft Farbenfabriken pharmaceutical company, later the Bayer company.

1906   The U.S. Congress passes the Pure Food and Drug Law, which places restrictions on "the manufacture, sale, or transportation of adulterated or misbranded or poisonous or deleterious foods, drugs, medicines, and liquors." The act also makes the earliest efforts to regulate the sale of so-called patent medicines. The law also led to the establishment of the Food and Drug Administration (FDA) that is the primary federal agency dealing with all forms of drugs in the United States today.

1909   The first international conference on the topic of the control of narcotic drugs is held in Shanghai, China. The conference laid the groundwork for the International Opium Convention, signed at The Hague, Netherlands, in 1912.

1909   The U.S. Congress passes the Smoking Opium Exclusion Act, which attempted to restrict the nonmedical use of the drug.

1912   The International Opium Convention is signed at The Hague, Netherlands, by delegates from China, France, Germany, Italy, Japan, the Netherlands, Persia (Iran), Portugal, Russia, Siam (Thailand), the United Kingdom, and the United States.

1914   Partly as a condition of the provisions of the International Opium Convention, the U.S. Congress adopts the Harrison Narcotic Act, which provided primarily for the licensing of individuals involved in the opium trade, along with taxes on the sale of the drug.

1914   The state of New York establishes what is probably the first effort to monitor transactions involving certain types of prescription drugs, requiring prescribers to use duplicate forms issued by the state and serialized for precise record-keeping.

1919   The International Opium Convention essentially goes into effect internationally when it becomes part of the Treaty of Versailles, which is signed by all of the world's major powers.

1922   The U.S. Congress adopts the Narcotic Drug Import and Export Act, which extends existing prohibitions on the importation of opium products, adds cocaine to the list of substances whose import is banned, and creates the Federal Narcotics Control Board, an early predecessor of today's Drug Enforcement Administration (DEA).

1924   The Heroin Act of 1924 bans the manufacture, importation, possession, and use of heroin for any reason whatsoever in the United States, including all medical applications.

1928   American physician Charles E. Terry and his wife, Mildred Pellens, publish one of the most comprehensive studies on opium in U.S. history, "The Opium Problem."

1932   German chemist Otto Eisleb (or Eislib) synthesizes the first synthetic opioid, pethidine (Dolantin, Demerol).

1932   The U.S. Congress passes the Uniform State Narcotic Act, designed to make state drug laws consistent with each other. All 50 states eventually adopted their own versions of the act, which has been amended and updated a number of times since 1932.

1938   The Federal Food, Drug, and Cosmetic Act of 1938 authorizes the FDA to develop regulations for the monitoring and control of synthetic chemicals developed for use in medicine. The act leads to a new regulation requiring the labeling of drugs that can be sold only by prescription.

1939   In one of the earliest programs designed to track drug prescriptions, the state of California introduces the California Triplicate Prescription Program, which requires that all prescriptions be written in triplicate, with one form remaining with the prescribing physician, a second form remaining with the dispensing pharmacist, and a third form being sent to a central state office (the attorney general's office, in the case of California).

1948   In the case of *United States v. Sullivan*, the U.S. Supreme Court rules that the FDA's requirement for the labeling of prescription drugs is constitutional and legal.

1951   The Boggs Act significantly increases the penalties for trafficking and use of narcotic drugs, to which marijuana is added for the first time in U.S. legislative history.

1951   The U.S. Congress adopts the Durham-Humphrey Amendment, an attempt to clarify the status of prescription drugs in the United States. The amendment specifies the types of drugs that are to be considered as "prescription" drugs and the mechanisms by which they can be ordered by physicians and sold by pharmacists.

1956   The Narcotic Control Act continues the trend of increasing the severity of federal penalties for trafficking and use of narcotic drugs and marijuana.

1965   The Drug Abuse Control Amendment imposes penalties for trafficking in and use of certain substances not listed as illegal to that point in history, such as stimulants, depressants, and hallucinogens.

1970   The U.S. Congress adopts the Controlled Substances Act of 1970, an act designed to update and consolidate the dozens of federal laws dealing with all aspects of a number of types of illicit drugs. A key provision of the law was the creation of five *schedules*, that is, categories of drugs, based on their potential for medical use and their potential harm to users.

1975   The National Institute of Drug Abuse contracts with researchers at the University of Michigan to conduct an annual survey of drug use by high school students, as well as their attitudes about various aspects of drug use. That study, called the Monitoring the Future study, has continued to the present day, increasing in size and complexity over the 40 years during which it has been conducted.

1991   The Medicare system introduces a program known as Patient Review and Restriction (or "lock-in") which allows states to limit a person's access to prescription drugs (as may be indicated by the patients nonmedical use of the drugs) without having an effect on the patient's other Medicare benefits.

2002   The U.S. Congress establishes the Harold Rogers Prescription Drug Monitoring Program, which provides grants to agencies for the development of prescription drug monitoring programs (PDMPs). The program provided significant emphasis for the adoption of PDMPs, which had, to that point, been almost entirely the responsibility of individual states and not the federal government.

2005   The U.S. Congress passes the National All Schedules Prescription Electronic Reporting Act of 2005, which requires the Secretary of Health and Human Services to develop a grant program for the establishment of controlled substances monitoring programs in all states.

2008   The FDA approves the release of immediate-release tapentasol, the first analgesic acting on the central nervous system approved in almost three decades in the United

States. Tapentadol has analgesic effects less than those of morphine, but more than a number of other opioids. It is listed as a schedule II drug and becomes commercially available in 2009.

2009 For the first time in history, the number of fatalities due to prescription drugs exceeds the number of deaths from vehicle accidents in the United States.

2010 The FDA approves the release of a reformulated version of the popular drug OxyContin that makes it more difficult to inhale of inject, thus reducing the risk of the drug's being used for nonmedical purposes. The drug manufacturer, Purdue Pharma, discontinues shipping the original OxyContin formulation to pharmacies.

2010 The FDA rescinds its approval of the drug propoxyphene (Darvon; Darvocet) because of its relatively high potential for misuse compared to its relatively modest efficacy as a pain-relieving medication.

2010 The U.S. Congress adopts the Secure and Responsible Drug Disposal Act of 2010, which outlines the circumstances under which a person "who has lawfully obtained a controlled substance in accordance with this title may, without being registered, deliver the controlled substance to another person for the purpose of disposal of the controlled substance."

2010 The state of Florida passes the nation's first pill-mill-type bill, setting standards for doctors who prescribe narcotics (H.B. 7095).

2010 The number of prescriptions written for opioid analgesics reaches 209.5 million, a nearly 300 percent increase over the number written only 20 years before in 1991 (75.5 million).

2011 In the publication "Epidemic: Responding to a America's Prescription Drug Abuse Crisis," the administration of President Barack Obama outlines the issues involved in the nation's prescription drug abuse crisis and the steps that need to be taken in order to deal with that crisis.

2012   The number of opioid analgesic prescriptions written in the United States drops by 19 percent over the number written two years earlier, and the number of deaths attributed to opioid overdose drops by 20 percent over the same period. Experts conclude that these changes reflect the ban on one form of opioid narcotic, propoxyphene, and an improved formulation of a second opioid, OxyContin, in 2010 (see **2010**). The problem with these encouraging data is that they are bracketed with comparable increases in morbidity and mortality data for heroin over the same period of time.

2012   The FDA announces a risk evaluation and mitigation strategy program for extended-release and long-acting drugs, which is designed to take actions that may help in reducing the extent to which such drugs are used for nonmedical purposes.

2014   Reflecting concerns about its use for nonmedical purposes, the DEA reschedules the drug hydrocodone from Schedule III to Schedule II in the National Schedules of Controlled Substances.

2015   Sixteen members of the U.S. Senate—14 Democrats and 2 Independents—send a letter to President Barack Obama asking that he significantly increase federal funding in the fight against prescription drug abuse. They recommend $68 million for monitoring individuals who are at risk for abusing prescription drugs, $25 million for a study of new treatments for opioid abuse, and $54 million for research on alternative forms of pain management that do not rely so heavily on opioids.

2015   An outbreak of HIV infections in rural Scott County, Indiana, is attributed to sharing of needles by individuals addicted to the opioid analgesic Opana (oxymorphone). As of mid-May 2015, more than 150 new cases of HIV had been diagnosed that could be traced to the nonmedical use of Opana. Indiana governor Mike Pence (Republican) reluctantly agrees to a needle exchange program, to which he had previously been opposed, as a possible way for ending the spread of the epidemic.

2015   DEA agents carry out raids in Alabama, Arkansas, Louisiana, and Mississippi targeting pharmacists, physicians, and street-dealers who are selling prescription drugs for non-medical purposes. More than 200 individuals are arrested as a result of the raids, which DEA officials call the "largest operation against illegal trafficking of prescription drugs" in U.S. history.

8   Glossary

Introduction

A study of prescription drug abuse issue often requires the use of specialized terminology. This chapter defines some of the most common terms used in such discussions. A list of some of the most common and important substances mentioned in a discussion of prescription drug abuse is also provided at the end of the glossary.

Addiction   A chronic, compulsive mental condition characterized by a persistent search for a substance or behavior that brings a sense of reward to the addicted individual, generally accompanied by significant and permanent changes in the brain.

Agonist   A chemical that binds to a receptor, usually in the central nervous system, and activates that receptor.

Analgesic   Any substance that reduces pain.

Antagonist   A chemical that binds to a receptor, usually in the central nervous system, and then blocks the action of that receptor.

Central nervous system (CNS)   The brain and spinal cord.

Chronic   Any condition that persists over long periods of time.

Comorbidity   The existence of two or more disorders or illnesses in an individual at the same time. Cases of comorbidity may require methods of treatment that differ from those used for each condition individually.

Dependence (drug; physical)   A condition in which the body functions normally only when it has access to some specific chemical substance, such as heroin or cocaine.

Dopamine   A neurotransmitter whose action is responsible for a number of mental states, including pleasure, feelings of emotion,   physical movements, and motivation to take action.

Endogenous   A substance that is produced within the body, including the brain.

Euphoria   A sense of happiness, ease, pleasure, joy, and/or well-being.

Exogenous   A substance that is produced outside a living body.

Exudate   A protein-rich fluid that seeps out of blood vessels or a bodily organ, often as the result of inflammation in the body, which then collects in nearby tissues.

Hallucination   A perception of some object or event that does not exist in reality.

Hallucinogen   A substance that causes hallucinations.

Materia medica   The whole body of knowledge available to the medical profession about the substances and procedures that can be used in the healing process.

Morbidity   Illness.

Mortality   Death.

Neurotransmitter   A chemical that carries a nerve message between two neurons (nerve cells), initiating some type of response at the receiving neuron.

Opioid receptor   A molecule or portion of a molecule that recognizes and binds to the opium molecule and other molecules similar in structure to it.

Over-the-counter drug   Any drug that can be sold without a prescription because it is regarded as having minimal negative health effects when used as intended.

Partial opioid agonist   A chemical that binds to a receptor, but that produces less of a response than is produced by a full agonist.

Pharmacopeia   A book that lists information about drugs available for health and medical purposes, along with their formulas, mode of action, and directions of use, usually published by a governmental agency or professional association.

Prescription drug   Any drug that can be purchased only with the presentation of a written order by a qualified medical professional for the treatment of some medical condition. The drug is considered to have sufficiently serious harmful side effects that it cannot be offered for general sale without specific instructions from a medical provider.

Psychoactive   Referring to a substance that can have a profound effect on mental functioning.

Psychotherapeutic   Anything that can improve one's mental function. The two major category of psychotherapeutics are drugs and behavioral training programs.

Receptor   A molecule in the body that is capable of recognizing certain characteristic substances, such as neurotransmitters or hormones, and then binding to those substances. The act of binding then sets off some other chemical or electrical process in a cell.

Reward   The pleasurable feeling that occurs when the body responds to some substance or action that it requires, as when it receives food at a point when it is hungry.

Tolerance   A condition in which the body requires ever-increasing amounts of a substance to produce the same effect once produced by smaller amounts of the substance.

Unsolicited reporting   The process by which an agency sends out information to end users (e.g., pharmacists and prescribing physicians) about possible prescription drug abusers, even though that information had not been requested by the end users.

Withdrawal A group of symptoms that develop when the body is deprived of access to some specific substance on which it has become dependent. Those symptoms may include headaches, nausea and vomiting, sweating, loss of appetite, fatigue, shakiness, insomnia, irritability, anxiety, depression, and hallucinations.

Prescription and Nonprescription Drugs

Adderall A combination of amphetamine and dextroamphetamine used primarily to treat attention deficit hyperactivity disorder and narcolepsy.

Barbiturate A chemical relative of barbituric acid that acts as a central nervous system depressant.

Benzodiazepines A family of compounds based on the benzodiazepine molecule, which consists of two rings and contains two nitrogen atoms, that act as central nervous system depressants.

Buprenorphine A semisynthetic derivative of the opioid thebaine used most commonly to treat opioid addiction.

Concerta The trade name for methylphenidate, a central nervous system stimulant.

Dextromethorphan A complex nitrogen-containing compound widely used in a number of over-the-counter cough and cold medications.

Methadone A long-acting synthetic opioid.

Opana The trade name for oxymorphone, an opioid pain medication that was implicated in the outbreak of an epidemic in Indiana in 2015 resulting from the sharing of needles by opioid addicts.

Opioid An opium-like substance that binds to opioid receptors in the body.

OxyContin An opioid narcotic used for the treatment of severe pain.

Percocet A narcotic analgesic that is a combination of acet-aminophen and oxycodone used primarily for the treatment of severe pain.

Ritalin The trade name for methylphenidate, a central ner-vous system stimulant.

Tramadol An opioid pain medication used for the treatment of moderate pain.

Valium The trade name for a benzodiazepine drug that acts as a central nervous system depressant.

Vicodin A combination of acetaminophen and hydrocodone used primarily to treat severe pain.

Xanax The trade name for a benzodiazepine drug that acts as a central nervous system depressant.

AARP Policy Institute, 207
Abbvie pharmaceuticals, 203
abdominal pain, 96, 97
Abilify, 48, 49
ACE inhibitors, 239
acetaminophen (Tylenol), 84,
    145, 152, 239, 263
acetylsalicylic acid, 193
    See also aspirin
acid-reducing medication, 47
ADD. *See* attention deficit
    disorder
Adderall (amphetamine and
    dextroamphetamine), 89,
    133, 145, 148–150, 241
Addiction. *See* drug addiction
addiction disorders, insurance
    coverage for, 171
addiction medicine, 171
addiction science, 211
ADHD. *See* attention deficit
    hyperactivity disorder
Advair Diskus (fluticasone
    propionate/salmetrol),
    47, 48
advertising,
    direct-to-consumer, 141

Advil (ibuprofen), 84, 152,
    240, 263
Affordable Care Act,
    153, 218
Afghanistan, prescription
    drug misuse in, 81
African Americans, 26, 73
agonists, 116–117, 325
    alpha, 239
    partial opioid, 117
Alaskan Natives, 73,
    215, 222
albuterol (Ventolin HFA), 47
alcohol, 146, 150, 157, 204
    regulation of sale of, 171
Alcohol, Drug Abuse,
    and Mental Health
    Administration
    (ADAMHA), 209,
    221–222
Alcoholics Anonymous, 206
alcoholism, 170
Alexander the Great, 314
Alka Seltzer Plus, 94
alkaloid chemistry, 16
alkaloids, 16
Allergan, 178

difference between medicinal and recreational use of, 86–87

direct-to-consumer advertising for, 141

diversion of, 102–104, 161, 203

evolution of, 41–45

extended-release, 322

global figures for, 48–49

illicit prescribing of, 102

information about, 211

long-acting, 322

medical uses of, 98–99

mortality and morbidity data, 76–77

most commonly abused, 48

most popular worldwide, 49

most profitable in U.S., 48

nonmedical use of, 3–4, 71–76, 79–80, 132, 142

nonmedical use of by categories, 83–84

percentage of use in the U.S., 46

perception of as "safer" than street drugs, 101, 132, 142, 241–242

proper disposal of, 111–112

reasons for nonmedical use of, 4–5, 100

selling, 102

side effects of, 50, 70, 87

sources of, 69, 101–104, 105

statistics, 233–242

storage and disposal of, 131

"sympathetic diversion" of, 142

top number of prescriptions written in U.S., 47–48

in the 21st century, 45–49

ubiquitous use of, 160

See also drugs; over-the-counter drugs

Prescription Monitoring Program, State of Oregon (2009), 258–260

prescription pad theft and forgery, 102, 108

prescription painkillers. See opioid analgesics (pain relievers); opioids; pain medications

prescriptions

ancient, 7

duplicate copies of, 110, 225, 319

e-prescriptions, 161

See also prescription drugs

"Prevent_Abuse" toolkit, 182

Preventing Abuse of Cough Treatments (PACT), 181

prevention of substance abuse. See drug abuse prevention

Principle of Addiction Medicine, 172

About the Author

David E. Newton holds an associate's degree in science from Grand Rapids (Michigan) Junior College, a BA in chemistry (with high distinction), an MA in education from the University of Michigan, and an EdD in science education from Harvard University. He is the author of more than 400 textbooks, encyclopedias, resource books, research manuals, laboratory manuals, trade books, and other educational materials. He taught mathematics, chemistry, and physical science in Grand Rapids, Michigan, for 13 years; was professor of chemistry and physics at Salem State College in Massachusetts for 15 years; and was adjunct professor in the College of Professional Studies at the University of San Francisco for 10 years.

The author's previous books for ABC CLIO include *Global Warming* (1993), *Gay and Lesbian Rights-A Resource Handbook* (1994, 2009), *The Ozone Dilemma* (1995), *Violence and the Mass Media* (1996), *Environmental Justice* (1996, 2009), *Encyclopedia of Cryptology* (1997), *Social Issues in Science and Technology: An Encyclopedia* (1999), *DNA Technology* (2009), *Sexual Health* (2010), *The Animal Experimentation Debate* (2013), *Marijuana* (2013), *World Energy Crisis* (2013), *Steroids and Doping in Sports* (2014), *GMO Food* (2014), *Science and Political Controversy* (2014), *Wind Energy* (2015), and *Fracking* (2015). His other recent books include *Physics: Oryx Frontiers of Science Series* (2000), *Sick!* (four volumes; 2000), *Science,*

Technology, and Society: The Impact of Science in the 19th Century (two volumes; 2001), *Encyclopedia of Fire* (2002), *Molecular Nanotechnology: Oryx Frontiers of Science Series* (2002), *Encyclopedia of Water* (2003), *Encyclopedia of Air* (2004), *The New Chemistry* (six volumes; 2007), *Nuclear Power* (2005), *Stem Cell Research* (2006), *Latinos in the Sciences, Math, and Professions* (2007), and *DNA Evidence and Forensic Science* (2008). He has also been an updating and consulting editor for a number of books and reference works, including *Chemical Compounds* (2005), *Chemical Elements* (2006), *Encyclopedia of Endangered Species* (2006), *World of Mathematics* (2006), *World of Chemistry* (2006), *World of Health* (2006), *UXL Encyclopedia of Science* (2007), *Alternative Medicine* (2008), *Grzimek's Animal Life Encyclopedia* (2009), *Community Health* (2009), *Genetic Medicine* (2009), *The Gale Encyclopedia of Medicine* (2010–2011), *The Gale Encyclopedia of Alternative Medicine* (2013), *Discoveries in Modern Science: Exploration, Invention, and Technology* (2013–2014), and *Science in Context* (2013–2014).